FROM POTSDAM
TO
POLAND

FROM POTSDAM
TO
POLAND

*American Policy Toward
Eastern Europe*

STEPHEN A. GARRETT

PRAEGER

New York
Westport, Connecticut
London

Library of Congress Cataloging-in-Publication Data

Garrett, Stephen A., 1939-
  From Potsdam to Poland.

  Bibliography: p.
  1. Europe, Eastern—Foreign relations—United
States. 2. United States—Foreign relations—Europe,
Eastern. 3. Europe, Eastern—Foreign relations—
1945- . 4. United States—Foreign relations—
1945- . I. Title.
DJK45.U5G37   1986   327.73047   86-20487
ISBN 0-275-92321-5 (alk. paper)

Copyright © 1986 by Stephen A. Garrett

All rights reserved. No portion of this book may be
reproduced, by any process or technique, without the
express written consent of the publisher.

Library of Congress Catalog Card Number: 86-20487
ISBN: 0-275-92321-5

First published in 1986

Praeger Publishers, 521 Fifth Avenue, New York, NY 10175
A division of Greenwood Press, Inc.

Printed in the United States of America

The paper used in this book complies with the Permanent
Paper Standard issued by the National Information Standards
Organization (Z39.48-1984).

10 9 8 7 6 5 4 3 2 1

Contents

120350

625742

Preface

This book examines certain problems in American foreign policy toward East Central Europe (or, alternatively, Eastern Europe), which, for present purposes, I take to include the countries of Poland, Czechoslovakia, Hungary, Romania, Bulgaria, Albania, and Yugoslavia. It makes no claim to being a systematic survey of the history of American relations with the region, nor is it an "area study" of the political, economic, and cultural circumstances of Eastern Europe itself. Instead, the focus is on specific issues in the development and execution of American diplomacy toward an important area of the world. The basic time frame covered is the period since 1945, and more particularly the last two decades, when American policy with respect to Eastern Europe has undergone significant change and been the subject of considerable debate.

One of the phenomena that has interested me as I have examined American foreign relations with Eastern Europe has been what seems to be a rather consistent gap between image and reality. Repeatedly, one comes across perceptions about American policy toward the region that on closer examination prove to have far less substance that might be supposed. I didn't design this book as an attack on "sacred cows"—indeed, I shared many of the above perceptions myself when I began work—but it has been a striking experience to have to constantly reevaluate former theories in the light of actual evidence.

I might give three very brief examples at this point. It is widely assumed that the substantial Eastern European ethnic community in the United States, which numbers anywhere from 12 to 15 million, has constantly pushed Washington to help in the "liberation" of Eastern Europe from Communist rule, and at the very least has provided a large obstacle to any normalization of relations between the United States and the regimes of the area. The reality is that the ethnic community has hardly been united on American diplomacy toward their lands of origin and that in general they have been manipulated more than manipulating as far as Washington's stance toward East Central Europe is concerned. Then there is the matter of American trade with Eastern Europe. Analysts from all points of the political spectrum have tended to see U.S. economic policy as a prime potential tool of leverage in East Central Europe. Some argue that such trade can lead to greater "understanding"; others say it can be used to force concessions, for example, on freedom of emigration. Again, the evidence is that this considerably overstates the rather marginal political effect that American trade can actually have. Finally, there is a perception that this country has always taken the lead in pressing the authorities in Eastern Europe on human rights questions, having at the same time to spur our more cautious and traditional European allies to join us in these humanitarian efforts. A study of the background of the Helsinki Final Act, however, which is the basis for almost all human rights discussion concerning Eastern Europe today, reveals that the United States lagged behind the West Europeans in insisting on human rights clauses in the Final Act. Indeed, it was not until almost two years after this document was signed that Washington finally began to make a public issue of human rights in Eastern Europe.

This study is divided into three parts, each of which represents a detailed examination of the above issues of perception and reality—and others as well. Part I deals with the Eastern European ethnic impact on the formulation of American foreign policy. Part II examines various matters arising out of American trade and economic policy more generally with East Central Europe. Finally, Part III considers the respective pull of "power and principle" in American diplomacy toward Eastern Europe, that is, American humanitarian as compared to geopolitical interests in the region.

My earlier comment to the effect that this book will question certain conventional wisdoms about the U.S. relationship with Eastern Europe may give the reader the impression that this will be essentially a negative exercise in "revisionist" scholarship. Actually, this book has a positive purpose. Perhaps the single most observable *leitmotif* in the evolution of American foreign policy toward East Central Europe since 1945 has been the relatively high level of frustration we have felt in attempting to develop a productive diplomacy toward the region. Without question at times the United States has had rather utopian notions of what it could accomplish in Eastern Europe. When these ideas proved beyond achievement, there was a tendency in some quarters to lapse into a resigned cynicism about the potential American role. What I attempt to argue here is that, even as we accept pragmatic limitations on our ability to transform the condition of Eastern Europe, there is no reason to lapse into passivity or fatalism about the relevance of American policy to the future of the region. There is a great deal that a carefully crafted American diplomacy can offer to those millions of East Europeans who aspire to a more promising economic and political future—and who so richly deserve it.

Some of the data and analysis contained in this book first appeared in journal articles by the author in the following publications: "Eastern European Ethnic Groups and American Foreign Policy," POLITICAL SCIENCE QUARTERLY

(Summer, 1978); "American Human Rights Policy Toward Eastern Europe," REVIEW OF POLITICS (October, 1981); and "The Carrot or the Stick: American Trade with Eastern Europe," EAST EUROPEAN QUARTERLY (Winter, 1981). Permission by the respective editors to use this material is gratefully acknowledged.

Finally, I wish to dedicate this book to my wife Marta, who provided the sort of home environment conducive to scholarly undertakings. For those who know her, it will come as no surprise that her steady encouragement and cheerful support were major ingredients in this project's finally being completed.

Part I.

THE TIES THAT BIND: EASTERN EUROPEAN ETHNICS AND AMERICAN FOREIGN POLICY

1.

The Eastern European
Ethnic Presence

It is hardly a novel observation that the United States is uniquely a nation of immigrants. As of the American bi-centennial in 1976, nearly 50 million people, representative of virtually all the world's nations, had migrated to these shores. Beginning early in the nineteenth century until about 1930, approximately 60 percent of total world migration was to the United States. The Census of 1970 revealed that one-sixth of the American population was either foreign-born or of foreign parentage. More than 30 million people claimed a foreign language as a mother tongue.[1]

Clearly the pluralistic character of American society has had a substantial influence on the course of American politics and on American foreign policy specifically. The special focus here is on the role that the Eastern European ethnic community has played in the development of American policy toward East Central Europe. What has been the overall role of that community in the development of American diplomacy toward their lands of origin? More broadly, how should or can the "national interest" be defined when influential ethnic minorities press for their particular version of that interest? May there not be a "general" interest that supersedes more particularistic definitions? On the other hand, is the concept of the "general" interest meaningful in an avowedly pluralistic society, even in terms of foreign policy? These are some of the questions to be considered, which necessarily involve an evaluation of (1) the present and past facts on the Eastern European ethnic presence in the United States; (2) the general nature of the foreign policy decision-making process in the United States, especially in terms of its susceptibility to pressure from specialized interests; and (3) the impact of the oft-remarked rising ethnic consciousness in the United States on future American relations with the countries of Eastern Europe.

EASTERN EUROPEAN ETHNICS IN THE UNITED STATES

The Eastern European ethnic presence in the United States goes back a long time. Tradition has it that two of Columbus's sailors were Ragusans from the port on the Adriatic that is now Dubrovnik. There were Poles among the first settlers at Jamestown, and Czechs were among those who came to New Amsterdam under the auspices of the Dutch West India Company in 1633. Substantial numbers of East Europeans arrived in this country, however, only with the advent of the new immigration of the late nineteenth and early twentieth centuries. Previously, the vast majority of immigrants were from Northern or Western Europe. In the decade 1871-80, for instance, approximately 74 percent of immigration fell into this category, whereas only 7 percent came from Southern and Eastern Europe, and the remainder from non-European areas.[2] Twenty years later these figures had almost reversed themselves. Poland, as one example, provided only about 12,000 immigrants in the years 1871-80, but in the last decade of the century this figure increased to approximately 100,000. The peak of the Polish migration came in the early 1920s before restrictive immigration laws put an end to the influx. For the decade as a whole some 228,000 Polish nationals took up residence in the United States, which produced a total first- and second-generation Polish population of approximately 2 million in this country. As of 1930, there were about a million Czechoslovaks, 320,000 Hungarians, 260,000 Yugoslavs, and 150,000 Romanians who also swelled the East European immigrant ranks.[3]

The new immigration was partly a function of unsettled conditions in the homeland and even more of opportunities created by the burgeoning U.S. industrial economy. The economy required a source of cheap labor, and the Eastern European immigration helped a great deal in fulfilling this need. Despite the obvious importance of the new immigrants to economic growth, however, their reception in this country was mixed at best. President Woodrow Wilson, the supposed champion of self-determination in Eastern Europe, reflected the views of many when he deplored the changing character of immigration to the United States:

There came multitudes of men of lowest class from the south of Italy and men of the meaner sort out of Hungary and Poland, men out of the ranks where there was neither skill nor energy nor any initiative or quick intelligence, and they came in numbers which increased from year to year, as if the countries of the south of Europe were disburdening themselves of the most sordid and hapless elements of their population.[4]

This attitude was to have its effect in subsequent years when politically organized Eastern European ethnic groups attempted to exert pressure on the United States to adopt supportive policies toward those left behind in the homeland. At all events, a rising popular clamor against the influx of Eastern Europeans with their strange languages, customs, and supposed clannishness led to the passage by Congress in 1924 of new laws that were openly designed to stem the flow of the new immigration. A quota system was established that took as a base year 1890, just prior to the upsurge of immigration from Eastern Europe. From this time forward, except for special legislative waivers granted, for example, to the Hungarian refugees of 1956, Eastern Europe has provided a relatively insignificant proportion of total immigration to this country. The Immigration and Naturalization Act of 1965 further reduced the number of individuals from the Eastern European countries (especially Poland and Hungary) gaining admittance to the United States.[5] Table 1 presents figures from the 1980 Census on the present American population with an Eastern European ancestry.

The data presented here are open to various interpretations as to what they say about the current Eastern European ethnic representation in the United States. Although it is obvious that even today significant numbers of Americans identify themselves as having an Eastern European ethnic background, it is also true that Americans of foreign stock (defined as first or second generation) are an increasingly smaller percentage of the total population. In 1940, for instance, the figure was 26 percent, but by 1970 it had fallen to an estimated 15 percent.[6] One factor that is particularly relevant to our subsequent discussion, however, is the change in calculation of the ethnic population by the Census Bureau as of the 1980 survey of population. In the 1970 Census, the government stressed figures on those who actually spoke the mother tongue of the land of origin, whether first or subsequent generations. In the 1980 Census, however, the key question was whether the individual involved identified himself or herself as being from a distinct ethnic background. The contrast between the earlier and later data is striking. Thus, some 963,000 people identified Czech as their "mother tongue" in 1970, whereas almost 2.7 million styled themselves as Czechoslovak in 1980. In the earlier census, approximately 2,438,000 considered Polish to be their native language, whereas in 1980 over 8 million people regarded their heritage as being

Table 1
Eastern European Ethnic Groups in the United States, 1980

Group	Total	Reporting Single Ancestry	Reporting Multiple Ancestry
Albanian	36,658	21,687	16,971
Bulgarian	42,504	21,489	21,015
Czechoslovak	2,669,262	1,150,108	1,519,154
Hungarian	1,776,902	727,223	1,049,679
Polish	8,228,037	3,805,740	4,422,297
Rumanian	315,258	141,675	173,583
Yugoslavic	840,748	420,977	419,601

Source: U.S. Department of Commerce, Bureau of the Census, *1980 Census of Population,* "Ancestry of the Population by State," Table 2 (Washington: Government Printing Office [GPO], 1980), p. 12.

Polish. The same contrast applies across all the ethnic groupings being considered here (e.g., 332,000 "Yugoslavics" in 1970 compared to 841,000 in 1980). Clearly a great many Americans who may have only the vaguest familiarity with the language of their land of origin nevertheless continue to feel at least some significant ethnic ties.[7]

Two other measures of the strength of the Eastern European ethnic presence are the number of foreign-language newspapers and periodicals published as well as various organizations specifically devoted to ethnic concerns, particularly organizations which for purposes of the present discussion demonstrate an interest in American foreign policy. Table 2 summarizes the current situation as far as the media are concerned. The circulation figures in the last column are taken from Louis Gerson's earlier study of ethnic influence on American politics and diplomacy.[8] He used 1958 as his reference year, and a comparison of the earlier figures with the later ones is revealing, particularly when census figures on the total number of Americans commanding the relevant mother tongue are included. Even if there has been some lessening of this ability since 1970, which was the last year in which we had reliable figures on speakers of languages other than English, the decline in the foreign-language media is dramatic.

The main point is that the data on foreign-language capability showed remarkably little variation between 1940 (the Census that Gerson employed in his own study) and the Census of 1970, when language aptitude was still a prime factor in the questions given to American citizens. Thus, in 1970 there were almost 2,440,000 Americans who claimed a knowledge of Polish, compared to 2,420,000 in 1940. The statistics for Hungarians were 447,000 in 1970, 453,000 in 1940;

Table 2

Foreign-Language Media of Eastern European Ethnic Groups in the United States, 1984

Language	Number of News-papers and Periodicals	Total Circulation Reported	1958 Reported Circulation
Albanian	--	--	2,015
Bulgarian	1	2,600	12,048
Czechoslovak	11	84,800	406,410
Hungarian	5	17,300	132,379
Polish	19	546,400	727,218
Romanian	1	4,500	11,207
Yugoslavic	6	95,800	106,248

Source: *The IMS 1984 Ayer Directory of Publications* (Fort Washington, Pa.: IMS Press, 1984).

for Romanians 56,000 in 1970, 65,000 in 1940; and for Czechs, 452,000 in 1970, 520,000 in 1940.[9] Given these results (a relatively modest decrease in the number of Americans able to read the foreign-language press), the declining circulation of foreign-language media is remarkable. To be sure, statements on circulation from these publications are often vague or missing altogether, and, as we have already noted, a decrease in readership of such media does not necessarily negate other ways in which ethnic consciousness can or is being maintained. Nevertheless, the relative decline of the Eastern European foreign-language press does have some implications, particularly in terms of the potential ability of ethnic organization leadership to communicate with their constituents and impress on them a given position on American policy toward the homeland. A leading student of the American Polonia lamented the fact that with "the near disappearance of the once vital Polonia press, the [Polish-American] Congress now finds itself without a vehicle with which to reach a large Polish American audience."[10]

If the foreign-language media are one indicator of ethnic consciousness in the United States, the number and variety of formal organizations (such as the Polish-American Congress) devoted to ethnic concerns are another. Of primary concern here are organizations with at least some announced interest in American policy toward the mother country or toward the Eastern European area as a whole. Many groups operate in the United States today whose prime function is social and cultural and which take little, if any, active part in communicating views to the Administration and Congress on American foreign policy. A spokesman for the Czechoslovak Society of Arts and Sciences (CSAS) for example, which has chapters throughout the United States, states that the purpose of the CSAS is to advance "Czechoslovak culture, research and scholarship." From its inception in 1958, the organization has "maintained its nonpolitical character, refusing to become an instrument of the so-called cold war."[11] Some organizations address themselves to both cultural and political matters. In a third category are groups that are avowedly almost entirely political. Their stated raison d'etre is to influence American policy.

Among the groups with a mixed function, perhaps the best known is the Polish-American Congress (PAC) referred to earlier. The Congress is an umbrella organization with divisions in thirty states and with more than 3,000 Polish-American cultural/fraternal organizations as affiliates.[12] It maintains an office in Washington and an office of the President (currently Aloysius Mazewski). The PAC was founded in 1944 to press for a free and independent postwar Poland. As it evolved, the Congress came to focus on three goals: freedom for Poland, the betterment of Polish-Americans in the United States, and anti-defamation activity.[13] The Polish National Alliance is by far the largest single constituent group within the Congress, with some 300,000 members, assets in excess of $171 million, over $400 million in insurance policies, and licensed affiliates in thirty-six states. The PNA, in accord with the general policies of the Congress, states that its functions are "to serve the best interests of the Polish immigrants" and "to help the land of our origin, Poland, in its struggle for freedom, independence and economic betterment."[14] The Alliance is straightforward in stating its basic premise:

What in our times excites so many sociologists, educators, and political scientists and activists, i.e., ethnicity, is nothing new to the Polish National Alliance. For nearly one hundred years, it has been proclaiming the inconsistencies of the so called "melting pot" theory, and in its place kept alive among its members, and generally, among Americans of Polish origin, the awareness of their ethnic heritage and its value to the pluralistic society and the culture of pluralism of the United States.[15]

Other ethnic organizations with a "mixed function" similar to that of the Polish-American Congress and Polish National Alliance include the American-Hungarian Federation, the Slovak League of America, the Romanian National Council, and the Free Albania Organization. Finally, some groups are specifically organized to sway American foreign policy, among which may be counted the Bulgarian National Front as well as the Bulgarian National Committee, the Croatian National Congress, the Czechoslovak Christian Democracy, the World Federation of Hungarian Freedom Fighters, and perhaps most prominent, the Assembly of Captive European Nations (ACEN).[16]

According to the organization's official literature, the ACEN was founded on September 20, 1954, "to provide an instrument for action on a sustained basis." The overall goal is the freedom and independence of the nations of East and Central Europe, which, the ACEN claims, had a tradition of "national sovereignty and parliamentary democracy." The Assembly is supported by tax deductible voluntary contributions, has an annual meeting in New York to elect officers of the organization, and features a Board of Directors composed of a representative from each of the captive nations as well as a Secretariat headed by a Secretary General who directs the work of the organization and implements its policy. The ACEN notes that it regularly submits "timely memoranda" to the Department of State and to Congress expressing its views, and that members of the Assembly have been invited on numerous occasions to testify before congressional committees concerning Eastern Europe. The ACEN also pursues its activities in Europe. It has contacts with the Council of Europe and has been accorded official observer status with the Parliamentary Assembly of the Council. It also participates in meetings of the Western European Union in Paris and those of the North Atlantic Assembly in Luxembourg. Of particular concern to ACEN is Captive Nations Week in the United States, established by Congress to fall annually in the third week of July until such time as the captive nations achieve their freedom. The President is directed by Congress to issue a proclamation noting Captive Nations Week, and various activities around the country are designed to stress the import of the Captive Nations Resolution. The ACEN claims that Captive Nations Week "is a continued proof of the moral support the American people give the captive nations in their quest for freedom."[17] Altogether the ACEN has probably been the most vocal of those groups pressing for a particular definition of the American national interest in Eastern Europe. How successful such efforts have been in the past and may be in the future is an interesting matter for consideration.

NOTES

1. Louis L. Gerson, "The Influence of Hyphenated Americans on U.S. Diplomacy," in ETHNICITY AND FOREIGN POLICY, ed. Abdul Aziz Said, rev. ed. (New York: Praeger, 1981), 21.

2. Marion T. Bennett, AMERICAN IMMIGRATION POLICIES (Washington, D.C.: Public Affairs Press, 1963), 31.

3. Victor Mamatey, THE UNITED STATES AND EAST CENTRAL EUROPE (Princeton: Princeton University Press, 1957), 24.

4. Woodrow Wilson, HISTORY OF THE AMERICAN PEOPLE (New York: Harper and Brothers, 1902), 212-213.

5. Roy Simon Bryce-Laporte, "The New Immigration: Its Origin, Visibility and Implications for Public Policy," in ETHNICITY AND PUBLIC POLICY, ed. Winston A. Van Horne (Madison: Board of Regents, University of Wisconsin System, 1982), 70.

6. Richard M. Scammon and Ben J. Wattenberg, THE REAL MAJORITY (New York: Coward, McCann and Geoghegan, 1970), 66.

7. For 1970 Census data on those speaking a given "mother tongue," see U.S. Department of Commerce, Bureau of the Census, 1970 CENSUS OF POPULATION. Subject Report 1A: "National Origins and Languages." Table 19 (Washington: GPO, 1970).

8. Louis L. Gerson, THE HYPHENATE IN AMERICAN POLITICS AND DIPLOMACY (Lawrence: University of Kansas Press, 1964).

9. The 1940 data are conveniently contained in Gerson, THE HYPHENATE, 264-265.

10. Donald Pienkos, "The Polish American Congress—An Appraisal," POLISH AMERICAN STUDIES, 36, no. 2 (1979), 26.

11. Czechoslovak Society of Arts and Sciences, BULLETIN (January 1983), 5.

12. NEW YORK TIMES, February 20, 1981, B1.

13. Pienkos, "The Polish American Congress," 1-9.

14. Polish National Alliance, IN THE MAINSTREAMS OF AMERICAN LIFE (Chicago: Alliance Publishers, 1976), 19.

15. Ibid., 6.

16. ASSEMBLY OF CAPTIVE EUROPEAN NATIONS (New York: Assembly of Captive European Nations, n.d.).

17. Ibid.

2.
The Failure
of a Lobby

The number of Americans with ethnic ties to Eastern Europe, the existence of a considerable if declining foreign-language media, and numerous political and cultural organizations devoted to ethnic concerns might lead one to conclude *prima facie* that American foreign policy toward East Central Europe has necessarily been heavily influenced by these factors. How important ethnic groups in general have been to American diplomacy is one question. Daniel Moynihan, for one, argues that they have been vital and that their influence is likely to increase. He writes that "the immigration process is the single most important determinant of American foreign policy," and he concludes that, even though foreign policy "responds to other things as well," it reacts "probably first of all to the primal facts of ethnicity."[1] Bernard Cohen is less certain. In surveying the opinions of high officials in the State Department, he notes that they do stress the multitude of their contacts with ethnic group demands. However, these contacts emerge as being frequently formalistic in character, designed to mute ethnic demands or to manipulate them rather than to respond positively to them. Cohen asserts that it "is hard to discover in these broad contacts much contemporary support for the view that ethnic groups exert a significant impact on American foreign policy."[2] The one exception that Cohen notes is the Jewish lobby vis-à-vis Israel. State Department officials were highly sensitive to the electoral power and political sophistication and organization of this group.

When we turn to ethnic lobbying on American foreign policy toward East Central Europe, however, it is hard not to conclude that at least in this particular case the evidence supports Cohen's overall thesis. Despite an infrastructure that ostensibly might lead to a significant role in the making of policy, Eastern European ethnic groups seemingly have had little direct influence on American diplomacy toward their homelands. This rather sweeping statement requires some elaboration and definition of terms. It would be fatuous to assert that Eastern European ethnics and their organizations have always been united in their specific proposals for U.S. policy toward East Central Europe (a point to be considered in greater detail later, especially with respect to the Polish-American Congress). Overall, however, the most prominent public spokespersons for the ethnic lobby historically stressed two minimum goals and aspired toward two maximum goals. The minimum goals were essentially negative: to prevent the United States from recognizing either formally or tacitly Soviet primacy in Eastern Europe and to restrict U.S. dealings with the "illegitimate" Communist regimes of Eastern Europe as much as possible. The maximum (more "positive") goals of the lobby have been to commit the United States to a conscious policy of liberating Eastern Europe from the hegemony of Moscow and to overturn the Communist regimes of the region.

Despite a brief bow in the direction of liberation in the Republican campaign platform of 1952, Washington has consistently resisted any serious program for detaching the Eastern European states from Russia's orbit by forceful means. There was a sort of comic-opera effort to parachute a resistance force into Albania in 1950, but following the total failure of this scheme, U.S. strategy in effect conceded that there would be no attempt to alter the status quo in Eastern Europe by violence.[3] As far as the minimum goals of the ethnic lobby are concerned, it might appear that at least for a time Washington did pursue quite a tough course reflective of ethnic desires. The United States protested strenuously, for example, at the establishment of the people's democracies in Eastern Europe on the Stalinist model following World War II. The postwar rhetoric continued on through the 1950s and early 1960s until President Johnson's "bridge-building" initiatives signaled a basic change in policy. ("Bridge-building" was an Administration term for the development of more positive relationships with individual Eastern European Communist countries.) Stringent economic measures were applied against the Communist regimes of Eastern Europe, with the exception of Yugoslavia and to a lesser extent of Poland, and the relevant governments were subject to as virulent an anti-Communist rhetoric as was their Soviet hegemon. To conclude that this policy was a reaction at least in part to domestic ethnic pressures, however, ignores the fact that to the degree U.S. policy was relatively tough in dealing with Eastern Europe, decisions on the U.S. stance were patently derived from a broad policy consensus in Washington concerning the nature of the threat to America's international position.

Thus, in the period 1945-48, the United States made much of Soviet policy in Eastern Europe precisely because Soviet behavior there was viewed as a test case for their willingness to cooperate on a whole range of international matters. Eastern Europe was adopted as a symbol of whether the wartime grand alliance could survive the war with Germany. Similarly in the 1950s—again with the exception of Yugoslavia and Poland—Washington showed little inclination to deal with the East European Communist regimes precisely because the notion of a unified Communist bloc was still taken seriously at that time. It was also felt that any sort of economic aid, for instance, to an individual Communist regime in the area would redound to the ultimate benefit of the Sino-Soviet bloc. The fact that certain ethnic groups applauded such rigidity—while at the same time calling for more aggressive actions—does not imply that their importunings were a serious factor in the policy design itself.

The most that the Eastern European ethnic lobby seemingly has been able to do in the years since 1945 has been to mount a sometimes effective delaying action against Administration plans to normalize relations with the Communist countries of East Central Europe, that is, plans that contemplated the abandonment of even the minimum goals of the ethnic lobby. One tactic employed in past years was economic reprisal. In response to President Johnson's tentative efforts at "bridge-building" to Eastern Europe in the middle 1960s, ethnic organizations in this country organized boycotts of goods imported into the United States from various East European countries. American cigarette manufacturers, for example, who attempted to use Yugoslav tobacco in their products felt the wrath of anti-Communist Yugoslav-Americans. A campaign against consumption of Polish hams undercut the Administration's opening to Warsaw. The Firestone Rubber Company was pressured into giving up an important contract with Romania. The temper of all these efforts was perhaps best caught in the slogan invented by a Florida chiropractor and placed in the local press, advising customers to "buy your Communist merchandise at 'Super Giant.' "[4]

George Kennan has spoken bitterly of his term as American Ambassador to Yugoslavia from 1961 to 1963 during which Croatian immigrant groups in the United States "never failed to oppose any move to better American-Yugoslav relations or to take advantage of any opportunity to make trouble between the two countries. And this they succeeded, with monotonous regularity, in doing."[5] The kind of obstructionism Kennan alluded to was responsible for temporarily denying most-favored-nation trade status to the Yugoslavs. Yet in the grand scheme of American foreign policy during these years a period of American-Yugoslav tension may have been unfortunate but was not a critical setback to the overall thrust of American diplomacy. What is important is that the efforts of the Croatian lobby to reverse basic American policy toward Yugoslavia—which since 1950 involved a tolerance of and even support for Belgrade's form of national communism—were almost totally futile.

A particularly compelling testament to the relative ineffectiveness of the Eastern European ethnic lobby in influencing American policy could be seen during the era of detente in the 1970s. The pattern of increased American trade and diplomatic interaction with Eastern Europe, accompanied by the opening to Moscow and a tacit consent to a Soviet sphere of influence in Eastern Europe, which were general features of the diplomacy of the Nixon, Ford, and Carter administrations, moved along with hardly so much as a bow in the direction of involved ethnic organizations. Moreover, the considerable electoral success enjoyed by, for example, President Nixon in the 1972 campaign among Americans of East European background testified to the fact that, while the leadership of the various groups may have been angered by the President's policy, this outrage seemingly did not extend to the rank and file, at least to the extent of causing any noticeable protest vote against Nixon's diplomacy.[6]

The evidence at the time in fact suggested that the ethnic lobby had become so fragmented that it perhaps faced dissolution as any sort of coherent force. A pamphlet issued by the ACEN indicated that of thirteen offices previously maintained by ACEN in various foreign countries, only one still remained active (in Denmark). The *ACEN News*, the bimonthly publication of the Plenary Assembly of the ACEN, ceased publication altogether.[7] Many of the political groupings of Eastern European ethnics referred to earlier seemed to have disappeared entirely. In one study which the present author undertook, an attempt was made to communicate with some twenty-four ethnic organizations which were listed in the *Encyclopedia of Associations* as having announced political or foreign policy interests. A listing in the *Encyclopedia*, however, seemed to be the extent of activity for many of these groups. Eight letters were returned indicating that the organization was no longer at its listed address and had no forwarding address; in all, only three responses were received. This decline in the ethnic lobby, incidentally, seems to have continued to the present day. The 1984 edition of the *Encyclopedia of Associations* lists formerly active groups such as the Hungarian Committee, the International Peasant Union, the National Committee for the Liberation of Czechoslovakia, the Pan-Albanian Federation, the American Bulgarian League, and the United American Croats as either being defunct or having no known address since the middle 1970s.

One of the responses to my earlier survey was in itself reflective of the decay of the ethnic lobby. It was from Ivan Docheff, president of the Bulgarian National Front since its founding in 1947, who lamented that in the past he was more optimistic about U.S. policy but that in recent years his optimism had faded. He stressed that the front was the "strongest Bulgarian anti-Communist organization in exile" and that its most effective technique of persuasion was "the mass demonstration and memorandums signed by thousands." The terms *strongest* and *most effective* seemed highly relative, however, in the context of Docheff's bitterness about the U.S. "sellout" of Bulgarian freedom and his concession that the front had been able to do little to prevent it. He ascribed this lack of success to "foreign and Communist infiltration" of the Washington decision-making apparatus. Docheff rather plaintively concluded that the only way the front could be effective in the future was to mobilize the power of the Bulgarian vote in the United States to pressure the politicians into greater sympathy toward the front's position (not, one would have thought, a very promising recipe for increased influence in Washington, given the scope of the Bulgarian vote).[8]

MANIPULATION OF THE ETHNIC LOBBY

The broad assertion that Eastern European ethnic groups have been largely absent from a position of influence in U.S. foreign policy does not mean, however, that they have not at certain times been perceived by various individuals and institutions in the Washington establishment as being a potentially powerful force. On the one hand, if genuinely aroused and united, they have been thought perhaps to have the ability seriously to disrupt current diplomatic maneuverings or even force policy in a direction not desired by the Administration. On the other hand, they have sometimes been seen as "targets of opportunity", providing real if perhaps unknowing support for a course of action Washington wanted to adopt in any case. The first perception has led to a variety of efforts to diffuse ethnic resentments. In many instances, this has involved—to put it bluntly—misleading and confusing the ethnic community. The second type of perception has resulted in episodes of outright manipulation.

For example, President Ford received a number of Eastern European ethnic leaders at the White House shortly before the 1976 election in order to assure them that he did recognize current Soviet domination of Eastern Europe (an attempt to clarify his statements in the debate with Jimmy Carter) but did not accept it as legitimate or valid. This meeting revealed the obvious concern that Ford and his advisers felt about an Eastern European foreign policy protest vote that might be decisive in the coming election—which in itself was an unexamined assumption—and his unembarrassed willingness to assert a policy position that some might argue was at considerable variance with his signing of the Helsinki accords ratifying postwar territorial arrangements in Europe.[9]

Perhaps the classic example of the ethnic community being misled and at the same time manipulated was the so-called liberation plank in the Republican party platform of 1952. Denouncing the "negative, futile, and immoral policy of containment that abandons countless human beings to a despotism and godless terrorism," the Republicans committed themselves to a strategy of liberating the "enslaved" countries of Eastern Europe from Soviet control. The methods by which this would be brought about were rather vaguely expressed, but the clear impression was left with ethnic voters that a Republican administration would be pursuing a much harder line in Eastern Europe than its Democratic predecessors. In actuality, Eisenhower almost immediately began backing away from the liberation plank. He stressed that liberation would only be pursued through peaceful means, and after a speech in Philadelphia in September, he virtually avoided mention of liberation altogether. The clear indication that Eisenhower Administration policy on Eastern Europe would in practice differ little from that already being pursued, however, was not widely perceived, given the initial attention and publicity extended to the liberation plank. It was also notable that other Republican spokespersons, particularly former Ambassador to Poland Arthur Lane, pursued the liberation theme aggressively throughout the campaign despite Eisenhower's tacit disavowal of it. Subsequent U.S. inaction vis-à-vis anti-regime uprisings in East Germany, Poland, and Hungary was testament to the essential duplicity in the talk of liberation in the 1952 campaign.[10]

The liberation plank was designed in part to deflect the presumed wrath of Eastern Europeans from the Republican party and focus it on the Democrats.

The assumption was that ethnic voters from East Europe were so angered by the course of events in the homeland that they would cast a potentially decisive protest vote in the 1952 elections against any who dared defend recent U.S. foreign policy. Yet the Republican strategists also saw liberation as a positive step that would help usher their party into the White House. Not only would the Republicans decry past events, but they would also promise a future policy that would and should bring a decisive electoral reward. In the event, it is questionable how great the reward was. To be sure, Eisenhower was able to cut into the Polish allegiance to the Democrats, whose share of the Polish vote decreased from approximately 70 percent in 1948 to about 50 percent in 1952.[11] Some of this switch to the Republicans may have been due to Eisenhower's putative commitment to liberation, but a general disillusionment with the Democrats played a major role as well. To the degree that foreign policy played a part in the electoral outcome, the evidence is that it was a general dissatisfaction with U.S. foreign policy, affecting both ethnic and nonethnic voter alike and centering around the stalemate in Korea, that was important. It might also be noted parenthetically that at the same time as the Republicans were supposedly calling for the liberation of Eastern Europe, their party platform supported new restrictions on immigration. At best, then, Eastern European ethnics faced mixed prospects for their interests in the event of a Republican triumph.

We have discussed the manipulation of the ethnic community in terms of U.S. political campaigns. The exploitation of ethnic groups in the interests of official policy ought to be considered as well. Washington has frequently seen such groups as quite useful for gaining any variety of goals. Such methods have not been applied exclusively to groups with an ethnic basis. President Roosevelt, for instance, encouraged the development of external pressure groups in 1940-41 devoted to U.S. aid to the British cause. Roosevelt, of course, was quite anxious to do what these groups would come to urge him to do, particularly convoying British ships with war materials across the Atlantic in the Spring of 1941. For purposes of public relations, however, he could cite the "pressure" from such organizations as a reason for agreeing to an important turn in U.S. policy.[12] Sometimes the process doesn't have to be quite so devious. On occasion, the Administration has looked to existing groups simply for allies in defending a new policy against possible opposition by, say, the Congress. A good example was the Polish aid program in 1957. In response to Wladyslaw Gomulka's successful defiance of Soviet attempts to crush the nascent Polish drive for autonomy in October 1956, the White House and State Department were resolved on a program of aid to support Gomulka's struggle for independence. Strong antagonism to this measure was anticipated from powerful segments of Congress. In order to blunt this opposition, the State Department called up "political reinforcements" in the guise of certain members of the Polish-American community in the United States. Polish ethnic groups were not totally enamored of Gomulka (who after all remained a Communist), but at least some of them did on balance favor U.S. support of him in his role as a defender of Polish autonomy against the Russians. As it turned out, the support of such groups for Administration policy was an important ingredient in its eventual passage.[13]

Sometimes policymakers have employed a domestic group, not simply as a tool for bringing general public opinion or the Congress along on an issue, but also as a device for pressuring foreign governments into accepting a position that Washington has seen as highly desirable in general foreign policy terms. A prime example was the Polish question in 1944-45. In terms of the geopolitical balance in Europe, Roosevelt and later Truman were greatly concerned about Poland's maintaining at least some independence from Soviet control. This necessitated a regime that, even though containing Communist representation, would not be dominated by it. The United States was also worried that Poland might be granted too much German territory in the West (as compensation for the readjustment of Poland's Eastern border). This would lead to an enduring German revanchism that necessarily would make Poland dependent on Soviet arms for protection. In sum, the question of the internal Polish regime and the Polish frontiers was seen as important to maintaining the European equilibrium, which in turn was linked to the overall U.S. security position.

In attempting to gain Stalin's assent to the U.S. approach to the Polish question, much was made of the pressures that the U.S. representatives supposedly felt from the Polish-American lobby in the United States. The implication was that, if Stalin forced the U.S. negotiators to accept an unfavorable settlement of the Polish issue, the electoral retaliation of Polish-Americans would be such that the Russians would have to deal with a far more unpalatable Republican Administration and Congress on future issues. At the Teheran Conference in 1943, for example, Roosevelt informed Stalin in a private meeting that as far as he personally was concerned, he "would like to see the Eastern border moved further to the West and the Western moved to the River Oder." He was quick to add, however, that he could not publicly take part in any such arrangement because of his fears of retaliation by American voters of Polish extraction in the 1944 elections, who could hardly be expected to be enthusiastic about loss of Polish territory in the East.[14] Similarly, on April 22, 1945, Truman told Soviet Foreign Minister Molotov that he simply had to have a representative government in Warsaw selected through free elections "because of the effect on American public opinion."[15] Now both Roosevelt and Truman were undoubtedly concerned about the Polish vote. Unmistakably, however, it was useful to stress the sanctions of U.S. ethnic opinion in attempting to persuade Stalin to accept a position that U.S. leaders would have adhered to in any case.

NOTES

1. Daniel P. Moynihan and Nathan Glazer, ETHNICITY: THEORY AND EXPERIENCE (Cambridge, Mass.: Harvard University Press, 1975), 22-23.

2. Bernard C. Cohen, THE PUBLIC'S IMPACT ON FOREIGN POLICY (Boston: Little, Brown and Co., 1973), 104.

3. The development and execution of the Albanian scheme are described by Kim Philby in MY SECRET WAR (New York: Dell, 1968). Philby was a high official in the British intelligence service who later defected to the Soviet Union after many years as an agent of Moscow. He admits in his book that his communications to his Soviet superiors may not have been totally unrelated to the failure of the Albanian plan.

4. John P. Leacacos, FIRES IN THE IN-BASKET (Cleveland: World Publishing Co., 1968), 234; William Chittick, STATE DEPARTMENT, PRESS AND PRESSURE GROUPS (New York: Wiley-Interscience, 1970), 224-225.

5. George F. Kennan, MEMOIRS 1950-1963 (Boston: Little, Brown and Co., 1972), 286-287.

6. Andrzej Korbonski, "The United States and East Europe," CURRENT HISTORY (May 1973), 226.

7. ASSEMBLY OF CAPTIVE EUROPEAN NATIONS (New York: Assembly of Captive European Nations, n.d.).

8. Personal communication from Ivan Docheff, president of the Bulgarian National Front, February 17, 1976.

9. NEW YORK TIMES, October 13, 1976, 24. Earlier, the President had personally called Aloysius Mazewski, head of the Polish-American Congress, to apologize for saying that there was "no Soviet domination of Eastern Europe."

10. Robert A. Divine, FOREIGN POLICY AND PRESIDENTIAL ELECTIONS, 1952-1960 (New York: New Viewpoints, 1974), 50-56.

11. Ibid., 84.

12. Robert Divine, ROOSEVELT AND WORLD WAR II (Baltimore: Johns Hopkins University Press, 1969), 42.

13. Stephen Kaplan, "United States Aid to Poland 1957-1964: Concerns, Objectives and Obstacles," WESTERN POLITICAL QUARTERLY 28, no. 1 (March 1975), 147-166.

14. Divine, ROOSEVELT AND WORLD WAR II, 92.

15. Stephen Ambrose, RISE TO GLOBALISM (Baltimore: Penguin Books, 1971), 113.

3.

The Reasons Why

It has been argued here that with regard to U.S. foreign policy Eastern European ethnic groups in this country have been exploited more often than they themselves have been exploitative and that their conscious efforts to influence diplomacy have been largely irrelevant and unavailing. Some comments on the overall social and political environment in which they have had to operate are now in order. In many respects, it is not the fact that the Eastern European ethnic lobby has failed that is so illuminating, but the circumstances surrounding and giving rise to this failure.

First, we have to recognize that an organization like the ACEN is in essence only one of a larger class of specialized interest groups that have traditionally attempted to influence American foreign policy. Most such groups have no particular ethnic identification. They can be based on common economic interest, on concern about a particular foreign policy issue (such as arms control), or on any of a variety of desiderata. Foreign policy lobbies can hope to bring their influences to bear in a number of ways. There is the traditional avenue whereby leaders or representative delegations from such groups send messages to or seek an audience with individuals within the official decision-making apparatus. Of a somewhat different character are approaches made not to career officials but to those in Congress or even to the President himself or to his aides who are concerned with protecting his political position. Failing to achieve a response in these arenas, the lobby can work within one or both of the major political parties, attempt to mobilize electoral power during given elections, and as a last resort appeal to general public opinion in the hope that a groundswell of support here will be reflected both at the polls and in the actions of government.

As far as the foreign policy professionals are concerned (the term *professionals* here referring to those with an official career involvement in foreign affairs), without question the State Department and various nongovernmental groups interested in foreign policy share to some extent a symbiotic relationship. As one authority has stated, the department "has a stake in reaching the American public and its constituent pressure groups with information about foreign policy; it also has an interest in finding out how its policies are affecting various groups in the domestic public."[1] The groups themselves, of course, have an interest in gathering information on department policies, passing this on to their members, and bringing their own views to the attention of officials.

Nevertheless, the evidence is that at least from the perspective of the State Department itself, the relationship between the professionals and the interest groups is far from an equal one. The department may welcome or at least tolerate delegations from various organizations and on occasion may work in concert with them, but the general pattern is for policy to be arrived at within a closed circle of officials based on some general notions of the overall national interest and shielded as much as possible from the importunings or pressures of some interested lobby. As a desk officer involved with Eastern European affairs once commented, "Our business is to figure out what the best policy is for the United States; it is not to let every group which has its own political interest in that policy have it."[2] Indeed, there is a general prejudice in the department against groups that are avowedly committed to a particular line in some policy area. To the degree that this position is constantly thrust on officials, it is generally given less and less heed. Former Secretary of State Dean Acheson neatly summarized the professionals' creed: "There are so many opportunities for special groups to profit at the general expense that we cannot expect concern for the public welfare to be sufficient as the sole restraint upon them."[3] It is of interest in this connection that when Congressman Edward Derwinski, a veteran of twenty-four years on the Hill and a prominent member of the House Foreign Affairs Committee, was appointed Counselor at the State Department in late 1982, he expressed considerable dismay at how little his State Department colleagues did take into account domestic political factors in making policy. He noted that the White House frequently would add such factors in before policy was finally determined, but

I've made the point here [the State Department] we should anticipate the White House concerns. Let's take Poland. Automatically the White House will think how will Polish-Americans react to this which isn't necessarily the reaction here. By the very nature of the process, the career diplomat would like not to have to take into account domestic political pressure.[4]

To be sure, there are interest groups and there are interest groups. The foreign policy professionals do distinguish between both the legitimacy and the practical political clout of various organizations. Such groups that do have influence, however, tend to share certain characteristics, and a review of these indicates that few, if any, Eastern European ethnic lobbies have enjoyed the requisite qualities. According to an analysis by the State Department itself, an effective lobbying organization has to be national in scope and importance, have an interest in diverse aspects of international affairs, have effective informational and educational media for the dissemination of knowledge about foreign affairs, and, perhaps most important of all, have a reputation from the perspective of the State Department and other Executive agencies of being "responsible" in their approach.[5] On each of these points it is clear that, fairly or unfairly, the ethnic lobby on Eastern Europe has been seen as wanting. The criteria of diversity of interests and reputation for responsibility have been particularly important in this regard. One State Department official commented, for instance, that most pressure groups in foreign policy, not excluding the ethnic lobby, "have a hobby horse which they beat to death; they use every opportunity to press their views." Another stated that he would be more inclined to solicit group views on policy matters if the relevant groups ever allowed him to forget them.[6] The reputation of Eastern European ethnic groups for tunnel vision has clearly worked to their disadvantage; there is an inherent benefit in seeming to be interested in all phases of foreign policy simply as concerned citizens. As far as the image of moderation and responsibility is concerned, the so-called lunatic fringe syndrome is operative. Proposals outside the current mainstream of American policy tend to have a difficult time getting a hearing, even if they have elements of logic and perhaps intellectual sophistication to recommend them. The protest against the Vietnam War in its early phase, for example, fell into this category and was accordingly ineffective.[7] The message of the ethnic lobby on Eastern Europe has suffered from the same disability. The impression one gets is that even relatively subtle and well-thought-out appeals from this group have been dismissed mainly because as a group they have been regarded as incorrigibly beyond the pale of respectable opinion.

A number of other factors are involved in the State Department's inclination not to take ethnic lobbies seriously—and in particular the appeals emanating from the Eastern European lobby. For one thing, most of them seem to lack any substantial power base. Not only are their numbers small in many cases, but, as I will discuss further on, the suspicion among the professionals is that for the rank and file of the ethnic community foreign policy questions are generally far less important than may be the case for the community leaders. The department's distinction between leaders and rank and file is in itself a major reason for the ineffectiveness of ethnic lobbying. Simply put, officials do not believe that ethnic leaders in many instances represent their supposed constituencies. They are often viewed as out of touch and more interested in their own positions, ego gratification, and possible governmental rewards than in substantive policy matters. The fact that the Bulgarian National Front has had only one president since 1947 does seem to indicate a certain lack of mass participation and vitality in the organization. Attitudes toward the leaders of the Polish-American Congress in 1944 are also of interest. As I have discussed, Poland was a major campaign issue that year, and the Polish-American Congress was the most visible and most vocal of the ethnic organizations lobbying the government on the matter. U.S. officials, however, viewed the executives of the Congress, particularly its president, Charles Rozmarek, as being interested less in the fate of the homeland than in the oppor-

120350

tunities "either to increase their power and hold over Polish-Americans or to obtain prominent positions in government."[8] It would be unfair to assert that ethnic leaders are invariably interested mainly in their own personal gratification. What is important, however, is that in many cases they are perceived in this fashion by those they are trying to influence.

Another reason for the State Department's lack of attentiveness to the ethnic lobby stems from the rather vague impression that it generally presents. The relevant groups are so fragmented and haphazard in the type of contacts they maintain with the department that it is hard for them to give a serious impression. Even Polish organizations, which are perhaps respected more than any other Eastern European group if only because of their relative influence in Congress, are viewed in this manner. As one department official commented,

While the Poles have lots of organizations, I have a feeling that they exist more on paper than anywhere else. . . . These people are numerous in key Midwest and Northeast industrial areas; they are a sought-after political group. But when it comes to anything other than elections, as for example to the bringing of influence to bear on a particular issue, it all gets rather amorphous.[9]

The very multitude of ethnic organizations as well as other nonethnic groups (especially those organized around a specific economic interest) in foreign policy is frequently welcomed by the State Department because under a system of countervailing influence the various groups often neutralize one another, leaving the department free to do what it wants. As one official commented, "We always welcome opposite views because that enables us to make a decision quite apart from these pressures."[10] The latter part of the statement once again reflects the overarching reason why the foreign policy professionals are generally unreceptive to ethnic pressures on foreign policy: their firmly held conviction that U.S. diplomacy should be developed in the context of what is in the overall national interest of the United States and that a determination of national interest is properly the preserve of career foreign policy specialists and not some interested minority group. This conviction is reinforced by the fact that historically the immigration process has not led to the United States having ethnic populations proportionate to the objective importance of the various foreign lands from whence they came. Thus, there are more Polish-Americans than Russian-Americans, but this hardly serves as a guide to the relative significance of Polish-American versus Soviet-American diplomatic interaction.

Another factor in professional disdain for ethnic interest group activity relates to the matter of information. The range of domestic problems is so vast that quite often a given interest group will have specialized information that will be taken seriously by executive departments as well as by Congress. In foreign policy, however, the professionals tend to feel that they usually possess more facts than the groups importuning them. As two authorities on this question have put it, "On foreign policy questions interest groups seem no better off than Congress in terms of the amount of information each has and in a considerably weaker position than either the State or the Defense Department."[11] If information is power, it is evident that on the range of issues associated with Eastern Europe, the "information" and analyses of ethnic groups have generally been regarded as limited in scope and quite frequently outdated or twisted by the ideological biases of those presenting them, especially since many of the most fervent representatives of such groups have not in fact been in their homelands for years or even decades.

The government is responsive to interest groups partially in terms of how directly such groups can demonstrate that a given policy or its alternative helps or hurts its interests. The American Trial Lawyer's Association, for example, may be able to do this with some effect as far as no-fault automobile insurance is concerned, but demonstrating a cause-and-effect relationship in foreign policy is generally much more difficult. As one of the leading students of interest group activity has stated, "Domestic politics often have direct economic consequences for citizens; these consequences are fairly easily demonstrable in a message. Foreign issues, on the other hand, usually have more indirect consequences (tariff questions excepted) and it is difficult to demonstrate in a message how a certain group might be hurt."[12] It is evident that successive administrations have indeed found it difficult to understand how the interests of Americans of Eastern European ethnic background were sufficiently damaged by the continuance of Communist regimes in Eastern Europe to warrant a fundamental change in American policy. To be sure, the existence of such regimes, particularly because of their subservience to Moscow, was a bitter disappointment. Whether this essentially abstract and emotional aversion warranted a course of American action that threatened a potentially catastrophic showdown with the Soviet Union was not something most policymakers have found difficult to resolve.

The theory has been advanced that "those issues that attract the attention of special publics, but that attract little general public attention, are more open to group influence than issues that attract wide and/or intense public scrutiny."[13] If this argument is accepted, it would presumably provide for a relatively significant Eastern European ethnic influence on American policy, since East Central Europe has been the object of little attention or knowledge on the part of the American public as a whole. This conclusion is largely negated, however, by two considerations. Carrying out the ultimate policy proposals of most of the relevant ethnic lobbies would have involved such serious consequences as to arouse and involve "general public attention." It was no doubt in recognition of this fact that successive administrations have deflected such proposals. In addition, over the past forty years on only a few occasions has the ethnic desire of liberating at least part of the homeland seemed within potential reach. The Hungarian uprising of 1956 was a prime example: this presumably was a promising time for restoring Hungary to the Western cause. Yet it is precisely in times of crisis such as this that various studies have shown the President and his advisers to have widest latitude. The country tends to rally around its leaders and to accept whatever judgments concerning the national interest they choose to make. The ironic result is that it has been exactly during the periods of what the ethnic lobby might consider maximum opportunity that various administrations have been most free from their special pressures.

It has been argued here that the foreign policy "professionals" are basically unsympathetic to giving ethnic groups a significant role in policy. A potential alternative open to these groups in such a case has been to redirect their efforts away from the career civil servants and the Executive branch generally, and instead to concentrate their efforts on the elected members of the Congress. Indeed, the separation-of-powers system and the pluralistic character of decision-making in the United States, present especially on matters of domestic import but also in foreign policy, theoretically give ethnic organizations a number of different opportunities for bringing influence to bear successfully. The record here is once again not a very impressive one.

To the extent that Eastern European groups have been able to have an effect in Congress, it has occurred substantially in the House, whose members face re-election every two years and some of whom must contend with large Eastern European ethnic concentrations in their districts. Certainly, some House members in this century have stood out as tireless representatives of ethnic concerns. Adolf Sabath (D.-Ill.), for instance, the first representative of the new immigrants in Congress, was instrumental in paving the way for a sympathetic Administration reception for Thomas Masaryk's trips to the United States to enlist U.S. support for an independent Czechoslovakia after World War I. Representative Charles Kersten (R.-Wis.) fought strenuously in the 1950s for an aggressive program of liberation of Eastern Europe from Soviet domination and for the breaking off of U.S. diplomatic relations with the Communist regimes of the area.[14] More recently, Congresswoman Mary Rose Oaker (D.-Ohio) took a leading role in attempting to frustrate the Carter Administration's plan to return the Crown of St. Stephen to Hungary as a step toward supposedly improving Hungarian-American relations. (The Crown, the symbol of the Hungarian nation, had been in American custody since 1945.) The activities of these three can be explained in part by their own heritage or by the ethnic composition of their particular districts. Oaker, for example, represents the Cleveland area with a large Hungarian-American constituency. Some congressmen of the current generation continue to carry the flag even without obvious motivations for so doing. When Senator Steve Symms (R.-Idaho) was serving in the House of Representatives, he distinguished himself by his support of Captive Nations Week, even though the number of Eastern European ethnics in Idaho is limited. Typical was his address before a World Anti-Communist League mass rally in Taipei in 1975 extolling the virtues of the Captive Nations Resolution and its importance for U.S. foreign policy.[15]

The above examples of congressional commitment to Eastern European ethnics, however, do not constitute evidence of a significant base of influence for pressuring the White House or the State Department. With the exception of Sabath, it is notable that those like Kersten who have boldly pushed specific measures for the ethnics rather than just harmless generalities have been deflected by the Executive branch and to a significant extent quarantined by fellow members of Congress. Thus, Kersten's efforts to swing the Congress behind a U.S. policy of liberating Eastern Europe were eventually muffled by his own peers. It appears that much of the sentiment previously ascribed to the State Department as far as ethnic influence on foreign policy is concerned also has something of a home in the Congress. At least among the foreign policy establishment of the Congress—concentrated especially in the two foreign relations committees—pressure groups seen as having an unduly narrow focus on a given policy issue have generally been shunted aside.

NOTES

1. William Chittick, STATE DEPARTMENT, PRESS AND PRESSURE GROUPS (New York: Wiley-Interscience, 1970), 220.

2. Bernard Cohen, THE PUBLIC'S IMPACT ON FOREIGN POLICY (Boston: Little, Brown and Co., 1973), 63.

3. Dean Acheson, POWER AND DIPLOMACY (Cambridge, Mass.: Harvard University Press, 1958), 28.

4. NEW YORK TIMES, July 1, 1983, A10.

5. Chittick, STATE DEPARTMENT, 224-225.

6. Ibid., 234.

7. Stephen A. Garrett, IDEALS AND REALITY: AN ANALYSIS OF THE DEBATE OVER VIETNAM (Washington: University Press of America, 1978).

8. Louis L. Gerson, THE HYPHENATE IN RECENT AMERICAN POLITICS AND DIPLOMACY (Lawrence: University of Kansas Press, 1964), 140.

9. Cohen, THE PUBLIC'S IMPACT ON FOREIGN POLICY, 105.

10. Chittick, STATE DEPARTMENT, 32.

11. John C. Spanier and Eric Uslaner, HOW AMERICAN FOREIGN POLICY IS MADE (New York: Praeger, 1974), 84.

12. Lester Milbrath, "Interest Groups and Foreign Policy," in DOMESTIC SOURCES OF FOREIGN POLICY, ed. James Rosenau (New York: Free Press, 1967), 241.

13. Ibid., 249.

14. Bennett Kovrig, THE MYTH OF LIBERATION (Baltimore: Johns Hopkins University Press, 1973), 102-105.

15. U.S. Congress, House of Representatives, CONGRESSIONAL RECORD, 94th Congress, 1st session (Washington: GPO, 1975), E4028.

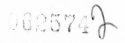

4.
Alternatives

If the Eastern European ethnic community has generally been unsuccessful in its dealings with the professional foreign policy establishment, this has not meant that the relevant groups necessarily had to abandon their attempt to influence American policy toward Eastern Europe. Two other avenues of influence were in theory available.

POWER OF THE BALLOT BOX

The first of these avenues involved using the political process itself to convey pressure for a change in policy. The desk officer in the State Department may not want to return the calls of an émigré organization demanding the liberation of Hungary, but he clearly does not perform his tasks in a total political vacuum. Even if the foreign policy "professionals" would prefer to define the national interest of the United States in analytical isolation, they still have some sense of domestic political realities (despite Derwinski's lament about their apolitical mode of operation). There is evidence, in fact, that the State Department is quite conscious of political forces in Congress and feels bound by these far more than by pressure applied directly from the outside by various interest organizations. An office director in the State Department has commented that "many of the higher-ups in the Department are sensitive to Congressional opinion. . . . They hesitate to recommend [a policy proposal] if they themselves think that it will go sour."[1] Our earlier point was that based on the past record the Eastern European ethnic lobby has not been able to make up in Congress what it has lost or never had in the State Department as far as concrete influence on policy was concerned. As one study put it, Eastern European ethnics have received for their labors in the legislative branch "little more than insertions into the Congressional Record of prepared speeches supporting their cause by members of the House and Senate."[2] At the same time, there has always been the theoretical possibility that through the electoral process, the ethnic lobby could create a much more responsive Congress which in turn would have a measurable effect on the deliberations of the State Department.

There is also the opinion at the White House itself. Direct orders from the President presumably have to be obeyed, even if they go against the consensus of professional judgment. Actually, this notion has to be qualified somewhat. There are myriad examples of the bureaucracy being able to deflect or even to smother seemingly precise foreign policy directives from the President.[3] Nevertheless, another option always open to Eastern European ethnic organizations was to employ electoral pressures to install not only a Congress but also a Presidency that would be responsive to their demands and would compel the State Department and other Executive agencies to conform to a new line despite their professional doubts.

At first glance, the prospects for using the vote to influence American policy toward Eastern Europe would seem to have been a promising course of action for Eastern European ethnic groups in the United States. There was the example of the Jewish vote and American support of Israel to offer encouragement. A great deal of evidence seemed to point to the fact that Jewish electoral power in certain large cities, particularly New York, exerted heavy pressure on successive administrations, particularly Democratic administrations, not to stray too far from uncritical support of Israel.[4] Moreover, the factor that gave the Jewish vote its supposed potency—that is, its concentration in swing states such as New York and New Jersey—also applied to the Eastern European ethnic population. Michigan, Illinois, Ohio, and Pennsylvania, for instance, had unusually large concentrations of Americans of Eastern European ethnic background. One study determined that the ten states with the most significant numbers of Polish-Americans represented 203 of the 270 electoral votes needed to elect a President. The same analysis pointed out that at least thirty-four congressional districts also had a large Polish-American constituency.[5] In the post-1945 period, an increasing number of congressmen were themselves of Eastern European heritage. At the end of the 1958 congressional campaign, for example, the Polish-American press exulted over the fact that an unprecedented thirteen Americans of Polish descent had been elected to Congress.[6]

Perhaps what should have been the most encouraging sign of all, however, was the fact that American politicians of both parties and at various levels of elective office took the "ethnic vote" seriously and designed their campaigns on the premise that ethnic identification was a key factor in voting choice. The late Theodore White, one of the best known chroniclers of contemporary American presidential elections, put the point vividly: "No subject is more intensely discussed in the privacy of any campaign headquarters, either state or national, than the ethnic origins of the American people and their block voting habits." White stressed that certain individuals build careers "on being (or claiming to be) experts on the Polish vote, the Jewish vote, the Negro vote, the Scandinavian vote, the Italian vote, and what the rights, expectations, offices and dignities of each of these blocs are."[7] A review of the measures which the national party organizations have taken to appeal to the various ethnic groupings is of interest in this regard.

Both the Republican and Democratic national committees currently have sections permanently established for appealing to Americans of diverse ethnic backgrounds. Among the Democrats, the Nationalities Division dates to 1932 and was at the time one of the campaign arms of the party. It is normally headed by a chairman who also bears the title of vice-chairman of the Democratic National Committee. The Nationalities Division is composed of twenty-four separate nationality sections ranging from Armenian to Yugoslav. Each has its own separate chairman. The division works closely with the presidents of the national ethnic organizations, with editors of ethnic newspapers, and with "opinion-molders" among the ethnics. The function of the division is twofold: to convey the views of ethnic groups to Democratic political candidates, and to advise these groups of the party positions on various domestic and foreign policy issues and the rationale for them.[8]

The Republicans lagged behind the Democrats in having a full-time nationalities division of the National Committee. To be sure, a heavy Republican appeal to the ethnic vote was made in past presidential campaigns, especially those of 1944, 1948, and 1952. These appeals, however, were essentially orchestrated by ad hoc sections of the National Committee, which ceased functioning once the campaign was concluded. In 1968 the Republican party finally established the National Republican Heritage (Nationalities) Groups Council as a permanent operating branch of the party's national committee. Its first chairman was Laszlo Pasztor, a Hungarian freedom fighter in 1956. Initially, some fifteen state Republican Nationalities Councils were set up under the overall supervision of the Heritage Groups Council (now expanded to twenty-five, in addition to more than thirty-three Nationality Federations organized across state boundaries). A GOP *Nationalities News* was first issued in October 1971 as a newsletter specifically directed toward ethnic concerns.[9] The establishment of the council demonstrated that the Nixon Administration for one now saw an historic opportunity to woo the ethnic vote away from its traditional Democratic affiliation. The President spoke directly to this point in a letter to Pasztor designed for distribution to the delegates to the first organizational meeting of the Heritage Groups Council. "The formation of this permanent auxiliary to the Republican Party represents a major landmark in our party's history," Nixon said. "To bring together the best of our rich and varied traditions and talents and direct them to the fulfillment of our common hopes is in the finest spirit of Republicans."[10]

The importance which the Republican party attaches to the ethnic vote has not diminished since then. Michael Sotirhos, current head of the Heritage Groups Council, proclaimed in 1983, for example, that "the Heritage Groups Council is a sleeping giant, ready to earn an even greater voice in the Republican Party and in the government of our country." The council issues a brochure explaining how to organize nationality clubs for specific candidates and ultimately for the Republican party itself, and gives specific guidelines for the nationality clubs on such matters as finances, membership, and even how to run a meeting according to standard parliamentary procedure.[11]

This brief discussion gives little hint of the intense competition the two parties have frequently waged for the Eastern European ethnic vote in presidential campaigns since 1944 and earlier. For present purposes, two key points should be made about this competition. First, presidential elections do not appear to have been an effective occasion for Eastern European ethnic groups to bring pressure to bear on American policy toward the homeland. Both national parties may have been conscious of the ethnic vote and have organized their campaigns with a view to appealing to this vote, not only on domestic but also on foreign policy grounds, but in actuality the foreign policy planks calculated to attract Eastern European ethnic support have, to put it politely, been somewhat misleading. Both parties have made promises to ethnic minorities which the leadership at least had little intention or interest in keeping (a phenomenon we have already discussed in another context).

To cite only one example, in 1944 President Roosevelt and his political aides were concerned that the large Polish-American vote in the United States might be alienated from the Democratic party because of concessions that the Administration had made or would likely make to the Soviet Union over the future territorial boundaries and regime of Poland. On the urging of his associates, Roosevelt agreed to see a delegation from the Polish-American Congress led by its chairman, Charles Rozmarek. The President

allowed photographers to take a picture of the delegation shaking hands with him in front of a large map of Poland on which the prewar boundaries extending far to the East into territory now held by Russia, were marked in heavy ink. In the remaining weeks of the campaign, Democrats arranged for the publication of this photograph in Polish-language papers across the nation, leading many to believe the President backed the London government in rejecting the Curzon line.[12]

But the Administration never had any serious intention of pressing for the prewar Polish boundaries, some of which extended almost 200 miles east of the Curzon line. Indeed, at the Teheran Conference, Roosevelt had more or less accepted the Curzon line as the legitimate eastern boundary for postwar Poland.

The second point to be considered with regard to presidential politics and American policy toward Eastern Europe is that for the mass of ethnic voters foreign policy does not seem to have been a decisive criterion in electoral choice. Party promises of a tough policy in Eastern Europe may have been important for ethnic group leadership—and at times may have been seen by the parties themselves as effective in swaying the mass of ethnic voters—but the evidence is that most voters have not in fact been especially influenced in this regard.

The Republicans, for instance, made a major effort to win over the Polish-American vote in 1944. Despite Roosevelt's guile on the Polish issue, Dewey and other Republican politicians ran a very intense and skillful campaign accusing the Administration of selling out Polish interests to the Soviets. The Republican strategy caused a great deal of concern in Democratic circles. Yet the Republican candidates did far worse in industrial districts with a high ethnic concentration than they had in 1940. What happened was perceived quite clearly by Senator Vandenberg in a letter to one of his constituents in Michigan: "I can fully understand that most of the Polish-Americans in our own Michigan area are also in the CIO and that these labor considerations were much too strong to be offset by any doubtful considerations in behalf of the old fatherland."[13]

Other considerations have on balance definitely outweighed foreign policy issues in the voting choices of Eastern European ethnics. These issues have fallen primarily in the economic realm, but in recent years the so-called social issue has also loomed important. For example, in 1972 concern about a deterioration in traditional American values forced measures of racial integration, and law and order moved ethnics to support Richard Nixon in record numbers. Among voters of Polish extraction Nixon increased his totals in various big cities compared to 1968 from 12 to 30 percent.[14] All this occurred despite the fact that the Republican platform was totally silent on the question of the "enslaved" Eastern European nations. The Democratic platform applauded steps toward normalizing American relations with the Soviet Union, but also called for a mobilization of world opinion to help the "oppressed peoples of Eastern Europe maintain their culture and religion." The Democrats also urged that pressure be brought to achieve liberalized emigration practices in these countries.[15] None of this, however, seemed to affect the rush of ethnic votes from the Democratic to the Republican camp. This swing was all the more striking in view of the fact that the Nixon Administration's policies, as noted earlier, had implied acquiescence in the Soviet sphere of influence in Eastern Europe.

The presidential campaign of 1980 provided additional evidence on this score. Ronald Reagan's victory was based in considerable part on the substantial defection of the "white ethnic vote" from Democratic to Republican ranks. Given Reagan's established anti-Communist credentials, as well as the dramatic development of the Solidarity trade union movement in Poland, one might have supposed that at least a modified version of the "liberation plank" of the 1952 campaign would have figured in Republican attempts to attract the Eastern European ethnics away from their traditional Democratic allegiance. In reality, the Republican party platform was notably barren of any plans for the future of East Central Europe, aside from a rote pledge of support for "the captive nations of Central and Eastern Europe in their hope to achieve self-determination." To the extent that the Republican platform addressed Eastern Europe, it concentrated on the dangers of the transfer of high technology to the "Eastern European satellites." The one specific suggestion given for a "new approach" to Eastern Europe was a greater emphasis on funding for Radio Free Europe, which was hardly a clarion call to arms. Ironically, the Democrats took appreciably greater note of the future of Eastern Europe in their own platform, promising to strengthen ties to the nations of the region and in particular to make a distinction between economic or diplomatic sanctions applied against the Soviet Union in contrast to Moscow's partners in the Warsaw Pact. The platform promised to treat "each of those nations [in Eastern Europe] with sensitivity to its individual situation" as long as they were willing "to maintain a constructive dialogue on issues of concern and significance to the United States."[16]

In the campaign itself, President Carter took special pains to try to sustain the Eastern European ethnic's traditional tie to the Democratic party. He stated that the ethnic "composition of American society is analogous to a beautiful mosaic," and boasted that it was his Administration that had established for the first time an Office of Ethnic Affairs. On September 20 he spoke at a dinner honoring the one hundredth anniversary of the Polish National Alliance and stressed that the United States remained committed to Poland's right to settle its own affairs free of outside influence (meaning the Soviet Union). This was the fourth speech Carter had given that week before an ethnic audience, and he was careful to point out the number of Americans of Polish background who had served in his Administration, including Secretary of State Edmund Muskie and National Security Adviser Zbigniew Brzezinski.[17] During the same period, the President announced with some fanfare that the United States had approved $670 million in new credits for Poland to purchase American grain and thus ameliorate the difficult food situation there. "This action is a significant proof of the solidarity between the American people and the Polish people," he said.[18] Ronald Reagan, for his part, combined ritual praise of the brave struggle of the Polish people for independence with a primary concentration on the supposed flaws of Carter Administration economic policy, with particular effects on American ethnics, and the general ineptness of Carter's leadership. Reagan's approach was perhaps best caught in remarks he made at an "ethnic picnic" in Jersey City, New Jersey, on September 1, where he was joined on the podium by Stanislaw Walesa, father of the leader of the Solidarity movement. Reagan claimed that Mr. Walesa's son provided the kind of leadership President Carter had failed to deliver.[19] The subsequent Republican landslide in November seemed to indicate that the specifics of President Carter's approach to Poland and Eastern Europe generally carried less impact with Eastern European ethnics than Reagan's abstract pledge of stronger leadership overall combined with a promise to generate more sustained economic growth, although perhaps it could be argued that Carter's relatively "soft" approach to East Central Europe was one factor that cost him votes.

APPEALS TO PUBLIC OPINION

Given the fact that Eastern European ethnic organizations had little influence on the foreign policy professionals, they had two principal alternative means by which they could seek to bring pressure for a change in policy. One of these involved using the power of the ballot, and the other pointed to a strategy of arousing public opinion in general against the present course of American diplomacy. The two modes of action were related—a groundswell of sentiment against American policy in Eastern Europe might have at least some repercussions at the polls. Yet appeals to the public as a whole had broader implications. Given the State Department's perception, for instance, of a wide public consensus for a certain stance, the credibility and impact of groups pressing for such a stance are bound to be greater. This suggests that the dismal picture painted so far of the Eastern European ethnic lobby's attempts to play a role in U.S. policy toward the homeland may in some sense have not been quite to the point. The emphasis in this book on the formal edge of the lobbying enterprise, that is, pressure applied to Congress and especially to the professional foreign policy apparatus in Washington, may give an unwarranted impression that the lobby's failure has been essentially a technical one, that is, an ineptness in the use of message and tactics in approaching the targets of influence. There have been consistent lapses of this sort in the Eastern European ethnic's vain effort to sway U.S. foreign policy. Nevertheless, the real story of the ethnic lobby's failure may lie not so much in mistakes made in Washington as in the general environment in which the lobby's activities have proceeded. Two different aspects of this environment merit attention: the attitudes, supportive or antagonistic, of the larger community of which the ethnic group is a part, and the cohesion and energy with which the ethnic group itself expresses a given foreign policy concern. Simply put, if the circumstances are right in both areas, even the most clumsy lobbying effort in Washington is bound to have an important effect; if they are not, even the most skilled approaches to government will likely prove unavailing. We will consider the second issue in due course; the first concerns us now.

Consider the so-called Israeli lobby. A standard Arab explanation for the U.S. commitment to Israel—a commitment going against what the Arabs see as overall U.S. interests in the Middle East—is that American Jews exercise a decisive influence over key institutions of this country, particularly the media and high finance. In reality, the Israeli lobby draws its effectiveness from two intertwining phenomena. Among the substantial Jewish community in the United States, the vast majority view the safety and prosperity of Israel not just as an abstract desideratum but as an absolutely fundamental goal. For American society as a whole, there is an equally large majority who consider that the United States does have a concrete moral commitment to Israel and that Israel as an entity has an unquestioned right to exist. In short, American Jews are close to united on a specific interest, and they are supported, if perhaps with less intensity, by their non-Jewish fellow citizens. In view of this combination, it is clear that no administration in Washington could abandon Israel to its fate even if it wanted to. (A considerable debate does exist, of course, on how much or whether the United States should commit its own forces to the defense of Israel.) The pro-Israel phenomenon in the United States, however, stands more or less by itself. The Eastern European ethnic lobby has not been able to demonstrate the same strength in either of the two environmental areas described here.

As one astute study has concluded, the efficacy of ethnic appeals to the American people has depended largely on the degree to which the relevant ethnic group could demonstrate that their appeal was basically an expression of American nationalism rather than, say, Polish or Hungarian nationalism. The message has to stress those values and ideals that Americans in fact consider as the essence of the American way of life. After World War II, for example, the Polish-American Congress (undoubtedly the most sophisticated of the ethnic lobbying organizations) insisted that it was fundamentally interested in the establishment in Poland of a free press, parliamentary institutions, secure civil liberties, and the free enterprise system. Whether in the absence of Soviet pressures in Poland such ideals would have been spread by the postwar Polish regime was not a question that under the circumstances had to be answered. Another important factor in the ethnic leadership's attempt to rally American public opinion at the time was their assurance that as far as they personally were concerned America was now their permanent home. They were not asking the American people to make sacrifices so that they could repatriate themselves to a more congenial Poland. On the contrary, what they were pressing for was a Poland that could provide at least some of the blessings of American life to those who had not had the good fortune to be able to emigrate to the United States.[20]

Perhaps the most notable, certainly the most visible, effort to stir American opinion concerning conditions in Eastern Europe has been the Captive Nations Resolution (CNR) mentioned earlier. Passed unanimously by Congress on July 17, 1959, it provided for the establishment of a "Captive Nations Week" to fall annually in the third week of July "until such time as freedom and independence shall have been achieved for all the captive nations of the world." Among the captive nations were cited not only all the Communist regimes of Eastern Europe but also such areas as Armenia, Azerbaijan, Byelorussia, Georgia, Idel-Ural, Cossackia, and Turkestan. On first impression, passage of the CNR would seem to have been indicative of considerable political clout among ethnic groups in Congress. In reality, it seems to have been passed without much thought as to its implications. The resolution itself was adopted verbatim from a draft submitted by Professor Lev Dobriansky of Georgetown University and was not even sent to the Senate Committee on Foreign Relations for approval. One commentator caught the flavor of the occasion in saying that the resolution had been churned out "along with other casual holiday proclamations, such as National Hot Dog Month."[21] It is apparent that few—or, in this instance, none—in the Congress wanted to be put on record as opposing freedom for the captive peoples.

The CNR was formalized as Public Law 86-90, and each July after a presidential proclamation of Captive Nations Week the public is invited to observe the week "with appropriate prayer, ceremonies and activities expressing their sympathy with and support for the just aspirations of the captive peoples." The actual character that Captive Nations Week (CNW) has assumed over the years may be summarized by reference to its observance during the height of detente in 1975

—marked especially by the signing of the Helsinki accords—and the attitude toward CNW on its twenty-fifth anniversary in 1983.

In July 1975 such congressmen as Clement Zablocki of Illinois and Herman Badillo of New York, and Senators Roman Hruska of Nebraska and Jesse Helms of North Carolina delivered remarks in the Congress on Captive Nations Week. In fealty to the call of the Captive Nations Resolution, the mayors of Providence, Rhode Island; New Haven, Connecticut; Mobile, Alabama; Youngstown, Ohio; and Elizabeth, New Jersey, all issued proclamations noting Captive Nations Week.[22] In New York City, Monsignor John Balkunas marked the opening of CNW with a mass at St. Patrick's Cathedral, and there was a round of speeches and parades in other parts of the city commemorating the occasion. Governor Meldrim Thompson of New Hampshire also issued a proclamation on Captive Nations Week. His statement accompanying the proclamation took his fellow governors to task for not giving the week the attention it deserved, and he assured the captive nations that "the people of New Hampshire share with them our aspirations for the recovery of their freedom and independence."[23]

In analyzing the impact of Captive Nations Week, several observations may be offered. Segments of the American public and some opinion leaders may have grown increasingly critical of aspects of detente, but this seemingly did not amount to a revived concern about the specific situation in Eastern Europe. Governor Thompson's complaint was echoed, for example, in a mournful editorial in the *New York Sunday News*, which said that "as far as official Washington is concerned . . . minimal, dutiful attention will be accorded to the occasion. Sad to relate, Captive Nations Week has come to be regarded by many of our leaders as a disquieting, embarrassing ghost from the past haunting detente banqueters."[24] Senator Helms took note of the very vague language of President Ford's proclamation of Captive Nations Week and pointed out a significant substitute of language in some presidential remarks shortly before Ford signed the Helsinki accords on European Security and Cooperation. The original draft of the President's speech noted that "United States policy supports the aspirations for freedom and national independence of the peoples of Eastern Europe by every peaceful means." This was changed in the actual address to "United States policy supports the aspirations for freedom and national independence of peoples everywhere." As Helms commented, this reduced the statement to a "bland generality of no significance whatsoever."[25] Also of interest was the fact that of those in Congress who did address themselves to Captive Nations Week, the message with respect to Eastern Europe was hardly in line with the original spirit of the CNR. Charles Whalen, Jr. (R.-Ohio), for example, insisted that "detente is a noble objective," and he saw evidence of an increasing Soviet inclination toward "reasonableness." His hope was that this inclination might gradually be extended to granting the right of "individual nationalities to determine their own destinies."[26]

The twenty-fifth anniversary of the proclamation of Captive Nations Week occurred during a period in which the avowedly anti-Communist Reagan Administration was in power, and one might have expected that, given the strongly anti-Soviet tenor of the times, unusual attention would be devoted to CNW on this particular occasion. The evidence, however, is that during July 1983 the message of the Captive Nations Resolution was viewed either with resigned melancholy or with barely concealed indifference. It is perhaps not without significance that the *New York Times* carried not a single story or even a casual reference to the occasion. Various members of Congress, it is true, offered remarks commemorating CNW, but the tenor of their comment could hardly have provided encouragement to those actively hoping for the liberation of the "Captive Nations." Congressman Samuel Stratton (R.-N.Y.), for example, noted that "the 25th anniversary is indeed a sad milestone and gives one pause to reflect on the magnitude of the problem." He confessed with some degree of candor that "we often wonder whether the speeches in this Chamber or speeches elsewhere can actually do the job." Another congressman from New York, Jerry Solomon, was frank in admitting that "few Americans realize that for the past 25 years part of July has been set aside for quiet lamentation over those who have been denied [their freedom] by their Communist oppressors." A basic contradiction in most congressional comment at this time concerning the CNW was the continuing complaint about the steady expansion of the Soviet Empire even as seeming hope was expressed about the inevitable coming of freedom to Eastern Europe. The one favorable sign that most could point to was the visit of Pope John to Poland and his ostensible rallying of Polish public opinion to the cause of independence.[27] The President himself, in a ceremony observing CNW at the White House on July 19, 1983, assured his audience, composed mostly of Eastern European ethnics, that "your dream is our dream. And someday, you, too, will be free." At the same time, Mr. Reagan took time out to praise what he saw as evidence of greater Soviet moderation at the review conference in Madrid concerning the Helsinki accords. His address was also notably devoid of any specific suggestions about how his Administration planned to create greater opportunities for freedom and liberation in Eastern Europe. Instead, the President spent much of his time urging ethnic support for his policies in Nicaragua and on the MX missile.[28]

In assessing the effectiveness of ethnic group attempts to mobilize public opinion in support of their position on Eastern Europe, several factors need to be stressed. A leading student of the relationship between American public opinion and foreign policy notes that "Americans of East European descent . . . assisted in the development and perpetuation of a strong anti-Russian policy in the 1940's and 1950's at a time when there were few domestic pressures for a more conciliatory policy."[29] An examination of the overall record since 1945 supports the notion that in those periods in which American opinion was generally disposed to be anti-Communist or anti-Soviet, the appeals of Eastern European ethnic groups have been received with some sympathy. This phenomenon may be considered equally applicable both to general public opinion and to what we have called the "foreign policy professionals." It is important to stress, however, that these groups by their efforts have only produced an added edge to the general viewpoint that already existed. At most, they have been able at times to focus attention on a specific issue in which Soviet behavior was perhaps most reprehensible and which might be made good if the United States "won" the Cold War. The exertions of the Polish-American Congress were effective in the late 1940s precisely because the American public was increasingly hostile to the Soviet Union for reasons above and beyond the situation in Eastern Europe. What the ethnic groups cannot do is to turn American opinion in a totally different direction, particularly if the Administration has put its own public relations apparatus behind a given line of policy. As Professor Milbrath comments,

The ability of interest groups specializing in foreign policy to affect broad public opinion on foreign policy is severely limited. Compared to the power of the President in this respect, their direct impact on opinion is miniscule. . . . The basic difficulty is that few people listen to group propaganda. Only as part of a concerted campaign, in close collaboration with public officials, are group propaganda efforts likely to attract sufficient attention to have even a slight effect.[30]

Even during periods in which the Eastern European ethnic lobby supposedly has found a receptive ear among the American public, there has been a striking ambivalence in attitudes on the part of the general populace quite in contrast to the type of support given to the cause of Israel. To be sure, during particularly dramatic periods in the history of Eastern Europe, U.S. public opinion has been affected by a flood of sentiment and support for the peoples of the area. When Louis Kossuth traveled to the United States in 1852, for example, following the failure of the Hungarian revolt several years earlier against Austrian and Russian oppression, he was greeted by vast crowds expressing their enthusiasm for his just struggle. Some 100,000 people lined the railroad tracks in Ohio as Kossuth made a triumphant procession to Columbus to address the Ohio legislature. Similarly, the Czech leader Thomas Masaryk was lionized in May 1918 during his travels in the United States to get support for an independent Czechoslovakia. When news of the attempted exodus of Czech prisoners of war from Bolshevik Russia reached the United States, the enthusiasm for the Czech cause swelled still further. The image of a small, oppressed country struggling against heavy odds to obtain self-determination obviously struck a highly responsive chord. Teddy Roosevelt reflected the feelings of many when he praised the Czech legion, "the extraordinary nature of whose great historic feat is literally unparalleled, so far as I know, in ancient or modern times."[31] More recently, the travails of the Hungarian freedom fighters during the events of October-November 1956 resulted in such an outpouring of sympathy in this country that Congress was moved to waive immigration restrictions to allow Hungarian exiles entry into the United States in large numbers. Also noticeable was the widespread sympathy in the United States for the Solidarity trade union movement in Poland as well as the considerable outrage at the subsequent repression of that movement by the regime in Warsaw.

Presumably, the above manifestations of public support should have proved invaluable in the efforts of Eastern European ethnic groups to pressure Washington on U.S. policy toward the homeland. Unfortunately for them, however, the U.S. public's enthusiasm for the Eastern European cause has been both episodic and abstract. There have been occasional outpourings of sympathy, but the more general pattern has been indifference or ignorance of the affairs of East Central Europe. Moreover, the quality of the sympathy expressed has drawn far more from the traditional American admiration of the underdog than it has from any concrete desire to expend American treasure or spill American blood to influence affairs in what, to paraphrase Neville Chamberlain concerning another East European crisis, was a faraway place of which Americans knew nothing (or very little). The amorphous quality of U.S. support for the East European cause was perhaps best caught some years ago in an editorial in the *New York Times* commenting on the so-called Williamsburg Declaration of June 1952. The declaration was a manifesto calling for the liberation of Eastern Europe from the Soviets and for a new political order in the region; it was drawn up by prominent émigré leaders. The *Times* declared that "these men at Williamsburg can be certain that opinion in this country and throughout the free world stands behind them."[32] In its own terms, this statement was unexceptional and no doubt correct. It hardly implied approval, however, of any measures strong enough to bring about the realization of the Williamsburg goals. Indeed, the *Times* in other contexts was just as fervent in its denunciation of an adventurous foreign policy as it was laudatory of the Williamsburg Declaration.

The gap between abstract support for Eastern European rights and a willingness to do something tangible to secure those rights has derived not just from the American people's typical instinct for moral gestures in foreign policy without supporting substance. The fact is that many Americans have had an idealized, uninformed picture of Eastern Europe that has not translated into an equal idealization of those who have emigrated to the United States from Eastern Europe. A certain irony is involved here. It was precisely the fact that the "new immigration" found it harder to assimilate than the older Western and Northern European immigrants that contributed to an enduring sense of ethnic identification in this country among Poles, Slovaks, and other Eastern Europeans. This ethnic bond fostered a continuing devotion to the fortunes of their countries of origin. The "separateness" characterizing many Eastern European ethnic communities in the United States, however, has proved to be a serious obstacle when ethnic organizations have made appeals to the general American public for support for the homeland. Bluntly put, a campaign organized to insure that there will always be an England falls on an audience that is likely to be receptive. A similar campaign for American help to the oppressed of Ruthenia or Bulgaria runs the risk of arousing the antagonisms that Ruthenians and Bulgarians themselves met when they came to the United States—and to some extent still experience.

One other factor bearing on the efforts of ethnic groups to mobilize opinion on Eastern Europe may be mentioned, and it concerns the relevant groups' relationship with the press. If a campaign to arouse the general public is to succeed, the relevant ethnic organizations have to find press outlets going beyond their own foreign-language media. To a large degree, however, they find the same obstacles to having their views represented, at least in the national press, as in the State Department. Most influential journalists and editors stress that their job is to inform the public generally and objectively. Their perception of the ethnic lobby is that it has only narrow interests and even these are presented in a warped fashion. Journalists are as wary of the "hobby horse mentality" displayed by the ethnic spokesmen as are official policymakers. Finally, the press has a general prejudice against the legitimacy of special interest groups, at least in foreign policy, since they seem to represent the particular as opposed to the general interest, which the press at least in theory is designed to serve.[33]

NOTES

1. Bernard Cohen, THE PUBLIC'S IMPACT ON FOREIGN POLICY (Boston: Little, Brown and Co., 1973), 152.

2. John C. Spanier and Eric Uslaner, HOW AMERICAN FOREIGN POLICY IS MADE (New York: Praeger, 1974), 87.

3. An excellent instance of this was the State Department's success in blunting the decision by the Kennedy White House on the "opening to the left" in Italy during the early 1960s. Kennedy's position was to encourage the left coalition efforts in Italy, but for a long time the State Department continued its previous support of conservative elements on the Italian scene. Arthur Schlesinger relates that it took almost two years for Kennedy's decision to be implemented. See A THOUSAND DAYS (Boston: Houghton Mifflin, 1965), 877-881.

4. An interesting discussion of the Jewish vote and the creation of Israel is John Snetsinger, TRUMAN, THE JEWISH VOTE AND THE CREATION OF ISRAEL (Stanford, Calif.: Hoover Institution Press, 1974).

5. Donald E. Pienkos, "The Polish American Congress—An Appraisal," POLISH AMERICAN STUDIES 36, no. 2 (1979), 37.

6. Perry L. Weed, THE WHITE ETHNIC MOVEMENT AND ETHNIC POLITICS (New York: Praeger, 1973), 131.

7. Theodore H. White, THE MAKING OF THE PRESIDENT 1960 (New York: Atheneum, 1964), 222.

8. Personal communication from Andrew Valuchek, Executive Director, Nationalities Division, Democratic National Committee, December 23, 1975.

9. Stephen A. Garrett, "Eastern European Ethnic Groups and American Foreign Policy," POLITICAL SCIENCE QUARTERLY (Summer 1978), 313.

10. Weed, THE WHITE ETHNIC MOVEMENT, 173.

11. The above material is drawn from several brochures provided to the author by the National Republican Heritage Groups (Nationalities) Council, including "A Handbook for Heritage Groups" and "Representing Ethnic Americans Within the Republican Party."

12. Robert Divine, FOREIGN POLICY AND PRESIDENTIAL ELECTIONS 1940-1948 (New York: New Viewpoints, 1974), 140.

13. Martin Weil, "Can the Blacks Do for Africa What the Jews Did for Israel?" FOREIGN POLICY (Summer 1974), 112.

14. Theodore H. White, THE MAKING OF THE PRESIDENT 1972 (New York: Atheneum, 1973), 369.

15. CONGRESSIONAL DIGEST (October 1972), 249.

16. Congressional Quarterly, HISTORIC DOCUMENTS OF 1980 (Washington: Congressional Quarterly Inc., 1981), 636-638, 758.

17. NEW YORK TIMES, September 21, 1980, 34.

18. NEW YORK TIMES, September 13, 1980, 1.

19. NEW YORK TIMES, September 2, 1980, 1.

20. Weil, "Can the Blacks Do for Africa," 117-118.

21. Louis Gerson, THE HYPHENATE IN RECENT AMERICAN POLITICS AND DIPLOMACY (Lawrence: University of Kansas Press, 1964), 26-27.

22. U.S. Congress, House of Representatives, CONGRESSIONAL RECORD, 94th Congress, 1st Session (July 23, 1975), H7358-7359.

23. U.S. Congress, Senate, CONGRESSIONAL RECORD, 94th Congress, 1st Session (July 29, 1975), S14120-14121.

24. U.S. Congress, House of Representatives, CONGRESSIONAL RECORD, 94th Congress, 1st Session (July 23, 1975), H 7359.

25. U.S. Congress, Senate, CONGRESSIONAL RECORD, 94th Congress, 1st Session (July 29, 1975), S14120.

26. U.S. Congress, CONGRESSIONAL RECORD, 94th Congress, 1st Session (July 22, 1975), E399.

27. U.S. Congress, House of Representatives, CONGRESSIONAL RECORD, 98th Congress, 1st Session (July 18, 1983), H5231-H5236.

28. U.S. Congress, CONGRESSIONAL RECORD, 98th Congress, 1st Session (July 20, 1983), E3592-E3593.

29. Ralph P. Levering, THE PUBLIC AND AMERICAN FOREIGN POLICY 1918-1978 (New York: William Morrow and Co., 1978), 26.

30. Lester W. Milbrath, "Interest Groups and Foreign Policy," in DOMESTIC SOURCES OF FOREIGN POLICY, ed. James Rosenau (New York: Free Press, 1967), 250-251.

31. THE LETTERS OF THEODORE ROOSEVELT, Vol. 3 (Cambridge, Mass.: Harvard University Press, 1954), 1364.

32. NEW YORK TIMES, June 13, 1952.

33. William Chittick, STATE DEPARTMENT, PRESS AND PRESSURE GROUPS (New York: Wiley-Interscience, 1970), 261-266.

5.
The Ethnic Lobby
Considered

Two critical matters relating to the impact of the Eastern European ethnic lobby on American foreign policy remain to be examined. One involves the kind of message the lobby has presented. The other concerns representativeness: what does a given ethnic community consist of and who is qualified to speak for it? Both of these points bear on judgments we may make on the legitimate or possible relationship between ethnicity and foreign policy.

In this connection it is necessary to reconsider the elements of ethnic consciousness in the United States. One distinguished authority has argued that "the ethnic consciousness of hyphenated Americans is less related to the winning of political power, the championing of the old country and the exaltation of culture and religion than it is to the achievement of dignity, equality, respectability, and unhampered access to American values and benefits."[1] Two theories have been proposed to explain the "new ethnicity" in this country. The "primordial" concept emphasizes the existence of deep-rooted historical instincts and associations that can be erased only with difficulty. The second theory concentrates on the "circumstantialist" notion, which holds that ethnic feelings are basically dependent on the surrounding environment and can wax or wane depending on that environment.[2] On balance, the second interpretation seems to reflect the weight of the evidence, and if so, such a conclusion has considerable significance for Eastern European ethnic influence on American diplomacy. The point is that contemporary American ethnicity may regard the specific fortunes of the homeland as only symbolic of a larger struggle for recognition, granting of integrity, and acceptance of an appropriate individual identity. Michael Novak asserts that "the new ethnicity does not stand for the balkanization of America. It stands for a true, real, multicultural cosmopolitanism."[3] From this perspective, the putative ethnic pressures on American diplomacy toward the old country are simply one version of a cry for respect. Consider the dubious phenomenon of so-called Polish jokes. One astute analyst of the Polish community in the United States has argued that "whatever the real and attributed reasons for their emergence, Polish jokes have had a profound influence on Polonia—more so, in fact, than all of Polonia's previous efforts at expanding the Polish-American and American knowledge of its Polish heritage."[4]

We have to face a fundamental issue in this context: why should the average ethnic devote a significant portion of his or her energies to U.S. foreign policy toward Eastern Europe? Because the bulk of immigrants from East Central Europe arrived prior to 1930, tangible memories of the homeland have clearly faded—and with them presumably whatever instinct may have existed for pressuring one's adopted land to intervene to secure the interests of those left behind. That such an instinct would be any stronger among successive generations born in the United States also seems doubtful. Moreover, many of the immigrants from Eastern Europe were distinguished not so much by loyalty to the regime from whence they came as to the local region or village, especially since they came from a largely peasant background.[5] A sentimental longing to revisit one's old surroundings may linger indefinitely without implying any passion about the political fortunes of the former, often vaguely felt, entity of state.

The irony seems to be, then, that "immigrant nationalism," a felt sense of commitment to the development of one's former homeland, may generally have been a function of experiences not in the old country but in this one. Two factors were paramount in this regard. There was the already mentioned sense of being "outcasts" in a new land, which inevitably led to an attempt to identify—and to sustain—the particular virtues of one's own culture. There was also the fact that most of the Eastern European immigration was pressed for the first time into a largely urban existence. The existence of various ethnic "ghettos" obviously facilitated the development of a sense of ethnic commonality and common purpose. In this regard it is of interest that the first newspaper published in the Lithuanian language appeared in this country and not in Lithuania itself, and that the birth of modern Czechoslovakia took place not in Prague but in Pittsburgh, Pennsylvania.[6]

Turning from the putative sources of Eastern European ethnic nationalism in the United States, it is important to recognize that the whole concept of a single "message" from an ethnic lobby presupposes a degree of unity within the relevant ethnic grouping that may be quite absent. Throughout our discussion we have used the phrase "Eastern European ethnic lobby," but when it comes down to it, we have been studying the activities mainly of those vocal organizations claiming to speak for the ethnic community. It is clear that two basic problems here are sociological and organizational: generational, economic, and social splits within an ethnic community that make it difficult to determine whether a consensus does in fact exist for a given foreign policy stance, and the existence of various formal lobbying groups that may or may not be reflective of the ethnic group generally and the leadership of which may or may not in fact be in touch with the membership itself.

In terms of social origin, it is necessary to recall that immigration from Eastern Europe at the end of the nineteenth and in the early twentieth centuries was composed primarily of the uneducated and the unskilled. Those involved were mainly from rural areas, and their interest in coming to the United States was essentially economic. By contrast, those who left Eastern Europe after 1945 were generally better educated and often held positions of relative prominence in their homeland, including political positions. It was natural that they should lead in bitter denunciations of events in Eastern Europe, and by virtue of their background they tended to assume leadership in those ethnic organizations actively interested in foreign policy.[7] An interesting analysis of the Polish-American Congress (PAC), for example, describes the tension that developed in the Congress after 1945 between the newer and older immigration. The newer element tended to play a dominant role in the state affiliates of the PAC, whereas Polish-Americans born in this country controlled the less politicized fraternal organizations. One issue that arose was whether PAC meetings should be held in Polish or English; another was the degree to which the organization should focus primarily on conditions in Poland itself. In evident exasperation at the demands of the more recent Polish immigration, PAC President Aloysius Mazewski, at the tenth convention of the PAC in 1976, criticized the "lunatic fringe" of the Congress who wanted to have nothing at all to do with the Polish regime, even including tourism by the Polish-American community.[8]

Moreover, to speak of the "Eastern European ethnic lobby" is to disguise the fact that in many instances nationalistic rivalries among various Eastern European ethnic groups were as important as the common bonds they shared. The Hungarian and Romanian communities in the United States, for example, may have agreed that the Soviets were not to be trusted, but at the same time they were in substantial disagreement over whether in the "post-liberation era" Hungary or Romania should have possession of Transylvania. The point is that old quarrels from Eastern Europe itself were carried to the United States and frequently made the notion of a united Eastern European ethnic lobby illusory.

Immigrants to the United States have also been solidly isolationist. After fleeing from hard experiences in their homeland, their instincts were to have the United States remain as free as possible from the corrupting influence of the Old World. These isolationist instincts, of course, varied in different parts of the country—the Midwest has generally been considered the heartland of isolationist feelings—but for our purposes what is important is that to the extent ethnic groups called on the American government to intervene in Eastern Europe, they were proposing just the sort of expansion of American involvement in the world that they resisted in other circumstances.[9]

Perhaps more fundamental to the dilemma of many East European ethnics, however, was the fact that their interests with regard to the homeland were twofold, and satisfaction of one could and did conflict with the other. Many of them were opposed to the internal Communist regimes of the area and would have welcomed their ouster in favor of governments supposedly more true to the will of the people. At the same time, they were also nationalists and thus committed to freedom of action for Eastern Europe vis-à-vis the Soviets. These strong nationalistic feelings were as strong or stronger than their anti-communism. One way to support national independence was to press American policymakers to extend economic and diplomatic support to the Eastern European regimes. The regimes could use this support to extend their independence from the Soviet Union (in the manner, say, of Yugoslavia). Aid to the regime, however, had the effect of strengthening its hold over its own people. The question then became, which was more important: greater freedom for the homeland from the Soviets or opposition to communism per se? One need only look at the debate among Americans of Yugoslav extraction following the start of American economic and military aid to Yugoslavia in 1950 to observe how difficult a choice this was. Tito undeniably remained a Marxist-Leninist, but at the same time there seemed little doubt that he was determined to chart a separate Yugoslav path to socialism and in particular to reserve to Yugoslav authorities themselves the ultimate choice as to political orientation in the country. A number of Americans of Yugoslavic background (Serbs, Slovenes, Croatians, and others) decided that Tito was the lesser of the evils they knew and supported Washington's aid program to Belgrade; others stressed Tito's unremitting commitment to authoritarian politics and argued loudly against American support of his regime.[10] The whole episode illustrated the complexity of the ethnic's relationship with his or her former homeland which was somewhat submerged in the ritual calls for liberation evident particularly in the 1950s.

Our reference to "calls for liberation" raises the question of whether the mass of Americans of Eastern European heritage were as "hard-line" in their approach to the Communist world (including Eastern Europe) as was implied by ethnic leaders during the height of the Cold War. It is of interest that many of the earlier Eastern European immigrants to the United States were radical in their politics. Many of them were socialists and even anarchists. The strident anti-Communist rhetoric of the most visible ethnic lobbying organizations in, say, the 1950s was hardly consistent with this tradition. An important segment of the earlier immigration was also Jewish, and as Jews they had little reason to desire a return by the Eastern European regimes to the quasi-fascist politics of the interwar years, when anti-Semitism was a common political theme. Many of the Communist elite in Eastern Europe in the early post-1945 years were themselves of Jewish background.

Various public opinion surveys suggest some interesting conclusions about the general political views of the Eastern European ethnic community. In August 1953, for example, the Roper survey found that 64 percent of East Europeans in the United States agreed with the statement that "while keeping up military strength, [the U.S. should] make every reasonable attempt to find a way to live peacefully with Russia."[11] This compared with a response of 68 percent from those of British heritage and 71 percent from Scandinavia (53 percent from Ireland and Italy). In 1964 the Survey Research Center at the University of Michigan discovered that 84 percent of American-Eastern Europeans (92 percent Polish-Americans) concurred with the notion that "our government should meet with Communist leaders to try to settle our differences" (compared to 68 percent for those from Britain and 74 percent for West Europeans generally). The same survey showed that more Americans of Eastern European heritage favored East-West trade than ethnic groups from any other country (including a number from Western Europe).[12] One possible explanation for the apparent paradox of the Eastern European ethnic community being widely regarded as stridently anti-Communist, even as polling data suggested a more moderate spectrum of private opinion, may be found once again in the relative insecurity that many Eastern European ethnics have felt in their adopted country. Because they have come from a region that is now itself Communist, there may be concern that by a process of association other Americans will perhaps view them as having suspect sympathies. At the very least, antagonisms created here could impede full acceptance into American society— all the more reason, then, for public protestations of a fervent anti-communism.

Whatever the real ideological leanings of Eastern European ethnics in this country, there is evidence that as a community they have felt far less comfortable in openly challenging American policy toward Eastern Europe than has been the case with their most vocal and visible leaders. Most immigrants did not come from democratic systems and thus were relatively cautious about directly attacking the "wisdom" of official judgments, especially in foreign policy. This instinct was ironically reinforced by the factor just mentioned: the fear of antagonizing a host society that was already perceived as in some ways hostile to these strange "visitors" from very different lands. One survey found that 68 percent of white ethnics (to be sure not all from Eastern Europe) agreed that "you have to respect authority and when you stop respecting authority, your situation isn't worth very much." Other studies established that 64 percent of ethnics concurred with the idea that if "you start to change things very much, you usually make them much worse," and 42 percent disagreed that "the minority should be free to criticize government decisions."[13]

What the above data suggest, in sum, is that the notion of a unified Eastern European ethnic lobby bent on pressuring the American government to a program of "liberating" the old homelands may have been fundamentally at odds with the reality of ethnic opinion. Not only has there been a considerable diversity in actual ethnic views on the desired political evolution of their countries of origin, but in general Eastern European ethnics have shown a propensity to follow the lead of legitimate authority in this country on foreign policy rather than attempting to challenge it. There is some rather interesting evidence that the mass of American ethnics regard the leaders of ethnic organizations, particularly those concerned basically with political questions, as "marginal" to their own group and thus unreliable as spokesmen/guides to the attitudes of their particular ethnic constituency. A particular case in point was the long career of Charles Rozmarek as head of the Polish-American Congress. During his tenure as president of PAC, extending from 1944 to 1968, Rozmarek came under increasing criticism for his arbitrary and authoritarian decision-making style. Particularly controversial was his open endorsement, in the name of the Congress, of the Republican candidates in the 1948 and 1952 presidential elections (the justification being that Dewey and Eisenhower were somehow more committed to Polish freedom and independence). When large numbers of Polish-Americans declined to accept Rozmarek's political guidance, the PAC president suffered a notable loss in prestige—and appeared to be substantially out of touch with his membership. Rozmarek had already set a precedent for these indiscretions when, with little consultation, he announced in 1947 that the Congress fully supported the political fortunes of Stanislaw Mikolajczyk in the contest for power in Poland itself, even though many Polish-Americans had affinities for other Polish figures to the left and right of Mikolajczyk.[14]

A key to Rozmarek's long tenure in office, despite his seemingly cavalier attitude toward consensual politics within the PAC, may be explained in part by a theory of elite selection among relatively deprived population groups. Such groups, among which many Eastern European ethnics would have to be counted, may select leaders whose economic success or professional attainments make them more "acceptable" to the outside world but who may, for this very reason, be relatively unrepresentative of the conditions and attitudes of the ethnic community they represent.[15] Despite the general Eastern European ethnic respect for authority, a survey of various ethnic groups in the mid-1970s (among which were included Poles, Slovaks, and Lithuanians) revealed that 65 percent felt that "public officials don't care much what people like me think."[16] If one assumes that the most prominent ethnic leaders may be viewed as "public officials," the data here suggest the ambiguous attitude of many ethnics toward their putative "leaders."

To summarize: the representatives of the so-called Eastern European ethnic lobby have never been able to project a credible image of the ethnic community as a whole solidly united behind one fundamental goal. The intensity of the Jewish commitment to the health of Israel finds no equivalent in the ranks of Eastern Europeans. I have discussed the *desiderata* supposedly established by the "ethnic lobby," but it must be stressed once again that these have been the ends articulated by a relatively tiny segment of the Eastern European immigrant population in this country, that is, the leadership of the various politically oriented ethnic organizations. Attempting to persuade the body of Eastern European ethnics that they should adopt these goals as their own and with a fervor equal to those propagating them has indeed been a primary problem of the ethnic lobby. Certainly the lobby has not been able to convince policymakers that the ethnic community generally felt as strongly about many issues as have the self-styled spokesmen of that community.

NOTES

1. Louis L. Gerson, "The Influence of Hyphenated Americans on U.S. Diplomacy," in ETHNICITY AND U.S. FOREIGN POLICY, ed. Abdul Aziz Said, revised edition (New York: Praeger, 1981), 31.

2. Nathan Glazer and Daniel P. Moynihan, "Introduction," in ETHNICITY: THEORY AND PRACTICE, eds. Nathan Glazer and Daniel P. Moynihan (Cambridge, Mass.: Harvard University Press, 1975), 19.

3. Michael Novak, "The New Ethnicity," in AMERICA AND THE NEW ETHNICITY, eds. David R. Colburn and George E. Pozzetta (Port Washington, N.Y.: Kennikat Press, 1979), 27.

4. Helena Znaniecki Lopata, "Polish America's Relations with the Rest of American Society," in AMERICA AND THE NEW ETHNICITY, Colburn and Pozzetta, eds., 151.

5. Gerson, "The Influence of Hyphenated Americans," 22.

6. Nathan Glazer, "Ethnic Groups in America: From National Culture to Ideology," in FREEDOM AND CONTROL IN MODERN SOCIETY, eds. Morroe Berger, Theodore Abel, and Charles Page (New York: D. Van Nostrand Co., 1954), 158-173.

7. Perry L. Weed, THE WHITE ETHNIC MOVEMENT AND ETHNIC POLITICS (New York: Praeger, 1973), 184.

8. Donald E. Pienkos, "The Polish American Congress—An Appraisal," POLISH AMERICAN STUDIES 36, No. 2 (1979), 17-18.

9. Paul Seabury, POWER, FREEDOM AND DIPLOMACY (New York: Vintage Books, 1967), 43-47.

10. Stephen A. Garrett, "On Dealing with National Communism: The Lessons of Yugoslavia," WESTERN POLITICAL QUARTERLY (September 1973).

11. Alfred Hero, AMERICAN RELIGIOUS GROUPS VIEW FOREIGN POLICY (Durham, N.C.: Duke University Press, 1967), 428.

12. Ibid., 430-431.

13. Thomas J. Pavlak, ETHNIC IDENTIFICATION AND POLITICAL BEHAVIOR (San Francisco: R&R Research Associates, 1976), 59-61.

14. Pienkos, "The Polish American Congress," 13-14.

15. John Higham, "Introduction: The Forms of Ethnic Leadership," in ETHNIC LEADERSHIP IN AMERICA, ed. John Higham (Baltimore: Johns Hopkins University Press, 1978), 2.

16. Pavlak, ETHNIC IDENTIFICATION, 67.

6.
The National Interest
and Other Interests

Whether Americans of Eastern European ethnic origin should have been given a larger voice in American diplomacy toward Eastern Europe is a matter that deserves some consideration. What after all is the legitimate role of various ethnic groups in the United States in the definition and pursuit of the national interest? One may accept the notion that a strong sense of ethnicity may be important in maintaining one's identity within American society without at the same time approving the injection of this ethnic consciousness into the foreign policy process. Many students of American diplomacy would continue to support the basic idea—if not the flamboyant language—of an item in the Democratic party's platform in the 1916 presidential election. The platform denounced "all alliances and combinations of individuals in this country, of whatever nationality or descent, who agree and conspire together for the purpose of embarrassing or weakening our government or of improperly influencing or coercing our public representatives in dealing or negotiating with any foreign power."[1]

A more contemporary—and perhaps even more acerbic—attack on ethnic influence over American diplomacy was contained in the analyses of political scientist G. Lowell Field. Professor Field admitted that he was interested in finding remedies "for the curse of ethnicity in American politics." He urged that the nationalities divisions of the major political parties be dissolved, and he also demanded the ostracism of politicians who appealed openly to the ethnic vote. Field went so far as to say that he denounced the notion that the "feelings of ethnic minorities are legitimate grounds for deciding whether or not . . . intervention by American power is possible or desirable."[2] Even if one questions the apparent stridency of Professor Field's views, it is hard to disagree with Charles Mayne's comment that there is a "possibility of very negative consequences following from a new intersection between American ethnicity and American foreign policy. . . . Ethnicity alone, divorced from larger foreign policy values or goals, can be a highly disruptive diplomatic wild card, working in unpredictable ways that can be destructive of national interests and priorities."[3]

It would be fatuous to pretend that we can resolve the complex problems related to ethnicity and foreign policy here. A few brief observations on how we might at least approach the problem can be offered, however. If the point of American foreign policy is to defend the national interest, that interest involves at least the following elements: the physical security of the United States, the protection and advancement of our economic well-being, the preservation of our democratic institutions, and, finally, the maintenance of what might be called the "national morale."

The concept of the "national morale" is perhaps the most amorphous element of the national interest, but this does not reduce its importance. National morale means general feelings of moral self-respect, confidence in the future, and pride in the country. It is obviously shaped by the course of domestic social, economic, and political events. It is also influenced by the nation's international situation, however, and it is in this particular respect that ethnic consciousness has its most evident role in determining American foreign policy, that is, of the American national interest. Judgments on what is necessary to secure the continued physical survival of the United States do not seem an appropriate object for ethnic pressures. However, if large ethnic populations consider the safety and welfare of their compatriots in the homeland to be important in their personal "morale," there is no inherent reason why American foreign policy should not give at least some attention to this fact, particularly when one of the supposed strengths of American society is precisely its rich pluralistic character. It seems inconsistent to praise this characteristic as important to the vitality and unique character of America while denying it any place in our foreign policy. Another leading student of ethnicity puts the point bluntly:

The right of ethnics to lobby for policies they desire no longer seems questionable. Why is the attempt by ethnic minorities to influence the direction of foreign policy any less legitimate than the lobbying efforts of any number of economic interest groups? Why should it be any less legitimate to vote from ethnic considerations than for economic or social reasons?[4]

This individual stresses once again that foreign policy "professionals" tend to stress military and economic interests in policy, but tend to ignore emotional factors like support for the downtrodden or impoverished, which is surely a valid goal of American diplomacy. As another writer, Lawrence Fuchs, has argued, foreign policy may be "too important to be left to the experts."[5]

Sticky problems do remain, however. There is the danger that ethnic groups in the United States, to the extent that they do have a measurable influence over foreign policy, may be regarded as "targets of opportunity" by political forces in the homeland that are either indifferent or hostile to basic American interests. Even if this should prove to be something of an illusory problem, there remains the question of just how American ethnic groups—and particularly Eastern European ethnic groups—can in fact assume a relevant and productive role in the determination and execution of American diplomacy toward the old country. Each of these points deserves separate attention.

MANIPULATION FROM THE HOMELAND

Shortly after the Republic was founded, none other than President George Washington sounded a warning about the possibly damaging implications of America's pluralistic character: "Against the insidious wiles of foreign influence (I conjure you to believe me, fellow citizens) the jealousy of a free people ought to be constantly awake, since history and experience prove that foreign influence is one of the most baneful foes of Republican Government."[6]

The evidence concerning the degree to which "foreign influence" has been a "baneful foe" of a republican foreign policy remains rather amorphous, but this does not mean that the issue President Washington raised is without significance. A more contemporary analysis reflects the same concern. "The persistent danger has been that some ethnic groups might place the desires of groups with which they have identified abroad ahead of consideration of the American national interest."[7] A review of American history presents various episodes in which ethnic groups in this country have been at least the putative targets of, and potentially compromised by, influence from abroad. There was, for example, the case of the large German-American community in the United States prior to and during World War I. German immigrants to this country had retained a keen interest in the struggle by the German nation to constitute itself a unified state. The famous German-American historian Carl Schurz spoke for many of his compatriots in a speech celebrating German Day at the Columbian Exposition in 1893: "What a glorious time! Every German heart, the wide world over, beat with admiration and gratitude for the kinsmen in the old home, and wherever the German mother tongue was heard, the joyful chorus resounded: At last the Germans have a Fatherland!"[8] The German-American Alliance was formed in 1901 to represent the German community in the United States, and by 1914 it claimed to have 2 million members. Originally designed to be an organization to defend German culture in this country, it acquired a reputation—fairly or unfairly—of having evolved into a movement controlled from Berlin. In any event, the Alliance lobbied strongly for American neutrality in the war, disputing the claims of British propaganda about German atrocities in the conflict and challenging the notion that Berlin represented a threat to American interests.[9]

Once the United States did enter the war, the backlash against the German-American community was substantial. Various streets and parks with German names were "Anglicized," sauerkraut became "liberty cabbage," the hamburger was restyled "the liberty burger," and even the inoffensive dachshund was converted to the "liberty dog." On a more serious note, some German-Americans were barred from school curricula, there were scattered instances of attacks on German-owned businesses, and some German-Americans went so far as to change their names in order to avoid persecution by the extremist patriotic fringe.[10]

In reaction to this painful experience, German-Americans generally retreated from involvement in the debate over foreign policy after World War I. The lesson they drew from the criticism heaped on them "was that other Americans would not tolerate groups who held themselves aloof; thus they should wholeheartedly adapt themselves to the national community."[11] The degree to which this premise was accepted by German-Americans was reflected in the widespread apathy and indifference that the community displayed toward the rise of Hitler and growing international tension in the 1930s. The notorious German-American Bund, openly pro-Hitler and supplied with funds from the German Embassy in Washington, never represented anything more than a small radical minority of the German-American presence in this country. The German Foreign Ministry itself "was frequently embarrassed by Bundist blunders and took all steps short of outright repudiation to control the organization."[12] At the time the German Ambassador to the United States, after trying for several years to drum up support for German policies among German-Americans, admitted to his superiors in Berlin that his efforts had been largely unavailing. Hardly one-third of the German-American community had any interest in the old country, he reported, and many of these were anti-Nazi.[13]

The Mussolini regime in Italy seemed to have had greater success in manipulating the Italian-American community during the same period. There was considerable admiration among many Italian-Americans for the "order" which Mussolini had brought to Italy, and the invasion of Ethiopia in 1936 aroused a good deal of enthusiasm. Rome was not loath to build on these sentiments. There was a major press and radio campaign to indoctrinate Americans of Italian ancestry. Mussolini wanted to counter anti-fascist sentiments within the Italian immigrant community, and he evidently also saw the 4 million Italian-Americans as a potential source of military manpower. In this connection, Italian consuls in the United States made a major effort to sustain and extend their influence over the Italian immigration, discouraging recent immigrants from becoming naturalized and attempting to intimidate any who spoke out against the fascist regime in Rome.[14] An effort of quite a different sort targeted at the Italian-American community came in 1948, when the democratic government in Rome was concerned about the prospect of a victory by the Italian Communist party in the national elections. Considerable effort—aided and abetted by American authorities themselves—was expended to convince Italian-Americans that they should communicate with family still in Italy, urging them to resist the siren song of Marxism (an effort that evidently paid some dividends, since the Communists failed to achieve power).

Two other groups merit attention in any discussion of the "manipulation" question, in part because they represent special aspects of the general issue. Prior to the achievement of Irish independence following World War I, people in this country commonly accepted the notion that the large Irish-American community had great potential importance in the struggle. As one authority has written, "the fires of Irish-American nationalism were repeatedly stoked by the visits of Irish

leaders who sought for Irish causes the pecuniary and moral assistance that the
Irish in America were uniquely qualified to give."[15] German efforts to keep the
United States neutral in World War I were directed not only at German-Americans but at the Irish in this country as well, an obvious strategy given the strong
anti-British sentiments of most Irish-Americans who resented continued British
control of the old country.

More recently, the Irish-American community has become a controversial aspect of the effort to achieve a political settlement in Northern Ireland, except
that in this case the players are somewhat different. Thus, the government of the
Republic of Ireland in Dublin has repeatedly urged Irish-Americans not to give
assistance or support to the Irish Republican Army (IRA), especially the Provi-
sionals, on the basis that such support constitutes a distinct barrier to peace in
the North. (Needless to say, the British government has made the same appeal,
although in their case the force of the argument may be somewhat muted.) Conversely, the IRA has made a documented effort to secure financial and political
support from Irish-Americans for their struggle against both the Protestants in
Northern Ireland and the British presence there. Spokesmen for the Irish Northern
Aid Committee (NORAID), one of the major Irish organizations in this country
concerned with the situation in Belfast, have repeatedly argued that their pecuniary help has been strictly for humanitarian aid for all victims of the struggle. The
argument might carry more weight if the IRA leaders did not regularly make trips
to the United States appealing to their compatriots for support for the "just rights"
of the people of Northern Ireland. In September 1982 Michael Flannery, founder
of NORAID, and three others were indicted in New York City for conspiring to
smuggle weapons to the IRA.[16] The evidence is that the Northern Ireland question has badly split the Irish-American community, and as a result it makes rather
marginal any potential influence of that community in the evolution of the situation. As one authority has commented, "Irish-Americans represent a significant
percentage of the electorate, but by the mid-1970s they neither shared a common
view on policy toward Ireland nor did they approach the issue with a high degree
of intensity. Accordingly, their ability to influence American policy toward Ireland
is questionable."[17]

Another controversial issue is the support by American Jews for the state of
Israel. The principal lobbying group for aid to Israel, the American-Israel Public
Affairs Committee (AIPAC), steadfastly maintains that it is an independent organization that receives no financial or political guidance from Israeli authorities.
This assertion is not easily judged. Former Senator William Fulbright (D.-Ark.)
was one of the sharpest voices decrying what he saw as an unnatural and disturb-
ing influence by Tel Aviv over a segment of the American population. He charged
that because of Israel's ability to arouse Jewish-American opinion, "in the Senate
the Israelis can count on 75 to 80 votes on anything they are interested in." One
incident during Fulbright's time in office is of interest in this connection. In 1975
the Administration proposed to sell a defensive missile system worth $256 million

to Jordan. The Israeli government denounced the intended sale and supposedly urged AIPAC to alert Jewish-Americans to the impending action. The director of AIPAC proceeded to distribute a memorandum discussing the sale to all members of both houses of Congress and to Jewish communities in 197 major and 200 smaller cities across the nation. The response was a deluge of calls and telegrams to the Congress urging rejection of the arms arrangement. It was in fact blocked by Congress.[18]

It may be tempting to conclude that various Israeli governments have been able to "use" Jewish-Americans to support Israel's interests, even if they could be considered contrary to broader American goals in the Middle East, especially good relations with the more moderate Arab governments. At the same time, it is important to recall a point made earlier, which is that the support Jewish-Americans give Israel is echoed with almost equal fervor by the clear majority of non-Jewish-Americans. The experience of German-Americans is instructive in this regard: they learned to their regret that given fundamentally different commitments in foreign policy by their fellow Americans it could be destructive, even dangerous, to try to insist on a fundamentally different line of diplomacy. This point brings us to the main focus of our analysis—Eastern European ethnics in the United States and their potential vulnerability to influence from the old homeland.

At least in the period since 1945 it would seem that such "vulnerability" would have been minimal. Given the generally high degree of tension between the United States and the Communist world in these years, it would have been futile—and, again, basically counterproductive—for Eastern European ethnics to push for a softer line toward the Communist bloc (the presumed goal of any manipulation from Prague, Budapest, or Sofia). In view of our previous discussion, the likelihood that most ethnics, in particular leaders of ethnic organizations, could have been persuaded by representatives of the homeland to do so appears in itself rather problematical. However, certain ambiguities in the situation here deserve some additional consideration.

It is instructive, in the first place, to recall that there have been definite episodes in which Eastern European ethnics in this country have been mobilized by representatives from the old country for political purposes. We have already referred to the activities of Thomas Masaryk in the Spring of 1918. Part of Masaryk's strategy to gain support for an independent Czechoslovakia was to cultivate his contacts in the Wilson Administration and in Congress. He also spent a good deal of time, however, appealing directly to the Czechoslovak community in the United States and made a particular point of trying to arouse their "consciousness" concerning the fate of the old country, which would then hopefully impact on their elected representatives. The activities of Masaryk were matched and even exceeded by those of Ignace Jan Paderewski, the world reknowned pianist and Polish nationalist, who came to the United States in 1915 as the unofficial representative of the Polish National Committee. Like Masaryk, Paderewski carefully nurtured contacts within the Administration and made a particular convert of Colonel

Edward House, perhaps President Wilson's most trusted adviser. At the same time, he appealed to the very large Polish-American community as the personification of Polish culture and patriotism. His success in mobilizing Polish-Americans behind the recreation of an independent Polish state extended even to many Americans of non-Polish background, who themselves saw Paderewski as the symbol of the new Poland. Paderewski's efforts played a considerable role in Wilson's decision to include a free Poland as one of his Fourteen Points.[19]

The coming of World War II raised the issue of the potential manipulation of the Eastern European ethnic community in a new form. *Fortune Magazine* warned in September 1942 that there is "dynamite on our shores," referring to the potential threat of divided loyalties among American ethnics.[20] The Office of Strategic Services and the Justice Department, employing the Alien Registration Section, seemed to take this warning to heart. Both organizations assembled considerable data on and analysis of nationality organizations, the foreign-language press, and the ethnic population generally. The State Department developed lists that classified various American ethnics as "loyal" or "disloyal."[21]

All of these activities took place in the pressured atmosphere of the wartime years, but there is some evidence that they were not simply an alarmist reaction to a phantom problem. Several organizations that purported to speak for American ethnics emerged at the time, and the indication was that the Soviet authorities played a not insignificant part in the formation and financing of these groups. The Polish American Labor Council, for instance, claimed to represent some 600,000 Polish workers in the United States and generally expressed enthusiasm for Stalin's positions concerning the postwar political settlement in Europe. Its president, Leo Krzycki, vigorously denounced the "divisive and vicious utterances of certain Polish misleaders [who had] no right to speak for all of us Americans of Polish origin or descent."[22] Krzycki's remarks were directed specifically at Charles Rozmarek, the president of the mainline Polish-American Congress.

More notorious was the American Slav Congress, which became an "important weapon of Moscow's political warfare against the United States."[23] The Congress was established in April 1942 and boasted that it represented the interests of over 15 million Slavs in the United States. Initially, the activities of the Congress were assisted by the fact that the Soviet Union was a wartime ally of the United States and was winning important victories against the bulk of the Germany Army. The American Slav Congress made a major effort to keep discussion of the Katyn Forest massacre off the public agenda. (Katyn was the site where over 4,000 Polish officers were slain by Soviet security forces.) It denounced the Polish government-in-exile in London as being unrepresentative of the views of Poles generally. The Congress also approved of Stalin's demand for the cession of thousands of square miles of territory in the eastern part of Poland to the Soviet Union at the conclusion of the war. These activities and others gradually alienated a number of Polish-American leaders and organizations as well as others, and as the Cold War developed the Congress became almost totally discredited. Whether during its heyday in World War II it may not have played some part in influencing the Roosevelt Administration's concessions on Eastern Europe at Teheran and Yalta is, however, an issue that remains ambiguous.[24]

Since 1945, evidence as to foreign penetration of the American Eastern European ethnic community has been extremely circumstantial, and given the general political orientation of at least the ethnic leadership, one might reasonably suppose that the question of overt or covert manipulation may not have been a major one. Nevertheless, there is scattered evidence that the issue cannot be entirely ignored. Thus, in the period after the rise of Gomulka to power in Poland in 1956 the Polish-American Congress combined general support for the Eisenhower Administration's policy of aiding the regime in Warsaw with expressed concerns about the potential of Communist infiltration of the organization, especially after many more Polish-Americans began to visit the old country following the relaxation of travel restrictions. This issue of possible subversion of the American Polonia became an extremely contentious one within the Congress and accounted for a general demoralization of its membership, to the point that during the early 1960s the Congress virtually faded from attention and the membership drastically declined.[25]

Even after the fortunes of the PAC revived under the leadership of Aloysius Malewzski, elected to the presidency of the organization in 1968, many still pointed out the continuing dilemma. Professor Piotr Wandycz of Harvard, for example, author of perhaps the leading study of Polish-American relations, noted that as the 1970s unfolded

the actual and potential contribution of the Polonia to American-Polish relations prompted the Warsaw government to cultivate it while asserting that it regarded the emigration as part of the American nation and had no wish to convert it to Communism. Warsaw has been seeking, however, to sustain and encourage the Polish Americans' interest in and attachment to the "old country." This policy has been rewarded with some success.

As far as the American Polonia is concerned, Wandycz argued, "the distinction between cooperating with Warsaw or being used by it has not always been clearly perceived."[26]

There has also been a continuing controversy about the putative manipulation of the large Croatian ethnic community in this country by the regime in Belgrade. Over the last ten years extremist Croatian elements in the United States have been involved in various actions, including airplane hijackings and bombings of Yugoslav government installations in Chicago and New York, to protest continued Yugoslav "oppression" of Croatian national rights. A charge made by some Croatian spokesmen is that the Yugoslav security service (UDBA) has been responsible for some of these activities in order to discredit the American Croatian population. Another accusation has been that the FBI has routinely provided information to the UDBA on dissident groups in this country, a charge that has been vehemently denied. The FBI claims that it "does not maintain any contact with the UDBA and has not furnished any information to that organization."[27] Whatever the real facts of the matter, it is of interest that in a draft report by the Senate Foreign Relations Committee, reference was made to an extensive network of Yugoslav secret police officials in this country whose prime function was to spy on Yugoslav-American groups and in some cases to engage in outright harassment.[28]

Finally, there are the interesting revelations of a Latvian, Imants Lesinskis, who was a Soviet KGB operative for twenty-three years before defecting to the United States in 1978. He described his work as one of "ethnic espionage." According to him, émigré mail from abroad is routinely intercepted by the Soviets; lists of Latvians living overseas are drawn up, with "files on almost all active immigrants." He goes on to say that "many people living in the West have ties to the old country and it is relatively easy for the KGB to use that nostalgia for the old country for their own purposes." One of the main goals of KGB activity is to organize Latvian support groups who will invite KGB people of the native country into the United States. The evident effectiveness of these efforts was caught in the statement of Aristids Lambergs, vice-chairman of the Boston-based American-Latvian Cultural Exchange Committee. "It dilutes our strength. It gets us to fight among ourselves. They are very effective." Moreover, Lambergs notes, "it is very difficult for the American government to counteract those ties because the American policy has been one of promoting human contact between émigrés and their homeland." Lesinskis himself claims that one West Coast-based Latvian group that he knows of has invited a number of persons with KGB connections to the United States.[29] The American Latvian community falls somewhat outside the ethnic groups being considered here, but Lesinskis' evidence nevertheless provides some striking confirmation that the overall issue of foreign manipulation of the Eastern European ethnic population remains a relevant one.

NOTES

1. NATIONAL PARTY PLATFORMS, 1840-1956, comp. Kirk H. Porter and Donald Bruce Johnson (Urbana: University of Illinois Press, 1956), 195-196.

2. G. Lowell Field, "Foreword," in THE HYPHENATE IN RECENT AMERICAN POLITICS AND DIPLOMACY by Louis Gerson (Lawrence: University of Kansas Press, 1964), xxvii; Field's views are also described in John Snetsinger's "Ethnicity and Foreign Policy," Vol. 1, ENCYCLOPEDIA OF AMERICAN FOREIGN POLICY, ed. Alexander De Conde (New York: Charles Scribner's Sons, 1978), 326.

3. Charles W. Maynes, "The Domestic Requirements of a Successful Foreign Policy," in PROCEEDINGS OF THE NATIONAL SECURITY AFFAIRS CONFERENCE, July 14-15, 1975 (Washington: National War College, 1975).

4. Snetsinger, "Ethnicity and Foreign Policy," 328.

5. Lawrence Fuchs, "Minority Groups and Foreign Policy," POLITICAL SCIENCE QUARTERLY 76 (1959), 161-75.

6. Howard Bahr, Bruce Chadwick, and Joseph Strauss, AMERICAN ETHNICITY (Lexington, Mass.: D.C. Heath and Co., 1979), 108.

7. Ralph P. Levering, THE PUBLIC AND AMERICAN FOREIGN POLICY 1918-1978 (New York: William Morrow and Co., 1978), 157.

8. Maldwyn A. Jones, THE OLD WORLD TIES OF AMERICAN ETHNIC GROUPS (London: H. K. Lewis and Co., 1976), 14.

9. Ibid., 15.

10. John Roche, "Immigration and Nationality: A Historical Overview of United States Policy," in ETHNIC RESURGENCE IN MODERN DEMOCRATIC STATES, ed. Uri Ra'anan (New York: Pergamon Press, 1980), 69.

11. Jones, THE OLD WORLD TIES, 17.

12. Frederick Luebke, "The Germans," in ETHNIC LEADERSHIP IN AMER-ICA, ed. John Higham (Baltimore: Johns Hopkins University Press, 1978), 84-85.

13. Joachim Remak, "'Friends of the New Germany': The Bund and German-American Relations," JOURNAL OF MODERN HISTORY, 29, no. 1 (March 1957), 41.

14. John P. Diggins, MUSSOLINI AND FASCISM; THE VIEW FROM AMER-ICA (Princeton: Princeton University Press, 1972), 78-110.

15. Jones, THE OLD WORLD TIES, 11.

16. NEW YORK TIMES, September 9, 1982, 44.

17. Snetsinger, "Ethnicity and Foreign Policy," 325.

18. NEW YORK TIMES, August 8, 1976, 2. For an extended treatment of both the Jewish-American and Arab-American lobbies in Washington, see Steven Spiegel, THE OTHER ARAB-ISRAELI CONFLICT: AMERICA'S MIDDLE EAST POLICY FROM TRUMAN TO REAGAN (Chicago: University of Chicago Press, 1985).

19. The overall issue of lobbying by Eastern European ethnics during the Wilson Administration is discussed by Mona Harrington, "Loyalties: Dual and Divided," in HARVARD ENCYCLOPEDIA OF AMERICAN ETHNIC GROUPS, ed. Stephen Thernstrom (Cambridge, Mass.: Harvard University Press, 1980).

20. Louis Gerson, "The Influence of Hyphenated Americans on U.S. Diplomacy," in ETHNICITY AND U.S. FOREIGN POLICY, ed. Abdul Azis Said, revised edition (New York: Praeger, 1981), 25.

21. Ibid.

22. Gerson, THE HYPHENATE IN RECENT AMERICAN POLITICS AND DIPLOMACY, 172.

23. Ibid., 171.

24. Ibid., 166-177.

25. Donald E. Pienkos, "The Polish American Congress—An Appraisal," POL-ISH AMERICAN STUDIES 36, no. 2 (1979), 5.

26. Piotr Wandycz, THE UNITED STATES AND POLAND (Cambridge, Mass.: Harvard University Press, 1980), 411.

27. NEW YORK TIMES, June 9, 1979, 8; Ibid., June 22, 1979, 3.

28. NEW YORK TIMES, August 9, 1979, 3.

29. CHRISTIAN SCIENCE MONITOR, June 14, 1984, 3-4.

7.

A Positive Role for Ethnics and American Foreign Policy

What is the appropriate role for Eastern European ethnics in determining American policy toward East Central Europe? In this connection, I would like to examine two relatively recent episodes that seem to demonstrate both the obstacles to and the potential for a positive role by the ethnic community in American diplomacy. The first concerns the controversy that arose over the Carter Administration's announced plan to return the Crown of St. Stephen to Hungary; the second involves the Polish-American community's position on American economic sanctions against Poland following the declaration of martial law in that country in December 1981.

THE RETURN OF THE CROWN OF ST. STEPHEN

The Holy Crown of St. Stephen is the most venerated symbol of Hungarian religious and national unity in existence. Tradition holds that Pope Sylvester II gave the Crown to St. Stephen, Hungary's first Christian king, in the year 1000. At the end of World War II, the Crown was handed over to American military units for safekeeping by its Hungarian custodians. Since 1945, there had been repeated discussions between Washington and Budapest as to its return. In early November 1977 the Administration of President Jimmy Carter announced that it had decided to return the Crown to Hungary, both as a testament to improved Hungarian-American relations and as a recognition of Hungary's increasing liberalization in domestic political and economic policy. The decision on the Crown was part of a more general American stance designed to encourage diversity within the Eastern European bloc.

The reaction of the Hungarian-American community in the United States was obviously a matter of some concern to the Carter Administration. Zbigniew Brzezinski, the President's National Security Adviser, supported the move as a positive way to encourage closer Hungarian-American relations, but was frank in saying that "after consulting the White House domestic advisers, I feared a negative reaction from voters of Eastern European origin."[1] The State Department claimed that it had attempted to survey the views of Hungarian-American ethnics on the matter, meeting or speaking with almost 100 leaders of Hungarian-American groups or with individuals representing only themselves.[2] As it turned out, Brzezinski's fears were well justified. On November 29, approximately 3,000 marchers representing thirty Hungarian-American organizations protested in the rain before the White House at the Crown's imminent return.[3] Later in December a large motorcade representing the same groups traveled from New York City to Independence Hall in Philadelphia in still another protest. Said one participant: "The Crown is a symbol of freedom of speech. But now it is being returned to the Communists against the wishes of most Hungarian Americans."[4]

On November 9, 1977, a Subcommittee of the House Committee on International Relations held hearings on the controversy surrounding the plan to return the Holy Crown of St. Stephen, and the testimony provided vivid evidence as to both the emotions and the contradictions inherent in the ethnic connection with American policy toward East Central Europe. Chairman Lee Hamilton repeatedly had to ask the audience to "refrain from demonstrations of either support or disapproval, even though I know [you] feel very strongly about this."[5] In the event, Congressman Hamilton's attempts at decorum were often defeated. Two prominent members of earlier Hungarian regimes, Major General Bela Kiraly, Commander in Chief of the National Guard, and Ferenc Nagy, former Prime Minister, spoke in favor of the Crown's return. One member of the audience denounced Kiraly as a "Benedict Arnold." Nagy was asked whether he was on the State Department's payroll (he had worked for Radio Free Europe). Another person shouted, "Mr. Chairman, how many more Munichs do we need?" The main burden of the criticism leveled by spokesmen for groups such as the World Federation of Hungarian Freedom Fighters was that the return of the Crown would represent a recognition of the Hungarian regime's "legitimacy" and would also ignore the lack of fundamental human rights in Hungary. Representative Mary Rose Oaker (D.-Ohio), representing a large Hungarian-American constituency in Cleveland, noted that she had introduced a bill (H.R. 7893) entitled "The Hungarian Crown of St. Stephen Protection Act" that would require the express approval of Congress before the Crown could be returned.[6]

Understandably, many members of the Hungarian-American community, particularly given the emotional significance attached to the Holy Crown of St. Stephen, would have misgivings about the implied message of its return to a regime that despite its relative "liberalism" was hardly an example of Jeffersonian democracy. At the same time, the unyielding resistance of various Hungarian-American groups and spokespersons to the Crown's return represents a classic example of the difficulties American ethnics have frequently had in establishing a constructive role in influencing the policy process. Three points in particular stand out when one examines the episode concerning the return of the Crown.

General Kiraly underlined one of these points when he asked whether the wishes of the 10 million people in Hungary themselves or the much smaller Hungarian-American émigré community should be paramount. As Kiraly eloquently put it:

There are émigrés who would hate to see the Holy Crown go back to Hungary because they can look at events in today's Hungary only with passionate loathing. I understand their sentiments, for there has been too much suffering for it to be easily forgotten. The issue, however, is whose wishes should have priority: those of a few thousand embittered émigrés or those of millions of Hungarians. I am sure the ten million Hungarians in Hungary desire to have the Holy Crown back. I respectfully recommend that their wishes be given priority.[7]

The ultimate issue, Kiraly argued, was "the limitation of passion by reason and commonsense."

Then there is the question that has been addressed at some length in this chapter, that is, who really speaks for the ethnic community? The State Department claimed that when it spoke to various leaders of the same Hungarian-American organization on a private basis their "individual views often varied from the stated public position of the group."[8] In view of the extremely charged atmosphere surrounding the House hearings on the return of the Crown, it is not surprising that Hungarian-Americans in support of the Carter Administration's policy should have felt some trepidation about testifying. One individual who did testify, Professor Ivan Volgyes, commented in this regard that the "best specialists have appeared here not as representatives of émigré groups, but as individual citizens who support the return of the Crown to Hungary."[9] Volgyes, a native-born Hungarian, fled Hungary following the revolution of 1956; such a background hardly made him sympathetic toward the Communist polity in Budapest. It should also be stressed that not all Hungarian-American groups were overtly opposed to the Crown's return. The largest Hungarian fraternal organization, the William Penn Association, went on record as supporting the return, on condition that the Crown remain in Hungary, that most-favored-nation trade status be given to the country, and that the Administration continue to champion human rights and religious freedom in Hungary.

Perhaps most important, by any objective evaluation, the Carter Administration's return of the Holy Crown of St. Stephen to Hungary represented an appropriate measure to advance both the pragmatic and the moral concerns of the United States. Any steps that succeed in furthering American influence in Eastern Europe—and by implication reducing Soviet domination over the region—seem almost self-evidently desirable. Policies that encourage greater "polycentrism" in the region fall into the same category. As several witnesses pointed out in the House hearings, the return of the Crown in no sense "legitimized" the Budapest regime; the United States already recognized its de facto legitimacy since it maintained diplomatic relations with the Hungarian government. The issue was whether

Washington should not pursue every avenue to move the Hungarian regime in a direction more palatable to Western definitions of pluralism. This also raises the question of American moral concerns. As Professor Volgyes rightly pointed out, the return of the Crown was evidence that the United States was in fact concerned about the future of Hungary: "In an age of increasing ethnic consciousness, close ties with Hungary must be a part of U.S. foreign policy that cannot and should not be neglected." Volgyes stated that the decision on the Crown was also related to America's own self-image. Clearly, the United States had no legal right to retain permanent custody over the Holy Crown of St. Stephen. Its return, therefore, was evidence that this country did respect legal norms as well as the sensitivities of the Hungarian people. "We should return the Crown to the people of Hungary, above all, for this reason," Volgyes concluded, "because it is their precious and cherished heritage and because it is the truly just thing to do."[10]

On January 6, 1978, Secretary of State Cyrus Vance led a U.S. delegation to Budapest composed of various governmental and private figures as part of the ceremony that marked the final return of the Holy Crown of St. Stephen to the Hungarian people. Hungarian-American relations have continued to develop since that time in a manner positive both for the citizens of Hungary and those of the United States. If the controversy over the Crown ultimately failed to derail this process, it nevertheless stands as a sobering example of the continuing difficulties some elements within one American ethnic group have in adopting a constructive approach to shaping American policy toward the homeland. Another recent case which has more positive connotations, however, involves Polish-Americans and the question of American economic sanctions against the regime of General Wojciech Jaruzelski.

THE POLISH SANCTIONS ISSUE

On December 13, 1981, the Polish government declared a state of martial law and outlawed the independent Solidarity trade union movement. The reaction of the Reagan Administration was swift. In a presidential address of December 23, Reagan promised that if the Polish regime decided to respect human rights as established by the Gdansk agreement of a year earlier, "we in America will gladly do our share to help the shattered Polish economy." In the absence of such a commitment, however, the United States was imposing a series of economic sanctions against the Warsaw regime. There would be no attempt to block food shipments to Poland undertaken through private humanitarian channels, but the President suspended all government-sponsored shipments of agricultural and dairy products to the Polish regime. "We must be sure that every bit of food provided by America goes to the Polish people, not their oppressors," Reagan said. Other sanctions included the suspension of Export-Import Bank credits, a ban on LOT (the Polish national airline) flights to the United States, the ending of Polish fishing rights in American waters, removal of Poland's most-favored-nation tariff status,

and American opposition to Polish membership in the International Monetary
Fund. The President stressed that these measures were "not directed against the
Polish people."[11]

If Hungarian-Americans were aroused over the issue of the Holy Crown of St.
Stephen, there was an equal, if not greater, fervor among Polish-Americans concerning developments in Poland both before and after the edict of martial law
was announced. The community of Wallington, New Jersey, for example, a suburb
of New York City, featured a population that was almost 85 percent Polish-American. As Solidarity struggled to maintain its independence in early 1981, the latest
news from Poland was the dominant topic of conversation. An extensive fund-
raising campaign was launched to provide resources to Solidarity. The majority
of men interviewed in Wallington by a visiting journalist indicated that they would
return to Poland to fight if the Soviets invaded.[12] In other areas of the American
Polonia, there was considerable excitement at the time about the relatively new
ease of communication between those in the old country and the Polish community in the United States. An editor of a leading Polish-American newspaper
in New York remarked that "there's a coming and going, an open door now between Poland and the West, like there never was before." The Kosciuszko Foundation, a major national organization for maintenance of the Polish cultural tradition, was particularly active in financing exchange programs for scholars, artists,
and students. In the previous year, the Foundation had sponsored almost 1,000
exchanges of Americans and Poles.[13]

It is against this background of pronounced optimism, even exhilaration, concerning developments in Poland that the subsequent evolution of Polonia's attitude toward American policy must be measured as an example of a notably mature and constructive application of ethnic political influence. One might have
expected that given the initial hopes of Polish-Americans that Poland had at last
achieved a real measure of freedom and independence, the subsequent disillusionment following martial law would have been strong indeed—and, in typical fashion,
would have resulted in an adamant stand against any dealings by Washington with
the Jaruzelski regime. The initial reaction by members of the ethnic community
reflected their strong feelings about developments in Poland. Various members
of Congress with a Polish background reported receiving a huge number of communications about the situation. Then-Congressman Edward Derwinski (R.-Ill.)
commented that "there's been an amazing interest in this whole Polish crisis."
Yet even in the first emotional weeks after the declaration of martial law, there
was evidence that the Polish-American community was not inclined to harness
all its energies and direct its entire policy toward sustaining an unyielding stance
by Washington vis-à-vis Jaruzelski. One interesting indicator at the time was the
experience of Congressman Dan Rostenkowski (D.-Ill.). In view of his own background and the large Polish-American segment of his constituency in the Chicago
area, Rostenkowski himself was braced to receive "an avalanche of calls" on the
Polish question. As it turned out, he received far fewer communications concerning

Poland than expected. One explanation was that people in his district realized that he was tied up in the debate over Social Security legislation—and this was of greater direct importance to them than events in Warsaw.[14]

The relative restraint—and realism—with which the Polonia regarded developments in Poland became increasingly manifest over the next several years. Few within the Polish-American community, or within American society generally, expressed anything other than outrage about the demise of the precious and brief freedoms that Poles had enjoyed during the heyday of the Solidarity movement. At the same time, the issue rather quickly became one not of whether Solidarity had any prospect of being restored to its previous position—Soviet pressure presumably eliminated this as a possibility—but whether there was any prospect that at least some of what Solidarity had fought for could be maintained. More specifically, how did American sanctions promote or deter this goal? An early analysis by one noted authority suggested a perhaps surprising conclusion in this regard, which was that Polish-Americans might well bring pressure to bear *against* continued sanctions, in part because the Polonia did not want the old country to be used as a pawn in the Soviet-American rivalry, and in part because full contacts with relatives in Poland would be significantly influenced by normalization of relations between Warsaw and Washington.[15]

This analysis proved to be perceptive. In November 1983 and January 1984 the Reagan Administration announced the removal of certain of the minor sanctions, including restoration of Polish fishing rights in American waters, permission to LOT to fly charter flights to the United States, and an agreement on talks concerning the rescheduling of Poland's massive official debt to the West. These steps aroused little enthusiasm among Polish-American leaders, but at the same time were not denounced by them. The question of sanctions was fully joined on July 21, 1984, when the Polish government announced a general amnesty for political prisoners seized during the initial period of martial law, which was one of the major prerequisites the Reagan Administration had established for normalization of its relations with the Polish regime. Administration officials indicated that the immediate American reaction would likely be to lift some additional sanctions, including the ban on regularly scheduled flights of LOT to the United States and American-financed scientific exchanges with Poland. Whether additional steps would be taken to lift other, more substantive economic sanctions would depend in part, it was said, on consultations with the major Polish-American groups.[16]

Less than two weeks later, the Administration announced that it had lifted the aforementioned sanctions, and the issue then became whether the United States ought to remove its opposition to Polish membership in the International Monetary Fund, whether Washington should once again confer most-favored-nation trade status on Poland, and whether American governmental credits for Polish purchase of food and other commodities should be restored. At this point the Polish-American Congress made an important decision, which was to reverse its previous coolness toward the lifting of sanctions and instead to press for a general dialogue with the Jaruzelski government as to the long-term implications of its announced amnesty for political prisoners. In particular, the Congress urged that discussions go forward on the question of Polish readmittance to the IMF, which was critical to Poland's future economic prospects. Aloysius Mazewski, president of the PAC, indicated that at the present he was opposed to renewal of U.S. commodity and Export-Import Bank credits, but his statements revealed two pragmatic considerations that are worthy of special attention. First, Mazewski referred to the opinion of those in Poland itself, especially the Catholic Church. He indicated that the Congress had been in close touch with Polish church authorities and had been persuaded by their argument that the lifting of at least some of the sanctions was in the Polish people's interest. (This position is in considerable contrast to the general lack of reference to Hungarian opinion itself by those Hungarian-Americans opposed to the return of the Holy Crown of St. Stephen.) Also of significance in this connection was the position of Solidarity leader Lech Walesa, who himself called for the lifting of American economic sanctions. Second, Mazewski recognized that, despite the continued objectionable features of the Jaruzelski government, a rigid American policy toward Warsaw would carry significant practical costs. Of particular concern was the possibility that the Polish regime might be pushed totally into the embrace of the Soviet Union and (barring Polish IMF membership) into surrendering any Western influence over the structuring of the Polish economy.[17]

There is a legitimate debate about whether American economic sanctions against Poland were effective in terms of moving the Jaruzelski regime in the desired direction, or whether the measured reduction in sanctions was not calculated to achieve the same purpose with greater efficiency. The important consideration for present purposes is the evident willingness of the Polish-American Congress to weigh its own policy stance remarkably free of emotion and temporarily satisfying expressions of outrage and opposition—on a question where such expressions would have been after all understandable—and instead struggle toward a position that reflected the complexities of their concerns regarding the old country. The position of the Congress represented only the culmination of an extended process of becoming a responsible and involved actor in the development of American policy toward Poland. As noted earlier, the Polish-American Congress, not without considerable soul searching, supported President Eisenhower's program of economic assistance to the Gomulka regime in 1957. It also gave general approval to President Johnson's "bridge-building" policy to Eastern Europe in the 1960s. Perhaps most symbolic, at the 1978 international Polonia conference in Canada, the president of the PAC argued for steadily increasing cultural exchanges between Poland and the United States so that involved individuals could debate the merits and drawbacks of the Polish system with Poles themselves.[18] All in all, then, the Polish-American Congress, perhaps more than any other Eastern European ethnic organization, has approached a solution of the perennial problem facing the ethnic community: an appropriate melding of idealism and realism.

CONCLUSION

In trying to establish a reasonable policy on the interaction between the Eastern European ethnic community and American diplomacy toward East Central Europe, one can accept the notion "that the goodwill that can be won by emphasizing the interrelationship between the ethnic group and policy toward the land of origin provides a compelling argument for encouraging such a relationship."[19] This observation is not as cynical as it sounds. In a democratic, pluralistic society, as the United States is proud to claim it is, due respect for the views of even relatively small segments of the total society is not only appropriate but perhaps necessary, not just on domestic matters but even in foreign policy. This need not—and should not—however, involve merely a concern about the potentially disruptive influence of the relevant ethnic group. On the contrary, the rich ethnic background of the American people provides manifold positive opportunities for a more efficacious foreign policy. A sensitive student of the relationship between Poland and the United States, for example, argues that "the Polish American elite can serve as an interpreter of the United States to Poland and vice versa. ... The actual and especially the potential role of the Polonia as a bridge between the two countries should not be underestimated." To be sure, there are dangers here. The same author cautions that the Polish-American elite must not "become a hybrid out of touch with both cultures operating within a miniculture of its own. This is a far more real danger than that of the 'hyphenate' being torn by conflicting loyalties."[20]

There is a real threat that Eastern European ethnic leaders—not to mention Eastern European ethnics generally—may find themselves lost between two cultures as they attempt to harness the energies of their new country in service to the old. Thus, any debate over the appropriate role of an American ethnic community in American diplomacy has to begin by defining and explicating that community itself. One of the tragedies of the Eastern European ethnic in American foreign policy has been that the voices that have spoken for the community— or at least have been perceived as speaking for it—have reflected only a partial measure of the insight and humanity of Eastern European ethnics as a whole. That Americans of Eastern European ethnic background should remain concerned about the conditions of their fellows in the homeland seems not only logical but also laudable. The problem has always been to place this concern within the context of the larger national interest of their adopted land. If we judge from the actions of spokespersons for certain of the most vocal ethnic groups of the 1950s and 1960s, this problem never approached solution. Given greater moderation and subtlety in the rhetoric—and perhaps a broader perspective as the more tangible memories of the homeland fade—it may yet be solved.

As far as the Eastern European ethnic community as a whole is concerned, however, there may be less conflict here than one might suppose. A theme enunciated earlier bears repeating for what it can tell us about the real implications of the influence of ethnicity on foreign policy. Gertrude Stein once said that every writer needs two countries: the country he or she lives in and a country of the imagination. Unlike Stein's Paris expatriates, Eastern European immigrants rarely wanted to leave America. "But, like them, they looked to the Old World to supply what America could not give, but what they felt they needed to restore the wholeness of their lives."[21] Ironically, then, the real purpose of Eastern European ethnic pressures on American foreign policy may have been to achieve greater dignity at home rather than a particular stance abroad.

NOTES

1. Zbigniew Brzezinski, POWER AND PRINCIPLE (New York: Farrar, Straus and Giroux, 1983), 299.

2. U.S. Congress, House of Representatives, Committee on International Relations, Subcommittee on Europe and the Middle East, THE HOLY CROWN OF ST. STEPHEN AND UNITED STATES-HUNGARIAN RELATIONS, Hearings, November 9, 1977, 95th Congress, 1st Session (Washington: GPO, 1978), 116 (hereafter cited as *Hearings*).

3. NEW YORK TIMES, November 30, 1977, B8.

4. NEW YORK TIMES, December 27, 1977, 3.

5. *Hearings*, 1.

6. *Hearings*, 2.

7. *Hearings*, 7.

8. *Hearings*, 8.

9. *Hearings*, 154.

10. Ibid.

11. Congressional Quarterly, HISTORIC DOCUMENTS OF 1981 (Washington: Congressional Quarterly Inc., 1982), 894-896.

12. NEW YORK TIMES, February 2, 1981, B1.

13. NEW YORK TIMES, February 20, 1981, B1.

14. NEW YORK TIMES, December 21, 1981, A17.

15. Jerry Hough, THE POLISH CRISIS: AMERICAN POLICY OPTIONS (Washington: Brookings Institution, 1982), 66.

16. NEW YORK TIMES, July 22, 1984, 7.

17. CHRISTIAN SCIENCE MONITOR, August 2, 1984, 1.

18. Donald E. Pienkos, "The Polish American Congress—An Appraisal," POLISH AMERICAN STUDIES 36, no. 2 (1979), 20-21.

19. John Snetsinger, "Ethnicity and Foreign Policy," in ENCYCLOPEDIA OF AMERICAN FOREIGN POLICY, vol. 1, ed. Alexander De Conde (New York: Charles Scribner's Sons, 1978), 327.

20. Piotr S. Wandycz, THE UNITED STATES AND POLAND (Cambridge, Mass.: Harvard University Press, 1980), 413.

21. Maldwyn A. Jones, THE OLD WORLD TIES OF AMERICAN ETHNIC GROUPS (London: H. K. Lewis and Co., 1976), 29.

Part II.

THE CARROT OR THE STICK: THE ECONOMICS AND POLITICS OF AMERICAN TRADE WITH EASTERN EUROPE

8.

Trade and Politics

In recent years, the subject of American trade with and investment in the Communist world has received increasing attention, particularly in the context of the general policy of detente and the erosion of detente during the Reagan years. Even though the issue of East-West economic relations figured prominently in earlier periods as well, the recent debate has probably been more intense than anything witnessed previously. Part of the reason for this, of course, is that an increasing Western trade with the Communist world presumably represents a fundamental rejection of the earlier premises and tools of the Cold War. Whether such a rejection is warranted generally has perhaps been the central theme of the foreign policy debate since at least the beginning of the Nixon Administration. In all the discussion on trade with the Communist regimes, however, the focus has been largely directed toward trade with the Soviet Union and, to a lesser extent, with the People's Republic of China. Relatively little has been offered on the more specific question of Western and especially American trade with the regimes of Eastern Europe. Although the latter question cannot be analyzed in isolation from the more general problem of East-West economic interchange, the issue of trade with the Communist countries of Eastern Europe does deserve separate and specialized consideration. The rationale for such trade, and the obstacles to its developing and having potentially productive side-effects, are in many instances distinct from those that obtain vis-à-vis the Soviet Union itself.

One can analyze American economic relations with Eastern Europe from a variety of perspectives. We might offer an essentially technical assessment of how important exports are to the American economy generally and what the past and future share of our exports Eastern Europe has absorbed and reasonably could be expected to absorb. The following discussion, however, is concerned largely with the political context of American trade with Eastern Europe, with trade as one facet of our overall policy stance toward the area. In this connection, it is striking how trade has been viewed by policymakers and, to some extent, by the general public as well as a significant tool of American policy. During earlier periods of that policy, trade was seen as a "stick" with which the United States could pummel and weaken the East European regimes; particularly during more recent periods, it has also been seen as a "carrot" that would facilitate a new American relationship with the countries of the region.

TRADE AS A STICK

Following the absorption of Eastern Europe into the Soviet orbit after World War II, the United States pursued a rather paradoxical commercial policy toward the region. On the one hand, we lamented the process by which the peoples of Eastern Europe had been subjected to Soviet domination. On the other hand, after 1948, we adopted a position on Eastern Europe that seemed designed to recognize no differences (or at least very few) between the dominated and the dominant. An economic embargo and boycott were established which treated the Soviet Union and the Eastern European states as equivalent. The general anti-Communist rhetoric emanating out of Washington condemned both Russian and East European leaders with fine impartiality. The United States broke diplomatic relations with several East European regimes (such as Albania and Bulgaria) and downgraded American diplomatic representation in several other countries (e.g., Hungary). The theory behind all this, of course, was that a unified Soviet bloc was in operation and that any assistance to or normalization with a member of that "bloc" would redound to the benefit of the total Communist monolith. Another important premise was that the "temporary" and "illegitimate" Communist regimes of Eastern Europe were not representative of the people they purported to serve, and thus any American dealings with these regimes would connive in the continued repression of those yearning for freedom.

A basic conclusion was that normal trade relations with the Eastern European countries was not in the interest of the United States. Two considerations underlay this judgment. On the one hand, imports by the Eastern European regimes of Western products, both agricultural and manufactured, would supposedly convey a series of benefits to the relevant governments. It would allow them to shift capital resources to military development, would strengthen the overall technological base of the system which in itself had military implications, and, perhaps most importantly, would save the Communist regimes from the consequences of the inherent flaws in their political-economic planning. The assumption was that the highly centralized nature of socialist decision-making, together with its emphasis on development of heavy industry, was bound to create a crisis in productivity and standards of living because of the inefficiencies inherent in such a system and the warping in allocation of resources. The result could only be a rising popular discontent with the prevailing regime, with potentially decisive political consequences. An embargo on trade with the Communist governments would thus impede their economic-military progress at the same time as it would accentuate a process of internal political instability. The existence of such instability would in itself contribute to the goal of weakening the regimes' economic infrastructure, in that it would severely limit the growth rates of the economies involved.[1]

The basic step by which the program of controls on trade with the Communist world generally and with Eastern Europe specifically was established was the Export Control Act of 1949. One purpose of the act was to protect our own domestic economy from an abnormal foreign demand for our products (which theoretically involved both Communist and non-Communist purchases). The real thrust of the Export Control Act, however, was to promote general foreign policy objectives of the United States and in particular to insure that American security was not undermined by export of what were styled "strategic goods." Under the act, virtually all American exports were subject to licensing. The General License, which allowed the export of certain classes of goods with the necessity of a special license for each transaction, involved primarily nonstrategic goods as defined in a published General License list. There was also a Validated License which applied to more sensitive items and which was issued only after the exporter certified the purposes for which the purchasing agent was acquiring the product. The Commerce Department maintained a "positive list" of goods regarded as strategic and thus generally denied to Communist countries. At the peak of the Cold War in the 1950s, there were around 1,000 items on this special list. In 1950 the United States, in cooperation with other major Western industrial countries and Japan, established the Consultative Group Coordinating Committee (COCOM) to insure unity in denying strategic goods to the Communist world. The Export Control Act of 1949 was supplemented by a series of subsequent pieces of legislation. The Mutual Defense Assistance Control Act (Battle Act) of 1951 forbade U.S. military, economic, or financial assistance to any country that permitted the sale of strategic goods to the Communist bloc in violation of the terms of the Export Control Act. Under the Agricultural Trade Development and Assistance Act of 1954 (PL 480), no exports of agricultural surpluses to any country dominated by international communism was allowed. (Yugoslavia was not regarded to be under such control.) Finally, in 1962 the Export Control Act was extended to proscribe the export of goods that had not just strategic but "economic significance" as well.[2]

At the same time as restrictions were being put on American exports to the Communist countries, obstacles were also placed on the import of goods from these regimes. The Trade Agreements Extension Act of 1951 withdrew most-favored-nation tariff status from the exports of the Communist world. These exports were henceforward subject to the extreme restrictions of the Smoot-Hawley Tariff Act of 1930. The act of 1951 also prohibited outright the import of certain specific items from various Communist countries (e.g., furs and skins from the Soviet Union). To further impede Communist trade with the United States, the Administration went beyond the practice of other Western countries in withholding regular diplomatic immunity and permanent resident status from Eastern

European trade organizations in this country. Commercial agents of the Communist nations were even restricted as to their travel and circulation while in the United States. Finally, for certain countries such as the People's Republic of China, North Vietnam, North Korea, and later Cuba, the American market was closed altogether by the Foreign Assets Control Regulations issued pursuant to the Trading with the Enemy Act of 1917. This boycott also applied to foreign firms, corporations, and business associations effectively controlled by Americans.[3]

TRADE AS A CARROT

A rather dramatic transition in American attitudes toward trade with Eastern Europe began to develop in the 1960s as part of a new American flexibility in dealing with the countries of the region. An important factor in understanding this transition is the historical American perception that Eastern Europe has always represented a potentially important market for American exports. It was the hope of tapping the Soviet market that contributed heavily to the American decision to recognize the Soviet regime in 1933. The same sentiments have applied, if perhaps with less intensity and consistency, to Eastern Europe. When one considers that, as of 1980, Eastern Europe (excluding the Soviet Union) had a combined Gross National Product of over $543 billion and a population exceeding 139 million, the idea that real economic opportunities have been present for the United States in the region does not seem frivolous.[4]

In any event, by the beginning of the decade, increasing doubts had come to be voiced about the rationale and effectiveness of the combination of embargo and boycott that the United States had employed since 1949, at least as it was directed toward the Soviet Union and Eastern Europe. (Few voices were calling for any changes in policy toward the People's Republic of China at this time.) Typical of the doubts now being expressed was the testimony given to a Sub-Committee on Foreign Economic Policy of the Joint Economic Committee of Congress during hearings in December 1961. One expert on international trade stated that, in pragmatic terms at least, export-import restrictions were rapidly becoming irrelevant. Professor Robert Allen commented that

it is my belief that the usefulness of the strategic embargo and discrimination against the Soviet Union and Eastern Europe is almost ended. The United States should consider the elimination of these measures in return for suitable concessions from state trading nations concerning their trading standards and practices. The interests of the United States can better be served by concentrating wholeheartedly on the achievement of worldwide economic stability and development through reduced trade barriers, enlarged capital flows, and more effective economic cooperation.[5]

Allen was hardly an optimist about any mellowing of the Communist challenge, but his remarks did reflect a growing consensus that in strict economic terms the United States would be better served by a change in previous policy. More to the point, however, as the decade advanced a number of others began to support liberalized trade with Eastern Europe, not just in terms of economic benefits to the United States, but in a much broader political context. Arguments were advanced that increased trade would help to reduce long-held suspicions, tensions, and frictions in the general American-East European relationship. It would also support the position of the relative "moderates" in the governments of Eastern Europe who were beginning to assert the benefits of normalized relations with the West. In addition, increased American-Eastern European trade would give the governments of the region an alternative to total economic reliance on the Soviet Union, and thus would contribute to a loosening of the Soviet-East European bloc structure as a whole, which—as we have noted earlier—has been a basic interest of the United States since World War II. Finally, Western trade could play a key role in encouraging and making possible a gradual decentralization of economic decision-making in Eastern Europe, which several of these governments were coming to favor. Such decentralization, of course, was bound to have at least some political consequences as more and more centers of at least partial decision-making autonomy were created. Samuel Pisar maintained that there was an "organic link" between internal economic reform in Eastern Europe and the latter's participation in the "international division of labor." In both cases, Pisar argued, "the stress is on efficiency. And efficiency has come to be identified with greater reliance on economic, as against political, considerations in the organization of production and commodity exchange."[6]

The new fusion of economics and politics as part of an American campaign of "bridge-building" to Eastern Europe was represented most notably in the Johnson Administration's submission of the East-West Trade Relations Act of 1966 to Congress. In his 1965 State of the Union address, the President had noted that in "Eastern Europe restless nations are slowly beginning to assert their identity. Your government, assisted by leaders in labor and business, is exploring ways to increase peaceful trade with these countries."[7] In a covering letter to the Trade Relations Act of 1966, the Administration argued more specifically that "the intimate engagement of peaceful trade, over a period of time, can influence Eastern European societies to develop along paths that are favorable to world peace."[8] The bill would have made possible the lowering of tariffs and even the granting of most-favored-nation trade status to certain Communist countries provided various rather vague conditions were met. As it happened, the bill died because of congressional opposition (fueled in part by the emotional issue of aid to North Vietnam being given by Communist states). It would have been only a modest step forward in any case, as the bill specifically did not constitute a direct revision of the Export Control Act of 1949 or the Battle Act of 1951.

Subsequent passage of the Export Administration Act of 1969, however, did represent a real change from previous legislation. Two major shifts in policy were provided for: it now became official American policy to encourage trade with *all* countries the United States had diplomatic or trading relations with, and export controls were now to focus only on *militarily* significant items as opposed to those with merely economic significance.[9] The proscriptions against certain exports were modified still further by a provision that a ban on export of a given item should not be maintained if it could be shown that Communist governments could purchase it from Western Europe or Japan. Only if it could be demonstrated that a sale by an American firm directly threatened U.S. national security was the ban to remain in effect. The Equal Export Opportunity Act of August 1972 broadened the terms of the earlier legislation, freeing over 1,500 items from restrictions under the terms of this act.[10]

Even in the absence of specific legislative provisions, the Johnson Administration undertook actions under Executive authority to ease restrictions on trade with Eastern Europe. On October 7, 1966, for instance, the President reduced export controls on several hundred nonstrategic items, and he signed a determination allowing extension of commercial credit guarantees to Poland, Hungary, Bulgaria, and Czechoslovakia.[11] Over the next several years stretching into the Nixon Administration, the process continued by which the Executive systematically reduced the number of items requiring a General License for export and transferred a number of others from the Validated License category to the General. Partly as a consequence of these actions, American trade with Eastern Europe in the period 1965-72 grew at a slow but steady pace. In 1965 American exports to Eastern Europe (considered here to include Bulgaria, Czechoslovakia, East Germany, Hungary, Poland, and Romania) amounted to only about $95 million, with imports from the area at the same level. By 1972 American exports had advanced to $272 million and imports from Eastern Europe to $226 million, an increase of 286 percent and 227 percent, respectively.[12]

American trade policy with Eastern Europe by the beginning of the 1970s had thus come almost (if not quite) full circle. At the end of World War II, there were great expectations about American penetration of the Eastern European market, and the figures for 1946 did give some credence to these hopes. (Exports to Czechoslovakia, for example, amounted to some $106 million and to Poland, $183 million.)[13] After this brief flush of enthusiasm, the United States switched into the embargo/boycott stance toward Eastern Europe that we have described. Now and for the past two decades, the general emphasis has been on a renewed economic relationship with the countries of the area. The question is whether the assumptions and expectations of the United States in any of these phases of policy toward Eastern Europe were or are valid, especially as far as the political importance attached to trade is concerned.

NOTES

1. A fuller treatment of the arguments for the embargo and boycott may be found in Thomas A. Wolf, U.S. EAST-WEST TRADE POLICY (Lexington, Mass.: D. C. Heath, 1975).

2. Marshall Goldman, DETENTE AND DOLLARS (New York: Basic Books, 1975), 48-50.

3. Samuel Pisar, COEXISTENCE AND COMMERCE (New York: McGraw-Hill, 1970), 94-107.

4. THE NEW BOOK OF WORLD RANKINGS, ed. George Kurian (New York: Facts on File, 1984), 96-97; International Institute of Strategic Studies, THE MILITARY BALANCE 1985-1986 (London: IISS, 1985), 31-67.

5. U.S. Congress, Joint Economic Committee, FOREIGN ECONOMIC POL-ICY, Hearings before the Subcommittee on Foreign Economic Policy, December 4-14, 1961 (Washington: GPO, 1962), 99.

6. Pisar, COEXISTENCE AND COMMERCE, 27-28.

7. DEPARTMENT OF STATE BULLETIN 52 (January 25, 1965), 96.

8. Ibid., 54 (May 30, 1966), 838.

9. James Henry Giffen, THE LEGAL AND PRACTICAL ASPECTS OF TRADE WITH THE SOVIET UNION (New York: Praeger, 1971), 102-103.

10. Goldman, DETENTE AND DOLLARS, 48-50.

11. Pisar, COEXISTENCE AND COMMERCE, 89-91.

12. U.S. Department of Commerce, Bureau of East-West Trade, SELECTED U.S.S.R. AND EASTERN EUROPEAN TRADE AND ECONOMIC DATA (Washington: GPO, May 1974).

13. U.S. Department of Commerce, Bureau of the Census, STATISTICAL ABSTRACT OF THE UNITED STATES 1947 (Washington: GPO, 1947).

9.
A General Evaluation

In formulating an answer to the last question, the initial step is to examine what the figures show as to the past and potential of American trade with Eastern Europe. Tables 3 and 4 present data on American exports to and imports from Bulgaria, Czechoslovakia, Hungary, Poland, Romania, and Yugoslavia for various years since 1938. The German Democratic Republic is excluded from subsequent calculations because it seems to fall into a special category as far as American policy toward Eastern Europe is concerned: prior to 1949, there was no such entity as the DDR, and in any case American policy toward the DDR has been formulated basically as a derivative of our approach to the "German question" generally, which to the United States has centered around the issues of West Berlin and German unification rather than the fate of East Europe as such.[1] Albania is also excluded here because the very small American economic interaction with that nation is conducted entirely through third-party intermediaries. The United States has had no regular diplomatic relations with Albania since June 1939.

At first glance, the data in the tables are rather impressive, at least insofar as they seem to demonstrate the developing potential of American-East European trade over time. Thus, American exports to Eastern Europe went from $68 million in 1938 to $86 million in 1959 to a figure of $2.62 billion by 1980. Imports advanced at a roughly similar rate: $50 million in 1938, $61 million in 1959, and about $1.38 billion in 1980. Perhaps more relevant than a mere recitation of raw dollar figures is a consideration of percentage increases in American trade with Eastern Europe. The data show that in the period 1970-75, for example, American exports to and imports from the countries of Eastern Europe increased in each instance close to 300 percent. The latter part of the decade witnessed a further increase in trade transactions of about 100 percent. Obviously, the more flexible trading policies initiated by the United States during the middle and late 1960s bore rather significant fruit, at least in terms of a greatly increased proportion of American trade with Eastern Europe and—the political optimists would

Table 3
U.S. Exports to Eastern Europe, Selected Years, 1938-84 (in millions of dollars)

	1938	1948	1959	1970	1975	1981	1982	1983	1984
Bulgaria	1	2	1	15	30	258	107	66	44
Czechoslovakia	27	22	3	23	53	83	84	59	58
Hungary	3	8	1	28	76	78	68	111	88
Poland	25	56	75	70	583	682	295	324	318
Romania	6	8	2	66	191	504	224	186	249
Yugoslavia	3	8	5	168	328	648	494	572	432

Table 4
U.S. Imports from Eastern Europe, Selected Years, 1938-84 (in millions of dollars)

	1938	1948	1959	1970	1975	1981	1982	1983	1984
Bulgaria	2	1	1	2	21	34	28	28	31
Czechoslovakia	26	22	12	23	31	67	62	62	96
Hungary	4	2	2	4	35	129	133	156	242
Poland	13	1	32	98	243	365	212	189	244
Rumania	3	1	1	13	133	561	348	513	969
Yugoslavia	4	5	5	96	261	437	360	386	527

Sources for Tables 3 and 4: U.S. Department of Commerce, Bureau of the Census, STATISTICAL ABSTRACT OF THE UNITED STATES 1974 (Washington: GPO, 1974); ibid., STATISTICAL ABSTRACT OF THE UNITED STATES 1979 (Washington: GPO, 1979); ibid., Industry and Trade Administration, OVERSEAS BUSINESS REPORTS. EAST-WEST TRADE UPDATE (Washington: GPO, September 1979); ibid., TRADE OF THE UNITED STATES WITH COMMUNIST COUNTRIES IN EASTERN EUROPE AND ASIA,. 1976-1978 (Washington: GPO, December 1979); ibid., International Trade Administration, OVERSEAS BUSINESS REPORTS. UNITED STATES FOREIGN TRADE ANNUAL 1973-1979 (Washington: GPO, July 1980); U.S. Department of State, THE BATTLE ACT REPORT 1963 (Washington: GPO, 1964); U.S. Department of Commerce, Bureau of the Census, STATISTICAL ABSTRACT OF THE UNITED STATES 1985 (Washington: GPO, 1985); U.S. Department of Commerce, BUSINESS AMERICA, Vol. 8, No. 5 (Washington: GPO, March 4, 1985).

hope—in an equivalent change in the overall American relationship with and impact on Eastern Europe.

A consideration of some other figures seems to offer a rather different perspective on the American economic relationship with Eastern Europe. Tables 5 and 6 show the percentage of total Eastern European exports and imports controlled by the United States in various years, as well as American trade with Eastern Europe as a portion of our overall trading picture. The data here lead to three conclusions: (1) In terms of American importance to the overall Eastern European economic

Table 5

U.S. Share of Eastern European Trade, Selected Years, 1938-82 (Exports and imports expressed in percentages)

	1938	1948	1959	1970	1975	1979	1980	1981	1982
Bulgaria	0.5	--	0.2	0.4	0.3	0.5	0.9	1.4	0.6
Czechoslovakia	9.8	3.0	0.5	0.6	0.5	1.2	0.8	0.5	0.5
Hungary	2.1	2.8	0.2	0.6	0.8	1.1	0.8	1.2	1.1
Poland	8.0	5.4	4.6	2.3	3.6	3.6	3.1	3.6	2.4
Rumania	2.9	--	0.3	2.0	3.2	4.0	4.1	4.8	3.1
Yugoslavia	2.9	1.9	0.8	5.7	5.4	5.8	4.1	4.1	3.6
Average for EE Countries Exports and Imports	4.6	3.3	1.1	1.9	2.3	2.7	2.3	2.6	1.9

Sources: United Nations, Department of Social and Economic Affairs, YEARBOOK OF INTERNATIONAL TRADE STATISTICS 1974, Vol. 1 (New York: UN, 1975); U.S. Department of Commerce, Domestic and International Business Administration, OVERSEAS BUSINESS REPORTS, EAST-WEST TRADE UPDATE (Washington: GPO, November 1976); U.S. Department of Commerce, Industry and Trade Administration, OVERSEAS BUSINESS REPORTS, EAST-WEST TRADE UPDATE (Washington: GPO, September 1979); U.S. Department of Commerce, International Trade Administration, OVERSEAS BUSINESS REPORTS, MARKETING IN YUGOSLAVIA (Washington: GPO, April 1980); U.S. Department of Commerce, STATISTICAL ABSTRACT OF THE UNITED STATES (Washington: GPO, 1985); Vienna Institute for Comparative Economic Studies, COMECON DATA 1983 (Westport, Conn.: Greenwood Press, 1984); United Nations, Department of Economic and Social Affairs, Statistical Office, STATISTICS YEARBOOK 1982 (New York: 1985).

Table 6

U.S. Exports/Imports with Eastern Europe as Percentage of Total U.S. Exports/Imports, Selected Years, 1938-83

	1938	1948	1959	1970	1975	1980	1981	1982	1983
Percentage of U.S. Exports to EE	2.0	0.8	0.5	0.8	0.9	1.2	1.0	0.6	0.7
Percentage of U.S. Imports from EE	2.6	0.4	0.3	0.5	0.7	0.6	0.6	0.5	0.5

Sources. U.S. Department of Commerce, Bureau of the Census, STATISTICAL ABSTRACT OF THE UNITED STATES 1946 (Washington: GPO, 1946); U.S. Department of Commerce, Bureau of the Census, STATISTICAL ABSTRACT OF THE UNITED STATES 1971 (Washington: GPO, 1971); U.S. Department of Commerce, Bureau of the Census, STATISTICAL ABSTRACT OF THE UNITED STATES 1975 (Washington: GPO, 1975); U.S. Department of Commerce, STATISTICAL ABSTRACT OF THE UNITED STATES 1985 (Washington: GPO, 1985).

situation, the highpoint was reached prior to World War II (our average share of Eastern European exports/imports being 4.6% in 1938 compared to 1.1% in 1959 and only 2.3% in 1980); (2) Eastern Europe has never been a significant factor in our general trade situation (exports to the area have never climbed above 2% since 1938 and for the most part have struggled to reach 1%, whereas imports since 1938 have remained at a level generally well below 1%); (3) to the extent that the United States has had any moderately significant trading relationships with Eastern Europe, these have focused on only three countries (Yugoslavia, Poland, and Romania). After the substantial percentage increases in U.S.-East European trade of the 1970s, there has been a distinct falling off in trade turnovers during more recent years, the American percentage of East European trade thus going from 2.7 percent in 1979 to only 1.9 percent in 1982.

A combination of factors have created and will continue to create tangible limits to the development of trading relations between the United States and Eastern Europe. Political judgments either to cut off trade or to encourage its expansion obviously have to be evaluated in light of this fact. The market in the United States for Eastern European exports has been and will likely continue to be so small that the Eastern European countries will not be able to sustain the inevitable balance of payments problems that a large expansion of American exports to Eastern Europe would entail. In 1984 Eastern Europe enjoyed a healthy surplus in its trading relationship with the United States, with exports exceeding imports by almost $1 billion. But this improved position had little effect on the level of imports from the United States, which fell from about $2.62 billion in 1980 to $1.19 billion in 1984. A critical factor in this situation was the East European concern about their hard currency debt, which suggested a strategy of continued limitation on purchases from the United States even as exports to this country expanded. It is well to reemphasize that there are significant limits to this strategy, however: substantial expansion of East European exports to the United States would probably have to be in the form of low-technology products which the United States has always feared as competition to its own marginal domestic industries.

Other factors limiting American-East European trade are the relative distance of the United States from the market, at least when compared to other potential exporters, and the overvalued American dollar which has priced many of our exports out of the reach of Eastern European countries. Overall, however, the basic obstacle has been the lack of complementarity in the two economic systems. Although the United States may have a number of goods that the Eastern European countries want, there is no equivalent U.S. interest in Eastern Europe's exports.[2]

One additional point should be made here about the realities of American trade with Eastern Europe. One of the prevailing theories in the debate over East-West trade is that the basic interest of the Communist countries in trade with the West stems from their interest in and need for our advanced technology, for example, third- and fourth-generation computers. While there is some truth to this proposi-

Table 7
Composition of U.S. Exports to Eastern Europe, 1983 (In millions of U.S. dollars)

Commodity	Bulgaria	Czechoslovakia	Hungary	Poland	Rumania
Foods, Live Animals, Beverages Tobaccos, etc.	36.32	7.15	52.70	131.12	3.53
Raw Materials and Primary Products	4.80	14.29	4.76	88.10	137.43
Chemicals, Manufactured Goods, Machinery and Transport Equipment	19.72	30.91	41.08	36.03	25.29
Items and Transactions N/Class	0.7	0.66	1.19	42.10	0.21
TOTAL:	60.91	53.01	99.73	297.35	166.46

Source: OECD, Department of Economics and Statistics, FOREIGN TRADE BY COMMODITIES. EXPORTS. Vol. 1, 1983 (Paris, 1985).

tion, at least in the case of the Eastern European countries being considered here, the actual composition of our exports has been heavily oriented toward food and raw materials. Table 7 presents data on the type of goods we exported to Eastern Europe in 1983. The first two categories ("Foods, Live Animals, etc." and "Raw Materials and Primary Products") accounted for 70 percent of our exports to the area. This pattern will likely continue, especially because it has been a regular phenomenon since the upsurge in American trade with Eastern Europe dating from the early 1970s. (The above two categories, for example, constituted about two-thirds of American exports to Eastern Europe in 1975.) The point is that the conventional wisdom about the appeal of American technology to the Communist countries should not overlook the fact that, in the instance of Eastern Europe as in other regions of the world, the question of using, for instance, American grain exports for both economic return and potentially for political advantage continues to be very important (the rubric that is applied being "food politics").

We have considered the general data here on American-East European trade. The next chapter focuses more specifically on the political implications and consequences of the past and future American economic relationship with Eastern Europe.

NOTES

1. The German Democratic Republic is not included among the responsibilities of the Office of Eastern European and Yugoslav Affairs in the Department of State. Instead, the DDR is assigned to the Office of Central European Affairs, together with the Federal Republic of Germany, Austria, and Switzerland. See Raymond Garthoff, "Eastern Europe in the Context of U.S.-Soviet Relations," in SOVIET POLICY IN EASTERN EUROPE, ed. Sarah Meiklejohn Terry (New Haven: Yale University Press, 1984), 323.

2. Committee for Economic Development, "A New Trade Policy Toward Communist Countries," in INTERNATIONAL TRADE AND FINANCE, eds. Robert E. Baldwin and J. David Richardson (Boston: Little, Brown and Co., 1974), 228-229.

10.
Political Mirages

Three general theories may be identified as to how international economic relationships may produce political benefits, and each of these has figured in the debate over American economic relations with Eastern Europe. First, there is the punitive approach, whereby a combination of embargo and boycott against one's principal adversaries supposedly will result in a net weakening of the enemy's economic and industrial base and indirectly therefore in its military potential. Second, there is what might be called the measured quid pro quo approach, in which economic relationships are not ruled out but in which decisions on specific trade and investment matters are conditioned by the target country's willingness to make certain specific political concessions in return for favorable treatment. Finally, there is the spillover strategy which assumes that maintaining and expanding economic relationships has general beneficial effects quite aside from any particular "concessions" the target country or countries may be moved to offer.

In analyzing the history of the American economic relationship with Eastern Europe since 1945, it is apparent that the debate in this country over which approach is most appropriate has come to focus almost entirely on the relative merits of the quid pro quo or spillover strategies. At least within politically relevant circles, there is an almost total absence today of any calls for a return to the punitive strategy of the 1950s. At first glance, the economic sanctions which the Reagan Administration announced in December 1981 against Poland might seem to contradict this assertion. In reality, however, the guiding premise behind the Polish sanctions was not punitive but specifically quid pro quo. The President stated quite clearly that in return for ending martial law, freeing political prisoners, and recognizing the right of free labor union activity in Poland, the United States would be prepared to end some or all of the sanctions. As we have already discussed, Washington in fact did reverse some of the measures imposed earlier in response to the Jaruzelski regime's declared amnesty for political prisoners and remission of martial law in 1984. At the same time, Washington held in reserve, for example, the restoring of most-favored-nation trading status to Poland until that government satisfied the remaining items on the Administration's agenda. The recent debate over American economic relations with Eastern Europe conveys a sense of *deja vu*: many of the basic arguments heard today were also offered at various times in the past, in practically the same terms. Another aspect of the discussion that commands attention is the way in which the different schools of thought present generalized assertions which they seem to regard as self-evident even in the absence of concrete empirical support. Take the spillover strategy, for example. The Commission on Security and Cooperation in Europe, the main congressional body established to monitor the evolution of the Helsinki accords of 1975, notes with apparent approval that the guiding principle behind Basket II of the Helsinki agreements was "the belief that mutually beneficial economic and scientific cooperation promotes understanding and harmonious relations between states, thereby contributing to the goals of security and co-operation." Even more than this, economic interdependence "would contribute to the process of detente by increasing the potential costs of East-West confron-tations."[1] The commission's stance was echoed in an analysis submitted to the Joint Economic Committee by Assistant Secretary of State Douglas Bennet in 1978. Bennet agreed that expanded trade with Eastern Europe would improve individual contacts and that such trade would give the countries involved a greater stake in a stable world economy and in general act as "an incentive for restraint in foreign relations." He went beyond the commission's assessment, moreover, in arguing that "expanded US trade relations with the countries of Eastern Europe provides these countries with an incentive and an opportunity to exercise more fully their national sovereignty."[2]

Advocates of a quid pro quo strategy in dealing with Eastern Europe have presented their views with equal vigor. It is instructive, for example, to examine certain opinions expressed in the late 1960s as the Johnson and Nixon adminis-trations attempted to persuade Congress of the wisdom of new and freer policies on American trade with the East. The late Senator Peter Dominick (R.-Colo.) spoke for many when, in a speech before Congress on July 21, 1968, he de-nounced the idea that expanding trade would help to reduce "misunderstandings" and in itself bring better relations. As Dominick put it, "Is trade for trade's sake the road to peace?" He was equally scornful of the notion that trade should be regarded mainly in terms of its pragmatic economic returns. Senator Dominick was careful to stress that he wasn't *per se* against expanded trade with Eastern Europe or the Soviet Union. The point was that "in order [for it] to be effective, and in order for the United States to receive the maximum benefit from trade with the East, our policies must demand political agreements as well as economic ones." Among the sort of quid pro quo's that Dominick had in mind was an in-creased flow of Western media into the Communist bloc, liberalized travel privi-leges for citizens of Communist regimes, and even assistance by the governments involved in helping to end the Vietnam War.[3]

In assessing the merits of these two approaches to American trade with Eastern Europe, as well as the now largely discredited "punitive" strategy of embargo and boycott, we may conclude that the utility of trade either as a "stick" or as a "carrot" has been greatly overrated. Ironically, both the "hawks" and the "doves" here seem equally to be the victims of what appears to be an illusion. Viewed historically, the potential or actual level of American economic exchange with Eastern Europe has never seemingly offered the prospect of having any decisive impact on the overall political equation. That trade should have been seen in various periods as an important tool for advancing American policy interests says a good deal about the propensity of this country to exaggerate the efficacy of particular tools of influence, and more especially to seize on a single such tool as the potential key to the achievement of broad policy goals.[4]

One caveat is in order here: it can be argued that other industrialized democracies have been and continue to be theoretically better situated to exploit trade relations with Eastern Europe for political gain, mainly because of their much higher share of East European trade turnover. At the height of detente in 1973, for example, thirteen non-Communist industrial countries (Canada, West Germany, United Kingdom, Belgium, Luxembourg, Sweden, Norway, Switzerland, Denmark, Austria, Netherlands, and Japan as well as the United States) enjoyed a total trade with Eastern Europe (excepting Yugoslavia but including the German Democratic Republic) of approximately $15.8 billion. Of this total, the American share was about $900 million, whereas West Germany commanded almost 40 percent of the total, with France, Italy, and Austria each having about 10 percent. For comparative purposes, East European trade among themselves and with the Soviet Union amounted to about $30 billion that year.[5]

Trade by the Federal Republic of Germany with various Eastern European countries has continued to expand even as American exports to and imports from Eastern Europe showed a marked decline in the early 1980s. Thus, West German trade with Hungary increased by 85 percent from 1975 to 1983, with Czechoslovakia by 48 percent, and with Bulgaria by 40 percent.[6] To the extent that the United States is successful, then, in developing a coordinated political-economic strategy among the major non-Communist countries on trade with Eastern Europe, the results may be a good deal more impressive than when only American trade is used as a counter. One fact that might give rise to some optimism about the potential of such a strategy is the relatively high percentage of East European GNP that is attributable to international trade. In 1982 trade comprised 17 percent of GNP for Czechoslovakia, 27 percent for Bulgaria, 24 percent for Romania, and 20 percent for Hungary.[7] The reality remains, however, that there are important obstacles to the development of a coordinated Western stance on East-West trade, which we will consider in greater detail below.

What seems to be the inherent validity of each of the three schools of thought on American trade with Eastern Europe, quite aside from the American ability either singly or in concert with others to carry out a particular economic strategy?

In other words, what do these theories have to recommend them in their own terms?

THE PUNITIVE STRATEGY

It is perhaps easiest to assess the merits of the punitive approach of embargo and boycott adhered to by the United States in the 1950s and early 1960s. Historically, economic boycotts have not generally been very effective. A recent study of seventy-eight different cases of economic sanctions in the twentieth century reveals that, whereas some effects were seen in about 40 percent of these cases, the latter all occurred under very special circumstances involving relatively modest policy goals. The overall finding was that "attempts to impair a foreign adversary's military potential, or otherwise change its policies in a major way, generally fail. . . . At most, there is a weak correlation between economic deprivation and political willingness to change."[8] Curiously, the longer the boycott is maintained, the more likely it is to lose whatever effectiveness it did have as the other party or parties makes appropriate adjustments. The interruption of trade has its most pronounced effect as a coercive measure if done shortly before an outbreak of actual military hostilities, which may require the target country to make rapid and sometimes abrupt changes in its procurement of needed materials. Even in this case, for economic sanctions to be effective a relatively rare set of criteria must be present: the boycotter must previously have had a very large share of the target country's international trade, that trade has to comprise a decisive portion of the country's GNP, and, for whatever reason, alternative markets and sources of supply are not available or very limited.[9]

None of the above factors applied to Eastern Europe during the 1950s. It was true that previously the countries of the area had relied on non-Communist sources for almost all their natural rubber and for much of their copper and titanium. Moreover, much of the trade of Eastern Europe had historically been oriented toward the West. Nevertheless, the Eastern European regimes were able to make needed adjustments, and indeed their GNP growth rates were impressive. In the period 1950-55, they ranged from an average of 6.3 percent for Hungary to 13.9 percent for Romania; the last five years of the decade showed a leveling off, but growth still averaged around 7.0 percent.[10] Of course, these figures are open to some interpretation: a good portion of the increased GNP was the result of the programs of forced industrialization undertaken during the period, and also represented a renewed use of productive capacity that had been underutilized in the immediate postwar years. The point is that Western economic pressures on Eastern Europe failed to accomplish one of their main purposes—they did not lead to a substantial destabilization of the target economies. There was economic unrest in Eastern Europe during these years, to be sure, which occasionally led to political outbursts (such as the events in East Berlin in June 1953 and in Poland in 1956), but this was a function not so much of the regimes not being able to satisfy demands for higher living standards because of the Western boycott as it was of the regime's conscious choice not to give primary focus to meeting consumer demands.

To a certain extent, the Eastern European countries were able to make "needed adjustments" in the face of trade restrictions imposed by the West through a large expansion of intra-East European trade under the aegis of COMECON (Council for Mutual Economic Assistance). More importantly, however, the East European regimes were required to depend on the Soviet Union for many of the imports previously obtained from the West and for purchases of East European exports. As late as 1948, Western Europe accounted for nearly half of East European trade; five years later, the figure ranged between 15 and 20 percent. During the same period the Soviet share of East European imports and exports increased sixfold.[11]
The Soviet Union favored the new orientation of Eastern European trade for its own purposes; in fact it was very much a function of Soviet pressure on the East European countries to restructure their trading relationships. The Western economic offensive against Eastern Europe contributed to and made more feasible an outcome which the Soviets wanted in any case. As one analyst remarked, "By its very scope or nature, the embargo has probably indirectly facilitated the strengthening of the central position of Russia in regard to the satellites, given the latter's increased dependence on Russia's deliveries of industrial raw materials and of even limited capital equipment, not obtainable from outside sources."[12]
Another interesting piece of testimony as to the actual effects of Western policy came from none other than Stalin himself. The Soviet leader, in *Economic Problems of Socialism in the USSR*, wrote that the Western powers had imposed "an economic blockade on the USSR, China and the European people's democracies, which did not join the 'Marshall plan' system, thinking thereby to strangle them." As it turned out, Stalin happily noted, "the effect, however, was not to strangle, but to strengthen the new world market [i.e., the intra-Communist trading system]."[13]

In sum, the very thing which the United States had always feared—Soviet control over the economic and ultimately military capabilities of Eastern Europe—was given a strong push by the adoption of a strategy that supposedly was designed to increase American leverage in Eastern Europe. The inescapable conclusion seems to be that the use of the "punitive approach" in the American economic relationship with Eastern Europe had little in the way of an objective foundation (i.e., major previous economic interaction) and was seriously flawed in its basic premises.

THE QUID PRO QUO STRATEGY

Some have argued for specific political concessions from East European countries in return for normalized economic relations with the West. In assessing the merits of such a position, we might begin by examining the evolution of the American relationship with Yugoslavia. Following President Tito's break with the Soviet Union in June 1948, a growing body of opinion within the Truman Administration suggested that it was in the American national interest to use economic levers to sustain Yugoslavia's new independent course. This question became increasingly important in the immediate years after the Yugoslav defection, after the European Communist countries almost totally severed trade relations with Belgrade and there was a series of natural disasters that drastically affected Yugoslav grain production. Eventually, the Administration formally proposed to Congress that the United States initiate a program of economic aid to Yugoslavia and also embark on a general effort to assist in reorientating Yugoslav trade toward the West.

In congressional hearings held to consider the Truman Administration's suggested new policy, members of Congress voiced considerable sentiment for linking any American aid or credits to specific political concessions from Belgrade, especially in the area of greater religious and civil liberties for the Yugoslav people. The assumption here was that the maintenance of Yugoslav independence was, for Tito, a *sine qua non*, that American support was critical to maintaining that independence and that as a consequence Tito would have little choice but to accede to the stated conditions of American aid. The Administration displayed little interest in testing the reality of these assumptions. Instead, it argued strenuously for the granting of aid without "strings." As a State Department spokesman commented, "Yugoslavia is a Communist state. It is a dictatorship. No attempt is being made to disguise these facts. . . . The issue here is a different one. Yugoslavia is resisting Soviet imperialism."[14]

In the event, the Yugoslav Emergency Relief Assistance Act of 1950 was enacted basically along Administration guidelines, that is, as an unencumbered effort to support Yugoslavia's economic position without qualifiers as to domestic political conditions in the country. This outcome, however, hardly ended the debate over the emerging relationship between Washington and Belgrade. One of the leading American scholars on Yugoslavia at the time, for example, argued that the Yugoslav people, "realizing that the regime has been in desperate need of Western aid," were not able to understand why the "Western powers, especially the United States, have given so freely without seeking some concessions for those who are the true friends of the West, of freedom and democracy. As time passes, it will be more difficult for Western leaders to evade the moral question."[15]

However "Western leaders" may have felt about the "moral" question in their dealings with Yugoslavia, the development of economic dealings between Washington and Belgrade over subsequent years was rather dramatic. In the period 1948-66, for example, total American economic aid to Yugoslavia was on the order of about $1.9 billion (some $1.2 billion in food aid, about $300 million in loans, and $390 million in grants).[16] Over this period, Yugoslav-U.S. trade also developed apace, spurred in part by Belgrade's enjoyment of most-favored-nation trade status (suspended only once in 1962). American exports to Yugoslavia went from only $8 million in 1948 to over $168 million by 1970 (imports from Yugoslavia expanding from $5 million to $96 million). By 1962 the United States absorbed 7.5 percent of total Yugoslav exports (which made it third among Belgrade's trading partners) and provided some 20 percent of Yugoslav imports (giving the United States first place in this regard).[17]

The consensus of informed opinion on Yugoslavia suggested that the above dealings in fact played a considerable role in solidifying Yugoslavia's sometimes tenuous independent course. One observer, referring to the immediate years after Belgrade's defection from Moscow, commented that, "it can be accepted as fact that the creaking economy of Yugoslavia was kept in motion largely because the United States . . . paid the bill for the essential raw materials."[18] Another study emphasized that during the rest of the 1950s and early 1960s the Yugoslavs also "projected United States aid into the national budget and their long-term planning in order to finance extensive industrialization projects, apparently assuming that year after year the gaping trade deficit would be covered by the allotment."[19]

Should, or *could*, the United States have exacted a "price" for the above economic interactions above and beyond the overall American interest in having Yugoslavia retain its posture outside the Soviet bloc? Of course, it is always difficult to demonstrate that an untried alternative would in fact have been more productive than what was decided on. As a general matter, however, it seems highly unlikely that a concerted program of demanding "quid pro quo's" from Tito in return for economic benefits would have produced measurable results. The fact is that the target regime in these cases will almost invariably reject the cruder sort of political blackmail which, for all its euphemistic language, would have been implicit in a quid pro quo economic policy toward Belgrade. In Yugoslavia's case, the alternatives to Western aid and trade after its expulsion from the Cominform were very bleak, but Tito's strong suit was precisely his pride in Yugoslav independence and his confidence in Yugoslavia's capacity for survival. A blunt demand of domestic reform in return for American assistance would have gone beyond the bounds of the sort of relationship Tito felt was acceptable with the West. A distinguished Balkan historian put the matter plainly: "The West had helped Tito by advancing aid without strings. But had the West attached strings, there is little doubt that he would have refused the aid, whatever the consequences."[20] It might be added here that part of the payoff which can come from normal economic relations by the West with individual Communist states is the image it conveys to the world of a pragmatic, tolerant Western leadership. This is sacrificed if the West openly insists on the recipient adjusting its system to suit Western desires. Tito himself had a straightforward attitude toward economic relations with the West. "It must be very clear to all that we do not wish to be the political appendage of anyone, that we have our own point of view and can judge things for ourselves. Those who don't approve our socialist system must know once and for all that we shall not renounce socialism and will never join up with capitalism. . . . Whoever wants to collaborate with us must accept us as we are."[21]

In considering specific pieces of evidence that suggest the doubtful utility of attaching conditions to American economic relations with Yugoslavia, one might usefully focus on the controversy surrounding Yugoslavia's most-favored-nation trade status which arose during the early Kennedy Administration. In 1961 Belgrade was host to a conference of the nonaligned nations. In the course of the discussion, President Tito continued his long-term policy of associating Yugoslavia with the views and interests of the Third World. The Yugoslav leader supported the rebels in Algeria, called for the abolition of foreign military bases, and the immediate cessation of nuclear testing by both the Soviet Union and the United States.[22] Washington's reaction to these positions was, to say the least, unenthusiastic. In commenting on the matter of continued economic assistance to Yugoslavia, President Kennedy said that "it is my belief that in the administration of these funds we should give great attention and consideration to those nations who have our view of the world crisis." Congress welcomed this expression of Executive opinion and in June of 1962 proceeded to ban all assistance to the Tito regime. A rider was also attached to the Trade Expansion Act of 1962 taking away most-favored-nation trade status for the Yugoslavs.[23] These measures only succeeded in solidifying Tito's determination to pursue his own course in world affairs, and he talked openly of reevaluating Belgrade's past ties with the United States. President Kennedy soon saw the apparent futility of using economic levers to shape Yugoslav foreign policy, and his Administration not only used an escape clause in the foreign aid bill to continue some economic aid to Yugoslavia but also pushed successfully for a restoration of most-favored-nation status for Belgrade the following year.

In discussing the modalities of the quid pro quo strategy in American economic dealings with Eastern Europe, other cases besides the American-Yugoslav relationship may be considered. One of these involves the Jackson-Vanik Amendment to the Trade Act of 1974, and another the efficacy of American economic sanctions against Poland after 1981.

Economics and Emigration

The Jackson-Vanik Amendment established the criteria under which most-favored-nation (MFN) tariff treatment could be extended to nonmarket economies which at the time of the Trade Act of 1974 did not yet enjoy such a privilege. The amendment tied granting of MFN status to a country's policy on emigration of its own citizens; it specifically denied MFN to any who imposed an immoderate tax on would-be emigrants or who in other ways placed significant obstacles in the way of free emigration. As a result of a compromise between the Congress and the Administration, the legislation allowed the President to waive by Executive order on an annual basis the above requirement in granting MFN status to an individual country if the President could report that such a waiver would substantially promote the objectives of the freedom-of-emigration provision. Also necessary to a waiver were assurances from the foreign country that its emigration practices would lead substantially to the achievement of the objectives of the statute. The President could make the initial waiver entirely on his own authority, but subsequent use required congressional acquiescence.[24] It was no secret that the main purpose of the amendment was to pressure the Soviet Union to liberalize its attitude toward emigration of Soviet Jews, but Jackson-Vanik also had application to every country in Eastern Europe except for Poland and Yugoslavia (both of which had received MFN rights before the legislation).

As it turned out, the Soviet Union (as well as other Eastern European countries such as Czechoslovakia and Bulgaria) found the Jackson-Vanik Amendment an "unacceptable interference" in its internal affairs. As a consequence, the USSR chose to abrogate the earlier Soviet-American Trade Agreement of 1972 when the Trade Act of which the amendment was a part became law in January 1975. (Another part of the Trade Act establishing severe limits on official credits to the Soviet Union also played a part in the decision.) The outcome was different, however, in the case of Romania and Hungary. On March 2, 1975, Romania and the United States signed a trade agreement which included reciprocal granting of MFN status. A little over three years later, in July 1978, a similar treaty was established with Hungary conferring MFN status on both countries in their trading relationships. In each instance, the relevant accords were supposedly arrived at pursuant to the provisions of Jackson-Vanik, but the political circumstances surrounding them were markedly different. In the case of Romania, a modest increase in current emigration allowed the Ford Administration to testify before Congress that Bucharest was conscious of its obligations under the Trade Act of 1974. Thus, the President was employing his waiver authority as contained in that act. In reality, however, granting MFN status to Romania was in the nature of a "reward" for Romania's relative independence in foreign policy and an encouragement to the Ceausescu regime to continue along the same path. (Substantial questions had been raised in 1975 about Romania's actual policy on free emigration of its citizens.) As far as Hungary was concerned, the later offering of MFN status by the United States (again by presidential waiver) was in effect a recognition of an accomplished reality, that is, Hungary's position as the most liberal of the Warsaw Pact members in its domestic social, economic, and human rights policy. As far as foreign policy was concerned, Hungary ironically was considerably more orthodox than the repressive Ceausescu regime.[25]

Since 1978, Hungary has each year received an MFN extension with relatively little difficulty. The same, however, cannot be said about Romania. The controversy over Romanian compliance with Jackson-Vanik came to a head in the Spring of 1983. For some years there had been growing impatience in Washington, especially in Congress, with the bleak human rights record of the Bucharest government. Even Romania's ostensible value as a foreign policy maverick in Eastern Europe failed to quell the criticism of Romanian domestic policy, in particular the Romanian crackdown on religious practice among Protestant sects and the occasional demonstration of labor unrest. (A major strike by miners in the Jiu Valley in western Romania in 1977 was crushed and many of its leaders jailed.) When the Ceausescu government decided on harsh new measures with respect to emigration policy, the Reagan Administration finally was moved to act. Late in 1982, the Romanian authorities announced that an "education tax" would henceforth be levied against would-be emigrants. This would have required affected individuals to reimburse the government between $4,000 and $5,000 (in hard currency) for each year of higher education they had received in Romania. Imposition of this law would drastically reduce even the relatively low level of emigration that had existed in the early 1980s (about 1,000 a year compared to earlier figures of around 4,000 each year). In response, in March 1983 the American Administration announced that it would revoke Romania's MFN privileges as of the following June.[26]

President Ceausescu, in a speech on March 4, reacted to Washington's statement by referring to violations of the "norms of international relations," and he castigated any use of "repressive economic and other kinds of sanctions" against governments as a consequence of their domestic policies. At the same time, he could hardly be unaware of the serious effects of losing MFN status in his trading relationship with the United States. One estimate was that its withdrawal could result in a halving of Romanian exports to the United States.[27] After some weeks of public recriminations between Washington and Bucharest, Romania eventually succumbed to American pressure. On June 3, President Reagan announced that he had "received assurances from the President of Romania that Romania will not require reimbursement to the state of educational costs as a precondition to emigration, and that Romania will not create economic or procedural barriers to emigration."[28] As a consequence of these assurances, the President said he was recommending the usual twelve-month extension of MFN rights for the Romanian regime. After often contentious congressional hearings on the matter, Romania did receive the recommended extension in September 1983.

Others besides the United States made a point of tying Romanian emigration policy to trade relations. The Federal Republic of Germany, for example, had long been concerned about the large Swabian German community in Romania and its right to emigrate to the FRG if it so chose. Foreign Minister Hans Dietrich Genscher paid a visit to Bucharest in late May 1983 to express his own concerns about the effect of the "educational tax" on German-Romanian economic relations. At the conclusion of his discussions with Romanian authorities, Genscher announced that a "satisfactory solution" to the emigration issue had been reached and that the FRG had agreed to proceed with the rescheduling of Romania's substantial bilateral debt with West Germany.[29]

Sanctions and Solidarity

The use (or threat) of the Jackson-Vanik Amendment in affecting Romanian policy on emigration is one instance in which the employment of the quid pro quo strategy seems to have had some success. The more typical result of such an approach, however, may be seen in the case of American economic sanctions against Poland after the declaration of martial law in December 1981.

In summary, these sanctions involved suspended consideration of new credits for Poland (including $100 million that had already been approved), a suspension of Polish civil aviation privileges in the United States, revocation of Polish fishing rights in American waters, the lapsing of ExImBank export credit insurance to Poland, suspension of delivery of remaining unshipped government-to-government agricultural aid, restrictions on export of American high technology, denial of Polish efforts to reschedule official debt, American opposition to Polish membership in the International Monetary Fund, and, finally, suspension of Poland's most-favored-nation tariff status with the United States.[30] In January 1982 all of the NATO countries except Greece agreed to impose their own sanctions, which were roughly equivalent in content to those of the United States. NATO members also agreed to cut off further government-guaranteed bank credits for exports to Poland, except for food. The U.S. International Trade Commission reported that this action "essentially stopped the export of Western spare parts and raw materials" to Poland.[31]

We have already referred to the ambitious list of items which the Reagan Administration stipulated as the basic conditions for ending some or all of the sanctions: the lifting of martial law in Poland, the release of imprisoned Solidarity leaders, restoration of the rights of the Polish people to free speech and association, and the beginning of a "process of dialogue and reconciliation with the [Roman Catholic] church and Solidarity."[32] From the beginning, moreover, American sanctions policy had a built-in ambiguity. Washington made a great effort to portray the sanctions as directed not at the Polish people but at the regime in Warsaw. As an official State Department comment had it, "the United States had no intention of making the Polish people suffer for the actions of the government."[33] Indeed, the United States spoke rather grandly of helping "to restore the shattered Polish economy" once appropriate political steps were undertaken by the Polish government. Two questions immediately presented themselves in this regard: how could the effect of economic sanctions be isolated from the Polish people themselves, and how realistic was it to expect that the Soviets would allow the Polish leaders, even if they had the desire, to pursue the sort of policies that Washington was demanding? In a startlingly cynical—and frank—answer to at least the first question, a Polish governmental spokesman publicly commented that whatever happened to the Polish masses the party elite would always be able "to eat their fill."

In judging the effect of the sanctions, we first need to focus on their economic effects but, more importantly for our purposes, on their evident political impact. Without question the strictly economic consequences were substantial, and the Jaruzelski regime went out of its way to stress the severity of this impact. Thus, Warsaw referred to some $10-12 billion in lost production and exports resulting from the first two and one-half years of the sanctions. This figure was certainly too high by a considerable margin. Polish authorities were able to cite only about $300 million in specific losses.[34] Nevertheless, Polish exports to the United States declined from a figure of around $415 million in 1980 to only about $100 million in the first six months of 1982. Revocation of MFN privileges for Poland was also of some significance. Textile exports to this country from Poland, for example, accounted for about 20 percent of total Polish exports to the United States; without MFN benefits, tariff rates for textiles went from 4 percent of each item's value to 35 percent.[35] That part of the sanctions package which froze new loans and credits was particularly damaging, although given Poland's already precarious credit position before the imposition of martial law, it is difficult to estimate how much in the way of new credit would have been forthcoming from the West even in the absence of sanctions.

An assessment of the political as opposed to the economic effect of Western sanctions policy on Poland is far more problematical. Secretary of State George Shultz commented on September 9, 1982, that the imposition of sanctions was "forcing the [Polish] regime to pay a heavy price for the suppression of human rights and freedom in Poland."[36] Even a superficial knowledge of the essential workings of the Marxist-Leninist regimes of Eastern Europe, however, should indicate that the regimes there are prepared to pay whatever price is necessary to sustain their general monopoly on power. It was precisely the fact that this monopoly was under challenge in Poland that moved the Jaruzelski government to declare martial law and outlaw Solidarity.

It is doubtful whether Western sanctions have had any measurable effect on the limited attempts by the Polish government to enter into a "dialogue" with their own people, in particular by the ending of martial law and the declaration of an amnesty for political prisoners in July 1984 (which was "rewarded" by an ending of certain relatively minor American measures such as the curtailment of Polish fishing rights in American waters and charter flights of the Polish airline LOT). Indeed, there is evidence to suggest that the sanctions may actually have slowed the Polish government's willingness to contemplate political concessions, since Warsaw was reluctant to be seen as caving in to Western pressures.[37] It is also well not to sustain any illusions as to the extent of the "concessions" that have been extended. The general pattern has been one in which the regime has paid lip-service to reform while at the same time its major efforts have been to continue the movement toward "normalization" of Polish society on the model experienced in Czechoslovakia after the Soviet invasion of 1968. Recently, for example, the government launched a frontal attack on the lingering autonomy of the Polish university community, which has long been a bastion of relatively independent political and economic thought within Polish life. The new policy stresses the necessity of ideological orthodoxy among university faculty. In the process, some sixty senior college staff members, including five rectors and several deans, were fired for lack of "correct" political orientation.[38]

Ironically, the imposition of sanctions, or at least the very broad scope they assumed, may be considered to have been not only ineffective politically but also counterproductive. Their existence allowed the government to blame much of the current Polish economic malaise not on past party mismanagement, where it properly belonged, but on "economic imperialism" by the West. At a more basic level, the Jaruzelski government was able to make some appeal to fundamental Polish patriotism against an attempt by outside powers to pressure the Polish regime. At the very least, the sanctions made the economic situation of the Polish masses more difficult, and this in turn aroused some perceptible resentment among this most pro-Western of the Eastern Europe nations. Such resentment was increased by the perception within Poland that the United States was basically punishing Poland for a situation imposed by the Soviet Union, which confronted a distinctly milder set of sanctions by the Western powers at the time.[39] As Jerry Hough has correctly observed, "the notion that the Polish people should be punished economically simply because they were suppressed politically is an uncomfortable one to live with."[40] In 1984, Solidarity leader Lech Walesa himself called for an easing of the sanctions because of their impact on the Polish people.

Even in strict economic terms there were counterproductive elements to the sanctions. The American refusal to engage in debt-rescheduling talks with Warsaw led the Polish government to stop all payments on its debts for the time being. The Polish regime must have also taken some satisfaction in the fact that the Reagan Administration was reluctant to go so far as to declare Poland officially in default on its debts, which would have had serious consequences in terms of Poland's future ability to secure new loans. Indeed, the Commodity Credit Corporation paid some $71.3 million to various Western banks that had extended corporation-guaranteed agricultural commodity loans to Poland precisely so that Poland would *not* be declared officially in default.[41] Western policy also pushed the Polish regime into ever greater reliance on the Soviet Union, exemplified by the agreement signed by General Jaruzelski on his trip to Moscow in May 1984, which tied the Polish economy more tightly to that of the Soviets.[42]

CONCLUSION

It would be overstating the case to argue that there are *never* any situations in which certain specific concessions from the target East European country may not be obtained as a consequence of Western decisions on economic policy. The Romanian emigration issue stands out as an obvious example. American threats to withdraw MFN status from Bucharest had a substantial effect on the Ceausescu regime's ultimate decision to revoke the education tax.

At the same time, an overall cautionary attitude toward using economic levers for political purposes seems eminently justified. In analyzing the Romanian case, for example, it is not hard to see special circumstances that made a quid pro quo policy effective in this instance, even though generally such an approach may be of doubtful utility. The withdrawal of MFN privileges was calculated to have a specially serious effect on Romanian exports to the United States. In the case of other East European countries, as is discussed in greater detail below, the MFN issue is less critical. In addition, by the early 1980s West German credits and economic dealings with Bucharest had achieved a particularly prominent role in the Romanian international trading position, which in turn provided Bonn with some measure of political leverage.

On balance, however, one is struck by the relatively meager success that has greeted the United States' overt attempts to manipulate economic relationships for political purposes. In most instances American economic dealings with Eastern Europe have been—and most likely will continue to be—too limited to provide much hope of converting them into political coinage. This conclusion seems particularly appropriate to the extent that general political changes in Eastern Europe are anticipated from manipulation of American economic policy. There is scant evidence that this sort of systemic alteration is achievable.

It is also well to reemphasize the theme, particularly prominent in our discussion on Polish sanctions, that adopting a quid pro quo approach can become counterproductive to both the general and the specific interests of the United States in Eastern Europe. A further case in point is the Soviet stance on Jewish emigration following the passage of the Jackson-Vanik Amendment. The amendment, far from spurring an increase in such emigration, seemed to have constrained it. In 1973, for example, the Soviet government approved almost 35,000 exit visas for Soviet Jews. In 1975 (following Soviet rejection of Jackson-Vanik), the number fell to a little over 13,000.[43] Although Jewish emigration from the Soviet Union gradually increased after that, reaching an all-time high of about 51,000 in 1979, few informed observers felt that the increase was due to Soviet hopes of achieving MFN status from the United States. The real motivation, to the extent that Western policy was a factor at all, probably arose out of Soviet attempts to woo Western European opinion by ostensibly "observing" provisions of the Helsinki accords on freedom of emigration. We might also recall the earlier discussion of the withholding of MFN privileges from Yugoslavia in 1962. Congressional action, rather than altering Yugoslav foreign policy, distinctly worsened Yugoslav-American relations and gave Belgrade even greater determination to pursue its own particular course. The American Ambassador to Yugoslavia at the time, George Kennan, was so distressed by what he saw as the obtuseness of American policy that he tendered his resignation.[44]

Those who have been most directly concerned with the technical realities of American-East European trade have generally been the most dubious about the opportunity to use that trade for political purposes. Congressional testimony in 1978 from both the Commerce and Treasury departments is a case in point. W. Michael Blumenthal, Secretary of the Treasury, thus commented that "economic bargaining pressure can be effective to only a limited extent to change or moderate [East European behavior]. Experience indicates that attempts to use economic pressure to obtain non-economic concessions are likely to be ineffective."[45] Commerce Secretary Juanita Kreps echoed this opinion. She stressed the relatively meager credits that the United States was able to offer its Eastern European trading partners, the fact that the question of MFN status hardly bore on the raw and semi-processed materials that most East European countries exported to the United States, and the reality that in the area of high technology a number of other countries (especially in Western Europe) would happily compensate for any American reluctance to trade in the relevant technologies. "The conclusion must be that [American] ability to use economic leverage unilaterally to achieve non-economic objectives is very sharply limited."[46]

A somewhat different approach to American trade with Eastern Europe was offered as the State Department position in the same congressional hearings, that is, that expanding American trade without insisting on specific concessions could in itself lead to greater "restraint" in East European foreign policy. The term we have employed here to characterize this sort of generalized political aspiration is the "spillover strategy." As a theory of the potential benefits to be had from increased American economic interaction with Eastern Europe, it is, of course, not confined to the halls of the State Department. The spillover strategy has received either tacit or explicit support from various segments of American society over the years, including important elements of the American business community itself. It is appropriate therefore to subject it to as careful an evaluation as we have applied to the embargo/boycott and quid pro quo strategies in American economic dealings with Eastern Europe. In concluding our analysis of the three schools of thought, it is also necessary to consider some further variables in the American-East European economic relationship that have so far not received adequate attention and that impact on each of the three approaches.

NOTES

1. U.S. Commission on Security and Cooperation in Europe, THE HELSINKI PROCESS AND EAST-WEST RELATIONS: PROGRESS IN PERSPECTIVE (Washington: GPO, March 1985), 32.

2. U.S. Congress, Joint Economic Committee, ISSUES IN EAST-WEST COMMERCIAL RELATIONS, 95th Congress, 2d Session (January 12, 1979), 288.

3. Philip D. Grub and Karel Holbik, eds., AMERICAN-EAST EUROPEAN TRADE (Washington: National Press, 1969), 14, 20.

4. A distinguished student of Eastern Europe thus referred to the "extraordinary opportunity" that trade provided "to affect the policy of the East European states." See Robert Byrne, "Before and After Helsinki," REVIEW OF POLITICS 37 (October 1975), 456.

5. U.S. Department of Commerce, THE UNITED STATES ROLE IN EAST-WEST TRADE (Washington: GPO, August 1975), C6-C9.

6. THE HELSINKI PROCESS AND EAST-WEST RELATIONS, 49.

7. Vienna Institute for Comparative Economic Studies, COMECON FOREIGN TRADE DATA 1982 (Westport, Conn.: Greenwood Press, 1983), 35.

8. Gary Clyde Hufbauer and Jeffrey J. Schott, ECONOMIC SANCTIONS IN SUPPORT OF FOREIGN POLICY GOALS. Policy Analyses in International Economics No. 6 (Washington: Institute for International Economics, October 1983), 75-76.

9. Marshall Goldman, DETENTE AND DOLLARS (New York: Basic Books, 1975), 45-48.

10. "Appendix: Comparative Statistical Data on Modernization and Development in Eastern Europe," compiled by Vernon Aspaturian, in THE POLITICS OF MODERNIZATION IN EASTERN EUROPE, ed. Charles Gati (New York: Praeger, 1974), 377.

11. Samuel Pisar, COEXISTENCE AND COMMERCE (New York: McGraw-Hill, 1970), 15.

12. Nicholas Spulber, "Problems of East-West Trade and Economics Trends in the European Satellites of Soviet Russia," in THE FATE OF EAST CENTRAL EUROPE, ed. Stephen Kertesz (Notre Dame, Ind.: University of Notre Dame Press, 1956), 568-589.

13. Gunnar Adler-Karlsson, WESTERN ECONOMIC WARFARE 1947-1967 (Stockholm: Almqvist and Wiksell, 1968), 17.

14. U.S. Congress, House of Representatives, Committee on Foreign Affairs, YUGOSLAV EMERGENCY RELIEF ASSISTANCE ACT OF 1950, Hearings Before the Eighty-First Congress, 2d Session, 3.

15. Alex N. Dragnich, TITO'S PROMISED LAND (New Brunswick, N.J.: Rutgers University Press, 1954), 310.

16. U.S. Agency for International Development, PROPOSED MUTUAL DEFENSE AND DEVELOPMENT PROGRAMS: FY 1966 (Washington: GPO, 1965), 228-234; U.S. Agency for International Development, OPERATIONS REPORT: FY 1966 (Washington: GPO, 1966).

17. George Macesich, YUGOSLAVIA: THE THEORY AND PRACTICE OF DEVELOPMENT PLANNING (Charlottesville: University Press of Virginia, 1964), 192.

18. M. S. Handler, "Dogma and Practice in Jugoslavia," FOREIGN AFFAIRS (April 1952), 434. Yugoslavia ran trade deficits of $100 million to $200 million in the immediate years after the split with Moscow. Another analysis supports the argument that these losses were basically compensated for by the combined Western program of economic aid. Rudolf Bicanic, ECONOMIC POLICY IN SOCIALIST YUGOSLAVIA (London: Cambridge University Press, 1973), 149-166.

19. George Bailey, "Where Titoism Was Tried," THE REPORTER (July 1, 1965), 13. Professor Fred Singleton notes that American aid to Yugoslavia up to 1962 was surpassed only by that given to Greece and Turkey. He also suggests that this "enormous volume of aid enabled Yugoslavia to run a massive trade deficit during a period of rapid industrialization." Fred Singleton, TWENTIETH-CENTURY YUGOSLAVIA (New York: Columbia University Press, 1976), 172.

20. Robert Lee Wolff, THE BALKANS IN OUR TIME (Cambridge, Mass.: Harvard University Press, 1956), 427.

21. Richard Stebbins, ed., THE UNITED STATES IN WORLD AFFAIRS 1954 (New York: Harper and Row, 1955), 184.

22. NEW YORK TIMES, September 6, 1961, 1.

23. Ibid., September 7, 1961, p. 5; George C. McGhee, "Eastern Europe: A Region in Ferment," DEPARTMENT OF STATE BULLETIN 51 (November 16, 1964), 712.

24. For a useful summary of the Jackson-Vanik Amendment and the overall Trade Act of 1974, see U.S. Senate, Committee on Finance, TRADE ACT OF 1974 (Washington: GPO, December 30, 1984).

25. Bennett Kovrig, "The United States: 'Peaceful Engagement' Revisited," in THE INTERNATIONAL POLITICS OF EASTERN EUROPE, ed. Charles Gati (New York: Praeger, 1976), 137.

26. U.S. Senate, Committee on Foreign Relations, HUMAN RIGHTS ISSUES IN UNITED STATES RELATIONS WITH ROMANIA AND CZECHOSLO-VAKIA, 98th Congress, 1st Session, April 1983, 3-8.

27. Eric Bourne, " 'Education tax' was only one of many Romanian human-rights abuses," CHRISTIAN SCIENCE MONITOR (March 8, 1983), 3.

28. U.S. Congress, Commission on Security and Cooperation in Europe, CSCE DIGEST (Washington: GPO, June 8, 1983), 10.

29. U.S. Commission on Security and Cooperation in Europe, CSCE DIGEST (Washington: GPO, June 8, 1983), 10-12.

30. U.S. Department of State, Bureau of Public Affairs, BACKGROUND NOTES POLAND (Washington: GPO, June 1983), 7.

31. "Suspension of Poland's Trade Status Sought," CONGRESSIONAL QUARTERLY WEEKLY REPORT (Washington: Congressional Quarterly Weekly Report, October 16, 1982), 2693.

32. Ibid., 2694.

33. BACKGROUND NOTES POLAND, 7.

34. Timothy Garton Ash, "Judging Polish Moves," NEW YORK TIMES (July 12, 1983).

35. "Suspension of Poland's Trade Status Sought," 2694.

36. Ibid.

37. Sarah Meiklejohn Terry, "The Soviet Union and Eastern Europe: Implications for American Policy," in SOVIET INTERNATIONAL BEHAVIOR AND U.S. POLICY OPTIONS, ed. Dan Caldwell (Lexington, Mass.: Lexington Books, 1985).

38. William Erickson, "Polish Leaders Clamp Down on Dissent in Education's Ivory Towers," CHRISTIAN SCIENCE MONITOR (December 18, 1985), 12.

39. A perceptive study of American policy choices in reacting to martial law in Poland is Charles Gati's "Polish Futures, Western Options," FOREIGN AFFAIRS (Winter 1982/83), especially 302-308.

40. Jerry Hough, THE POLISH CRISIS: AMERICAN POLICY OPTIONS (Washington: Brookings Institution, 1982), 66.

41. "Suspension of Poland's Trade Status Sought," 2694.

42. NEW YORK TIMES, May 5, 1984.

43. U.S. Department of State, Bureau of Public Affairs, "Soviet Jewish Emigration," GIST (Washington: GPO, July 1977). An interesting study of the Jackson-Vanik Amendment, including its actual effect on Jewish emigration from the

Soviet Union, is Paula Stern's WATER'S EDGE (Westport, Conn.: Greenwood Press, 1979).

44. Kennan discusses his bittersweet experience as American Ambassador to Yugoslavia in MEMOIRS 1950-1963, Vol. 2 (Boston: Little, Brown, and Co., 1972), 267-318.

45. ISSUES IN EAST-WEST COMMERCIAL RELATIONS, 292.

46. Ibid., 296-297.

11.
The Spillover Strategy

It will be recalled that the "spillover strategy" as an approach to American economic policy toward Eastern Europe posits that certain desirable political results may constitute derivatives of an expanded Western economic relationship with the countries of the area. Such a strategy avoids, or at least is highly dubious of, demanding specific political commitments from East European states in return for various economic overtures from the West. Instead, the spillover strategy is based on a general theory of the relationship between politics and economics, applied in this case to the dynamics of East-West trade.

The ostensible political utilities of such trade may be summarized as follows: (1) It will contribute to greater "understanding" and empathy between the societies and countries involved, the assumption being that conflict in international affairs is often the result of ignorance and misperception more than objective factors. (2) It will result in a much greater "linkage" of the socialist economies of Eastern Europe with the international economic system and in this sense create a basic interest of the Eastern European states in having stable and expanding world economic relationships. (3) Partly as a function of the last effect, East-West trade will lead to growing restraint in foreign policy decision-making by the Communist countries involved, since their economic interests may be put at risk by "adventurism" in international affairs. (4) With specific reference to the nations of Eastern Europe, an expanding economic relationship with the West will allow the regimes involved to develop greater independence in both the economic and political realms and a corresponding reduction in their dependence on the Soviet hegemon. (5) Finally, economic ties with the West may contribute to greater decentralization in economic planning within the Eastern European countries and a concomitant increase in overall "liberalization" of the regime in not only the economic but also the political area.

This list of potential benefits to be gained from Western economic dealings with Eastern Europe is fairly ambitious. What does the evidence suggest as to the reality of the basic arguments? The evidence is ambiguous and at times seemingly contradictory. For instance, as already noted, American trade and aid with Yugoslavia increased substantially in the 1950s and 1960s at the same time as the Belgrade regime was developing more independent policies in both the domestic and foreign sphere. Over the last two decades, American economic interaction with Romania and Hungary has also increased substantially. Bucharest has pursued a distinct foreign policy while remaining rigidly authoritarian at home, whereas Budapest has liberalized its domestic practices even while adhering to a conventional pro-Soviet international stance. To the extent that American economic policy has had any "spillover" effect in these three countries, it seems to have produced strikingly different results.

In developing a general response to adherents of the spillover strategy, and in particular to the notion that increased East European economic interaction with the West will lead to "restraint" in foreign policy, it may not be unfair to recall the intellectual precedent of Norman Angell's "The Great Illusion." This treatise, published in 1909, created something of a sensation within the European peace movement prior to World War I, and Angell himself was later to receive the Nobel Peace Prize in 1933 as a recognition of his writings on questions of war and peace. Angell's essential argument in "The Great Illusion" was that, despite the expectations of various governments, modern war did not convey any economic benefits to the victor. Angell's hope was that his essay could help persuade the European powers that economic prosperity would follow entirely from maintaining and expanding peaceful commercial relations among the principal European actors.[1] Angell's goal of preventing a major war by demonstrating that war would not be economically rational itself proved to be a great illusion. Whether or not any European statesman ever accepted his basic thesis is unclear; even if they had, fundamental social, political, and psychological factors combined to make a great military confrontation in Europe at least highly probable.

This is not to say that the spillover strategy is totally without merit. I have argued previously that the embargo/boycott and quid pro quo approach to American economic dealings with Eastern Europe greatly exaggerated the effects of different American trading policies with Eastern Europe. I would suggest, however, that to the extent that any tangible political benefits can be anticipated from taking a particular economic line toward Eastern Europe, the approach of the spillover theorists does have something marginal to recommend it. The point is not to engage in an "illusion" as to what a trade turnover between the United States and Eastern Europe on the order of a few billion dollars is going to achieve in terms of a new ideological or even psychological affinity and progress toward political rapprochement.

One positive element in considering the credibility of spillover theory is America's highly concentrated trade with Eastern Europe (Romania, Yugoslavia, and Poland). This circumstance does offer, at least in theory, some encouragement to an American strategy of persuading these countries via economic relationships to maintain a relatively independent stance from the Soviet Union in either foreign or domestic policy, or both. Even at the level of Eastern Europe as a whole, one analysis suggests that closer integration in COMECON—presumably not in the Western interest—seems to vary in direct proportion to levels of Eastern European economic exchange with the West.[2] This conclusion also provides the United States, or at least the United States together with its Western European allies, with a concrete motivation for expanded trade.

At the same time, it is critical here to consider the whole issue of cause and effect. Expanded trade between Eastern Europe and the West has historically been very much a function of the overall political environment. In this sense, increased economic exchanges have been more a consequence of than a contributor to detente. Thus, a major factor in the greatly increased East European trade with the United States in the early 1970s was the general warming of relations between Washington and the Communist world, especially the Soviet bloc. Conversely, one likely element in the decline in such trade in the early 1980s was the worsening international climate, in particular relations between the Soviet Union and the United States, which tended to reduce Moscow's tolerance for separate political or economic overtures to the West by the East European regimes. (The only countervailing factor is the Soviet interest in the Eastern Europeans acquiring hard currency through additional exports in order to pay in future for Soviet raw materials shipments, e.g., oil, in convertible currency.)[3]

The issue of cause and effect also applies to the domestic scene in Eastern Europe. There is substantial reason to question whether Western economic influence plays any real role in regime decisions on economic decentralization or general liberalization of the society. An analysis of the Hungarian economic reforms initiated in the late 1960s and pursued with varying degrees of vigor since then demonstrates that the relative percentages of Hungarian trade with Communist and non-Communist sources remained pretty much unconnected to the internal reorganization of the Hungarian economy.[4] A more general study of foreign and domestic policy "deviations" in Eastern Europe argues that such have occurred only "under the auspices of a cohesive communist regime in full control of its domestic situation" and, more to our point, have never been the result of "a Western initiative; on the contrary, all of the regimes involved have specifically rejected such influence and have sought to legitimize their departures from Soviet orthodoxy in Marxist-Leninist terms." The only real impact the West has been able to exert, concludes the argument, is to offer support for the changes *ex post facto*, that is, to help sustain them rather than create them.[5]

The Yugoslav experience testifies to the truth of the last proposition. As discussed earlier, an overt strategy of demanding quid pro quo's from Belgrade in return for a favorable economic relationship with the United States did not produce many returns (on the few occasions in which it was tried) and by the nature of the situation could not be expected to succeed. Were there, however, more subtle "spillover" effects of the forthcoming American economic policy toward

Yugoslavia that contributed to Belgrade's independent foreign policy and relatively liberal domestic regime?

Several points seem to stand out in addressing this question. In the first place, for several years following the Soviet-Yugoslav schism in 1948—and regardless of the gradual warming of relations between Belgrade and the West—Yugoslav domestic policy became even more Stalinist than before. There were large-scale and violent purges of "disloyal" elements within the country, and harsh collectivization of agriculture as well as emphasis on heavy industrialization at the expense of consumer needs was accelerated. Only in the early 1950s did Yugoslav policy gradually begin to turn toward "liberal" reforms. All the evidence suggests, however, that this change in direction was almost entirely a result of Tito's own conclusions about necessary directions in the Yugoslav economy and society. It seemingly had little to do with putative Western influence on his thinking. A critical element in Tito's ability to reverse previous domestic policy, moreover, was his unquestioned dominance of the political scene in Yugoslavia, which obviously gave him confidence that he could push through the relevant measures. It was the cohesion of the Yugoslav political elite, far more than any supposed influence from the West, that was decisive in this instance.

American and other Western trade and aid facilitated a process that Tito was committed to in any case. Take, for example, the matter of economic decentralization in which substantial independent power was given to local Workers' Councils. A fair amount of economic disarray initially resulted from this program, but the developing Yugoslav-Western economic relationship helped to mitigate its effects. As one analysis had it, American trade and especially aid "not only became an integral part of the economy but also was a key element of national economic progress."[6] An economic cycle was created, which had important political effects. Western aid supported decentralization, which in turn led not only to increased unemployment, but also to a balance of payments problem. In response, the Yugoslav regime encouraged several hundred thousand of its workers to find jobs abroad, mostly in Northern Europe; the government also adopted a program of attracting foreign tourism. Both policies were designed to attract hard currency to pay for continued imports, and both were calculated to increase at least indirectly the pressure for further liberalization (not least from returning workers who had had experience in the West).[7]

On the foreign policy front, as already argued, Tito's pursuit of nonalignment was a function of his analysis as to how to maximize the Yugoslav role in international affairs. Here too there is little, if any, evidence that he was moved in this direction because of an evolution in his personal ideology deriving out of contacts with the West. On the contrary, as already noted, Tito never tired of explaining that he remained a committed Marxist-Leninist and was simply pursuing his own version of national communism. During a period of U.S. disillusionment with Yugoslav foreign policy, a joint Columbia-Harvard research group offered a dose of realism as to the "spillover" possibilities of Western economic and political dealings with the countries of the Communist world, including Yugoslavia. Such dealings, the group concluded, could bring "marginal alleviation" in the difficult relationship that inherently existed, but it was "necessary for the United States to be prudent both in not pressing for more than the traffic can bear and also in not succumbing to the happy belief that exchanges can somehow dissolve the political and moral differences dividing us and the Soviet bloc."[8]

THREE INITIATIVES

To the extent that an expansion of American economic interaction with Eastern Europe can bring even marginal political benefits, three areas of policy seem particularly relevant to prospects for a modest "spillover."

Industrial Cooperation Agreements

The first of these initiatives involves the potential of what are generically called Industrial Cooperation Agreements (ICAs). Such arrangements "denote a long-term deal involving the transfer of technology, know-how, capital and/or marketing services from one partner to another, the payment for which may be realized in a finished, resultant product. Thus, licensing, the supply of complete plants and joint ventures of all types can be classified as forms of industrial cooperation."[9] Co-production schemes are a particularly prominent form of ICAs. The American firm in this instance provides the technical knowledge, capital goods, managerial skills, and foreign sales outlets; the East European country offers labor, raw materials, basic plant facilities, and so on. The American company in theory is thus able to acquire finished goods at well below their potential cost of manufacture elsewhere, and the Eastern Europeans, by paying for the acquired technology and equipment out of production, are able to conserve precious foreign exchange.[10]

The development of various types of ICAs has been a special feature of the evolving economic relationship between the Eastern European countries and the West since at least the early 1970s. As of 1975, for instance, some 250 agreements, particularly in the co-production sphere, had been realized. Corning Glass took the lead in entering into an equity joint venture agreement with the Hungarian authorities. In Yugoslavia by the middle of the decade there were more than twenty Yugoslav-American joint business enterprises, including a $700 million petrochemical complex.[11] Various Eastern European governments at the time took specific measures to encourage the further development of ICAs. Budapest, for example, issued legislation in May 1977 that allowed a variety of joint ventures between Western and Hungarian enterprises, and even provided for a majority equity on the part of the Western investor. The Romanian government took steps in the same direction, although in this case direct foreign investment was limited to 49 percent of equity.[12] At the present time, it is estimated that over a thousand ICAs have been established between Eastern Europe and Western concerns.

As suggested above, the expansion of ICAs has been substantially a result of pressure from and the perceived interests of the Eastern European countries themselves. Three factors seem to have been uppermost in the calculations of the relevant governments and enterprises. ICAs facilitate technology transfer and in a manner that may avoid some of the sensitive political controversies involved in direct sales of technology from the West. Acquisition of modern technology in this way can assist East European enterprises in overcoming the chronic problems of inefficiency associated with their centrally planned economies, especially if the relevant technology is accompanied by Western managerial expertise. ICAs also theoretically promote a continued expansion of East European exports to the West, an important consideration in view of the difficulties that relatively low-quality East European manufactures have historically had in penetrating the Western market. A survey undertaken in 1974 revealed that managers from Poland, Hungary, and Czechoslovakia felt that only about a quarter of the products manufactured in their own firms conformed to Western standards.[13] Finally, as noted, ICAs obviously allow the Eastern European countries to deal at least in part with the severe balance of payments problems that all have faced over the last decade to the degree that they have made extensive hard currency purchases of technology and industrial goods from the West.

Even if the expansion of the ICA phenomenon is more a reflection of Eastern European than of Western interests, the ICAs currently in existence have their own logic even from the West's point of view. From a spillover theorist's perspective, for example, the considerable personal contact and interchange that are an essential part of the typical Industrial Cooperation Agreement potentially represent just the sort of increase in empathy and cross-cultural understanding that is so basic to this school of thought. Moreover, ICAs may represent a much-needed alternative to traditional trading relations between East and West, particularly given the economic difficulties of the Eastern European regimes in the 1980s. As two leading students of such agreements remark, "East-West industrial cooperation could provide support for ordinary trade by setting up long-term relations and ties at the enterprise level, thereby enabling East-West relations to further expand."[14]

At the same time, some caution is appropriate as to the broader political and economic implications of Industrial Cooperation Agreements. ICAs may defeat one of the prime aspirations of the spillover school by allowing the Eastern European regimes to avoid economic decentralization and perhaps an accompanying political liberalization. It is precisely because such agreements provide a way for the relevant regimes to gain access to more efficient technology in a manner easier than straight purchase from the West that make them so attractive. (The assumption is that, in the absence of such transfers, the regimes might seriously have to consider relatively unpalatable domestic reform programs.) It is also necessary to stress that Western commercial interests have distinct misgivings of their own concerning the rise of ICAs, particularly as they involve Eastern European demands that Western investment be founded on a 100 percent counter-trade arrangement (not uncommon in current circumstances). Many governmental entities and private enterprises in the West, if they had a choice, would prefer to follow standard norms of commercial transaction rather than the sometimes doubtful potential of ICAs.

Various concerns in the West are willing to entertain the "potential of ICAs" because it has increasingly become the only alternative to a general severing or at least substantial diminution of economic relations with various Eastern European Communist countries. On a more positive note, some Western business organizations find such agreements at least moderately attractive because of their capacity for overcoming the artificial and cumbersome separation between domestic economic and foreign trade policy so common in the socialist bloc.[15] A balanced assessment would seem to be that ICAs are likely to play an increasingly important role in the evolving relationship between the West, including the United States, and the Eastern European economies—in some ways a positive development, in other ways much more uncertain. Perhaps the very ambiguity of this relatively new phenomenon in itself reflects the general ambiguity attendant on the Western democracies' economic overtures to the East.

Financing

Assuming that an expansion of American-East European trade has at least some beneficial political effects—not to mention positive economic returns—it is necessary to consider the United States' traditional and contemporary attitude toward the financing of that trade. The picture is fairly straightforward: particularly when compared to its Western European allies, the United States has generally pursued a restrictive policy on credits that would facilitate trade between this country and the East European regimes. This has applied in both the public and private sectors. Under the Johnson Debt Default Act of 1934, for example, which is still in effect, it is illegal for any private American person or corporation to lend money or to buy the bonds of a country defaulting on its debts to the U.S. government. The act was a response to the failure of many countries to repay World War I debts, but eventually it came to affect the Communist countries hardest, because it was later amended to exclude members of the World Bank or the International Monetary Fund. A subsequent ruling did hold that private commercial credits for up to 180 days were allowed under the Johnson Act, which helped at least in the sale of American agricultural products. The negative impact of the Johnson legislation in Eastern Europe has been further reduced by the fact that first Yugoslavia, later Romania and most recently Poland have joined the IMF (Albania and Bulgaria were determined not to be in default on their debts and thus have never been subject to the provisions of the Johnson Act). Nevertheless, the Act continues to provide a definite obstacle to expanded American trade with Hungary and Czechoslovakia.[16]

It is at the level of official credits, however, that the restrictive American policy is most pronounced. The two institutions most relevant in this regard are the Export-Import Bank (Eximbank) and the Commodity Credit Corporation (CCC). Under the Jackson-Vanik Amendment to the Trade Act of 1974, both most-favored-nation status *and* American governmental credits were tied to the Communist countries' policy on free emigration. The result is that not only the Soviet Union but also several of the Eastern European regimes are officially ineligible for favorable consideration by the Eximbank and CCC (Romania, Hungary, and Yugoslavia being the exceptions). Again, the American position on financing of trade with Eastern Europe stands in marked contrast to the practices of the Western European countries, which regard official credits as a normal prerequisite for doing business in the area. Indeed, the West Europeans historically have not only extended substantial credits but have also engaged in a wide range of government-supported direct or indirect subsidies in this respect, effectively reducing the interest charged to 4 or 5 percent below prevailing world market rates. The argument has been that such arrangements are preferable to alternative barter deals and are a significant benefit to West European capital goods exporters.[17] One analysis has suggested that the net size of Western subsidies to the Soviet bloc was over $3 billion in 1981, accounting for approximately 20 percent of the total value of new OECD loans to the Communist countries in that year.[18] Washington has been particularly critical of the West Europeans' predilection for offering credit subsidies. Indeed, there is reason to question whether such a policy represents a net plus for the domestic economies of the European countries themselves or contributes materially to increased trade with the Communist nations.[19] Under a recent agreement, the International Export Credit Arrangement, the Europeans have agreed to a general policy of eliminating such subsidies. Private American firms continue to feel, however, that their competitors in Western Europe are not entirely living up to this agreement and that, as a result, they are at a still greater disadvantage in attempting to sell to the East European market.[20]

An uncritical granting of massive credits to the East European regimes in past years has, of course, had serious consequences. (We will discuss the East European debt crisis in greater detail below.) At the same time, it is difficult to understand a unilateral American policy on credits which goes against the practices of virtually all of our allies and, as noted above, places American firms at a distinct disadvantage in the competition for East European markets. A detailed study of the current economic situation in Romania and Hungary stresses the importance of American policy on credits as those two countries attempt to deal with the economic "shocks" of the last several years. The analysis focuses on the importance of continued official U.S. export credits, as well as credit guarantees, for the economic plans of Romania and Hungary. Also of importance is the American willingness to engage in negotiations on rescheduling official credit obligations if the private financial markets are to be encouraged to do so. Informal U.S. pressures on private lenders can also be of importance in the credit position of the two regimes. Of course, none of these steps can be taken in a political vacuum. The high levels of tension between the United States and the Soviet Union in the early 1980s presumably discouraged the private capital markets from further business in Eastern Europe and, as already noted, made Moscow less tolerant of economic openings to the West by its East European associates.[21] The appropriate conclusion, then, would seem to be that a more realistic credit policy on the part of the United States is important in any strategy for increasing American-East European economic interaction. At the same time, a revised policy on financing trade will not have its full effect unless progress is made in other noneconomic areas of the East-West relationship.

Most-Favored-Nation Status

Normally, granting most-favored-nation benefits is not regarded as an important policy decision within the international trading system. The United States itself routinely grants MFN status to well over one hundred of its current trading partners, the socialist camp being the only major group that faces discriminatory treatment in this regard. The West Europeans, by contrast, make few if any distinctions between the differing ideological blocs in granting MFN. Moreover, the Helsinki accords of 1975 made a point of stressing "the beneficial effects which can result from the application of most-favoured-nation treatment."[22]

The American policy of regarding most-favored-nation benefits in a basically political context, at least as they are related to the Communist world, dates back to 1951. In that year, the United States reversed its previous tradition of unconditional and unlimited application of MFN treatment to its trading partners by suspending, pursuant to the Trade Agreements Extension Act, the MFN status of all Communist countries except Yugoslavia. This action ran counter to certain other international obligations that Washington had already assumed. Thus, under the terms of the General Agreement on Tariffs and Trade (GATT), all of the original signatories were guaranteed nondiscriminatory commercial treatment from the other members. Czechoslovakia was an original signatory to GATT (in 1947), and the United States was put in the rather awkward position of petitioning the contracting parties of GATT for special permission to suspend American MFN privileges for Prague.[23]

The restrictive American approach to MFN terms for the Communist countries continued unabated for the next two decades (although Poland did receive MFN status in December 1960 through a special dispensation). Ostensibly, the Trade Act of 1974 provided new opportunities for several Eastern European countries at last to acquire MFN privileges, but as we have discussed the linking of MFN to emigration practices meant that the old policies were continued in a different framework. Evidence that this was the case could be seen not only in the emigration criteria established for MFN status among nonmarket (i.e., Communist) countries, but also in a special provision of the Trade Act relating once again to Czechoslovakia. Section 408 required that the agreement concerning the settlement of claims by American citizens against the Czechoslovak government, initialed on July 5, 1974, be renegotiated and submitted to Congress as part of any granting of MFN status to Prague. In effect, Congress was linking an increase in the levels of compensation to American citizens for properties expropriated by Czechoslovakia in the late 1940s to the awarding of MFN rights to that country.[24] The matter was finally settled in January 1982, but to date Czechoslovakia has still not received MFN privileges, basically because the regime refuses to offer the required guarantees as to freedom of emigration for Czech citizens.

Now it would be idle to expect that even if MFN status was applied without exception to all the members of COMECON, including the Soviet Union, that exports by those countries to the United States would invariably expand substantially. Interestingly, Moscow has made much of the fact that its lack of MFN privileges has contributed greatly to the imbalance in its trade with the United States. A more realistic assessment would be that many of the primary products that the Soviet Union now exports to the United States are already exempt from the onerous provisions of the 1930 Smoot-Hawley tariff. The Soviet manufactures that would benefit from MFN treatment are, because of their poor quality, not likely to make much of a dent in the American market even in the best of circumstances. The same applies to the export position of certain East European countries.

There is considerable evidence, nevertheless, that the acquisition of MFN status would make at least some difference in the ability of several of the Eastern European economies to penetrate the American market. This applies with particular force to a country like Czechoslovakia, whose exports of highly fabricated goods have been severely affected by the absence of MFN privileges. Thus, in 1972 fully 87 percent of Czech exports to the United States were subject to the severe tariff standards of Smoot-Hawley.[25] An econometric study done under the auspices of the Department of Commerce in 1976 suggested that with MFN treatment the exports of Bulgaria, Czechoslovakia, and the German Democratic Republic to the United States would have increased 41 percent, 169 percent, and 250 percent, respectively.[26] After Hungary received MFN status in 1978, it might be noted, its exports to the United States increased by 64 percent the following year, and it has maintained a trading surplus with the United States ever since.[27]

Quite aside from the potential economic effects of an altered American approach to the MFN question for Eastern Europe, current American MFN policy has important political ramifications. There is considerable evidence that the East Europeans see the discriminatory American attitude toward MFN privileges as constituting a denial of their very political legitimacy. A congressional delegation that visited various East European countries in 1984 summarized its findings as follows: "The lack of most-favored-nation treatment is clearly the major barrier preventing normalization of trade. In addition to making products of these countries noncompetitive in the U.S. market, trade officials in the region believe our trade law discriminates against their countries because of their political system."[28] At least from the perspective of spillover theorists, this finding is of some importance, for the object of trade in this definition is not to alter regimes as such but rather to contribute to their gradual evolution toward more humane standards and, not least, to permit a gradual improvement in American relations with the relevant governments. What presumably is also of some bemusement to East European leaders is the somewhat quixotic manner in which Washington has applied political criteria to granting of MFN privileges. Thus, both Romania and Hungary have received MFN benefits under the Trade Act of 1974. However, Romania, with one of the most repressive regimes in Eastern Europe, received MFN status almost three years before Hungary, which has a demonstrably more liberal internal order. Whether American values were represented more openly in Romania than in Hungary was an interesting question.

The logical conclusion of this discussion is that the benefits of the United States adopting a traditional, that is, nonpolitical, approach to granting MFN status to all of its trading partners in the Communist or non-Communist world would seem to outweigh the potential disadvantages of such a policy. Ironically, taking a "nonpolitical" approach to the MFN issue in itself conveys the best prospect of achieving at least some modest political benefits. Both the Ford and Carter administrations made some effort to persuade Congress to modify the terms of the Trade Act of 1974, specifically with respect to the Jackson-Vanik Amendment. In April 1975 Secretary of Treasury William Simon affirmed to Soviet officials the administration's "determination to work with Congress in obtaining enactment of legislation to hasten the normalization of trade and financial relationships." The final Communique of the 1979 Vienna summit placed the Carter Administration on record as recognizing "the necessity of working toward the elimination of obstacles to mutually beneficial trade."[29] The Soviet invasion of Afghanistan effectively brought this rather desultory effort to a halt. A more recent suggestion has been that the Trade Act of 1974 be amended to allow the granting of MFN privileges on a multi-year basis, at least to countries such as Hungary, which find the yearly necessity of renewed congressional approval for their MFN status both politically and economically obstructive. Washington's future attitude on the MFN question seems likely to stand as a prime test case of its ability to draw appropriate conclusions about the possible interaction of political and economic variables in trade policy toward Eastern Europe.

NOTES

1. Norman Angell, THE GREAT ILLUSION (New York: Garland Publishing, 1972).

2. Andrezej Korbonski, "Detente, East-West Trade and the Future of Economic Integration in Eastern Europe," WORLD POLITICS (July 1976), 568-569.

3. William Zimmerman, "Soviet-East European Relations in the 1980's and the Changing International System," in EAST-WEST RELATIONS AND THE

FUTURE OF EASTERN EUROPE, eds. Morris Bernstein, Zvi Gitelman, and William Zimmerman (London: George Allen and Unwin, 1981), 101.

4. David Granick, "The Hungarian Economic Reform," WORLD POLITICS (April 1973), 414-429.

5. Sarah Meiklejohn Terry, "The Soviet Union and Eastern Europe: Implications for American Policy," in SOVIET INTERNATIONAL BEHAVIOR AND U.S. POLICY OPTIONS, ed. Dan Caldwell (Lexington, Mass.: Lexington Books, 1985), 36.

6. George Bailey, "Where Titoism Was Tried," THE REPORTER (July 1, 1965), 14.

7. For example, in 1964 Yugoslavia gained some $200 million in hard currency from earnings of Yugoslavs abroad as well as from tourism.

8. U.S. Senate, Committee on Foreign Relations, UNITED STATES FOREIGN POLICY, USSR AND EASTERN EUROPE, Committee Print Prepared by a Columbia-Harvard Research Group, 86th Congress, 2d Session (Washington: GPO, 1960), 73.

9. U.S. Commission on Security and Cooperation in Europe, THE HELSINKI PROCESS AND EAST-WEST RELATIONS: PROGRESS IN PERSPECTIVE (Washington: GPO, March 1985), 79.

10. Samuel Pisar, COEXISTENCE AND COMMERCE (New York: McGraw-Hill, 1970), 39.

11. Thomas Magner, "Yugoslavia and Tito: The Long Farewell," CURRENT HISTORY (April 1978), 157.

12. PROGRESS IN PERSPECTIVE, 82-83.

13. Friedrich Levcik and Jan Stankovsky, INDUSTRIAL COOPERATION BETWEEN EAST AND WEST (White Plains, N.Y.: M. E. Sharpe, 1979), 50.

14. Ibid., 226.

15. Ibid., 226-229.

16. Marshall Goldman, DETENTE AND DOLLARS (New York: Basic Books, 1975), 51-54.

17. Gary K. Bertsch and John R. McIntyre, "The Western Alliance and East-West Trade: In Pursuit of an Integrated Strategy," in THE POLITICS OF EAST-WEST TRADE, ed. Gordon B. Smith (Boulder, Colo.: Westview Press, 1984), 218.

18. Daniel F. Kohler, ECONOMICS COSTS AND BENEFITS OF SUBSIDIZING WESTERN CREDITS TO THE EAST (Santa Monica, Calif.: Rand Corporation, July 1984).

19. Ibid.

20. U.S. Congress, Joint Economic Committee, EAST-WEST TECHNOLOGY TRANSFER: A CONGRESSIONAL DIALOG WITH THE REAGAN ADMINISTRATION, A dialog prepared for the use of the Joint Economic Committee. December 19, 1984, 98th Congress, 2d Session, 102.

21. Laura D'Andrea Tyson, ECONOMIC ADJUSTMENT IN EASTERN EUROPE (Santa Monica, Calif.: Rand Corporation, September 1984), v-ix.

22. PROGRESS IN PERSPECTIVE, 43.

23. U.S. Congress, Joint Economic Committee, EAST-EUROPEAN ECONOMIC ASSESSMENT, Part 2—Regional Assessments. July 10, 1981. 97th Congress, 1st Session (Washington: GPO, 1981), 668, 671.

24. Ibid., 670.

25. Goldman, 59.

26. EAST EUROPEAN ECONOMIC ASSESSMENT, 643.

27. PROGRESS IN PERSPECTIVE, 43.

28. U.S. Congress, House of Representatives, Committee on Ways and Means, Subcommittee on Trade, REPORT ON TRADE MISSION TO CENTRAL AND EASTERN EUROPE, 98th Congress, 2d Session (Washington: GPO, March 29, 1984), vi.

29. U.S. Department of Commerce, International Trade Administration, MOST FAVORED NATION TRADE STATUS (Washington: GPO, n.d.), 3.

12.

Final Complications

In concluding this discussion of the American economic relationship with the countries of Eastern Europe, two issues merit separate and more extended consideration. The first of these concerns the greatly changed Eastern European economic situation in the 1980s; the second involves the question of America's relationships with its allies in deciding on economic policy toward Eastern Europe, particularly as it involves controls on the export of strategic technology.

EASTERN EUROPEAN ECONOMIES IN TRANSITION

The great expansion of American trade with Eastern Europe during the 1970s took place in a general environment of economic growth and expanding consumer consumption among the East European societies. Indeed, this environment was a prime contributor to expanded trade. The pattern was not a totally unbroken one: particularly at the time of the massive increases in oil prices in 1973-74, both the West and the East were subject to substantial economic dislocations and recessionary pressures. On balance, however, the 1970s can be seen as a generally positive decade both for GNP growth rates in Eastern Europe and for an increasing Western economic presence in the region.

The experience of the last several years, however, has been a distinctly different one. The "second oil price shock" of 1979 had particularly severe consequences in Eastern Europe. In a more fundamental sense, the inherent inefficiencies and contradictions in standard socialist economic planning finally came together to create a general malaise, if not crisis, in the economic situation of all the East European systems. The basic contributing factor in this crisis, aside from the external elements of oil prices and Western economic recession, was a familiar one to students of Eastern Europe's economic performance: overly rigid central planning, resulting in a continuing lack of productivity. The signs of the new economic "crisis" in Eastern Europe were manifold. There was nonfulfillment of virtually all stated economic plans, living standards began to decline after a decade of

111

improvement, and East European debt grew to alarming proportions. The general response of the East European governments to these developments was broadly similar: a conscious effort to restrict imports, especially from hard currency sources, a campaign to increase exports at all costs, pressures for more counter-trade arrangements in East-West economic dealings, demands for further Western credits to service the already very large debt. One important aspect of the regimes' attempt to deal with the crisis was their reluctance to impose draconian reductions in consumer consumption in order to meet the new economic circumstances. As noted above, living standards did decline, but overall the basic emphasis was on reducing domestic investment rather than consumption, the rationale for this being fear of the political consequences of a drastic lowering of consumer expectations. The ironic result was that the adjustments needed to modernize the ailing East European economies were largely postponed, especially modernization of the production base.[1]

The changing economic circumstances of Eastern Europe presented the United States specifically and the West more generally with some complex and delicate issues of policy. At least two stood out as having potentially significant implications.

The Question of the East European Debt

A great deal of attention has been given in recent years to the debt load incurred by the East European regimes, particularly Poland, Romania, and Yugoslavia, from both official and especially private Western lenders. The issue attained prominence primarily because, given their other economic difficulties, it became increasingly uncertain as to how or whether the East European countries would be able to service this debt. In this sense, the East European debt crisis was no different from that obtaining in, say, Latin America. In fact, the roots of the problem extended some time back, just as it did in the case of other regions of the world.

The basic circumstances giving rise to the debt problem in Eastern Europe were essentially threefold: (1) Private Western financial institutions in the 1970s had a surfeit of petrodollars resulting from the oil price hikes and eagerly sought lending opportunities to maximize use of these funds. (2) Given the relative optimism about the state of the Eastern European economies, the countries of the region seemed to be good credit risks. (3) Ambitious projections about the potential of ever-increasing East-West trade made both public and private Western lenders anxious to supply credits to spur this development. The net result of the coming together of these factors was a dramatic increase in the Eastern European debt load. In only three years, from 1974 to 1977, for example, the net outstanding debt of the countries of COMECON rose about $13 billion to over $46 billion. Some 62 percent of this debt was held by Western commercial banks.[2] By 1980 six non-Soviet COMECON countries (East Germany, Poland, Czechoslovakia, Hungary, Bulgaria, and Romania) had by themselves reached the $46 billion level in obligations.

Concern was expressed even in the early 1970s about the economic and political wisdom of the socialist bloc's amassing such a high indebtedness as a consequence of the relatively uncritical Western granting of credits. Secretary of State Henry Kissinger warned, for example, that the huge debt involved "complications." The socialist bloc, he said, "must not be permitted to use their centrally directed systems for unfair advantage; nor should they be permitted to play off the industrial democracies against each other through selective political pressures." He warned against the East's "possible efforts" "to misuse economic relations for political purposes" inimical to the interests of the West.[3]

The potential political implications of a very large debt obligation by the Eastern European countries remain. We have argued previously that American credit policy has historically been unduly restrictive, particularly in terms of placing American exporters at a distinct disadvantage compared to their European counterparts, and the reality is that the American portion of the East European debt obligation is minimal compared to that of our allies. At the same time, any consideration of a change in American attitudes toward credits has to take into appropriate consideration some of the broader questions inherent in Western lending policies to the socialist camp. The case of Poland stands as a prime example. In response to Warsaw's declaration of martial law in December 1981, the Reagan Administration, as already noted, instituted a ban on further credits in an attempt to pressure the Jaruzelski regime into political concessions. An American attempt was also made to develop a coordinated stance on the Polish situation with its West European allies. Given the extremely high involvement of private and public Western financial institutions in loans to the Polish government (of a total Polish debt of some $28 billion, a roughly equal amount was owed to private and governmental sources) there was considerable reluctance on the part of the Europeans to contemplate declaring Poland in default because of its effects on the Western banking system. In the absence of a formal rescheduling agreement with its lenders, Poland itself refused to make further payments, even on interest. The effect then was an implicit subsidy to the Polish economy by the West. (Warsaw included some $3 billion in unpaid debt in its 1983 budget as a savings.)[4]

There seems little prospect that the Polish financial crisis will measurably improve in the foreseeable future. The only new business that most institutions will now consider with Poland must be based on secured letters of credit. The Polish Parliament at one point estimated that total Polish debt would rise to over $32 billion by 1985.[5] As it turned out, this appears to have been somewhat excessive: the debt load was about $26 billion at the end of 1984. One factor here was that in many countries a substantial share of Polish loans had in effect been written off. It is also true that by 1985 virtually all of the Polish debt to private commercial institutions had been renegotiated, relieving for a brief period the crushing burden on Poland of payments on its private bank obligations. However, much of the debt originally renegotiated will fall due in 1986, which will once again raise the problem of debt maturities.[6] The crux of the Polish crisis is that the country needs a considerable expansion of exports in order to service its existing debt, but an improved export position depends heavily on continued imports of needed raw materials to process the relevant manufactures. Given this "noncompressable" import requirement, together with Western reluctance to offer any substantial new credits to pay for such imports, it is difficult to envision any substantial change in the Polish financial situation even into the 1990s.

The general East European debt crisis has leveled off considerably in the last several years. The six non-Soviet members of COMECON thus reduced their overall debt load from about $46 billion in 1980 to around $33 billion by the end of 1984. Romania, for instance, one of the major debtor nations in the region, benefited from debt reschedulings in 1982 and 1983 but was able to meet its 1984 obligations without further assistance. Year-end hard currency debt was about $7.9 billion, down from the 1981 high of $12 billion. Bulgarian debt also declined from a high of $4 billion in 1979 to something over $1 billion by 1984.[7] The overall situation for the East European region was that most countries were far from bankrupt and were increasingly able to service their debt without undue difficulty. Projections for the middle 1980s, for example, showed a quite reasonable debt service ratio of 15 percent for Bulgaria, 20 percent for Czechoslovakia, 32 percent for Hungary, and 43 percent for Romania.[8] Going against this pattern, however, is the continued difficulty which Yugoslavia finds itself in—total debt of about $20 billion as of 1985—and, of course, the Polish situation. Since Poland and Yugoslavia are two of the critical focal points of overall American policy in Eastern Europe, the economic and political ramifications of the debt question do not seem about to go away.

The Soviet Economic Relationship With Eastern Europe

The Soviet economic relationship with the countries of Eastern Europe has been widely misperceived for some years. In the Stalinist period Eastern Europe represented a prime zone of economic exploitation for the Soviets. As the Soviet-East European relationship matured, however, based both on COMECON and the Warsaw Pact, the Soviets gradually came to acquire as many, if not more, obligations to Eastern Europe in a material sense as rewards from it. In order to maintain a coordinated and cohesive social-economic bloc, for example, the Soviet Union was forced at times to devote disproportionate capital investment to the development of industrial raw materials that the Eastern European countries were now dependent on. Moreover, the type of finished goods that the Soviet Union received in return from Eastern Europe often were of inferior quality since they did not have to compete on the world market. In something of an irony, the relationship between Moscow and its Eastern European allies, at least in the economic sphere, came to resemble classical Marxist-Leninist theory about the exploitation of the less developed world by the cosmopolitan (colonial) powers, with Russia playing the role of the LDC as a cheap source of raw materials as well as a "dumping ground" for the manufactures of the "exploiter." Presumably Moscow did not view the relationship in these terms, but there was no mistaking the fundamental change in the economic position. As one scholar observed, "In contrast to the earlier post-World War II period, Eastern Europe no longer represented an economic asset that could be exploited for the benefit of the U.S.S.R. but a burden that had to be carried by the hegemonic power."[9]

A key element in the evolving Soviet-East European economic relationship was the willingness, however reluctant, of the Soviets to supply Eastern Europe with quantities of oil and other raw materials at well below world market prices. Again, such a policy was adopted for broader policy purposes—to maintain a degree of economic and thus political stability in Eastern Europe—but it carried heavy costs, particularly in the case of petroleum products, which could always be sold to the Western market for badly needed hard currency. The question in recent years has been how long and to what degree the Soviet Union would continue to be willing to absorb the costs of being the leader of an alliance—and what the consequences of a change in past policy would be.

The evidence on this score is of some interest, particularly given the fact that continued Soviet subsidies presumably have been of even greater significance to the economies of Eastern Europe during their time of troubles in the 1980s. The overall picture is one of an increasing Soviet reluctance to continue the generous economic policies of the past. The average ruble price of Soviet oil sales to Eastern Europe, for example, increased anywhere from 25 percent to 28 percent in 1981, and another 21 percent to 27 percent in 1982. Increasingly, the East European regimes have been forced to launch out onto the world market, especially in the Middle East, to satisfy their energy requirements. In addition, overall terms of trade between the Soviet Union and its East European allies declined on the average by roughly 7 percent annually in both 1981 and 1982.[10]

At the same time as the Soviet leaders are taking a generally tougher stance in their economic dealings with Eastern Europe, they are also pursuing a sophisticated policy of differentiation in economic policy with respect to individual countries of the region. In the case of Hungary, for instance, which is relatively liberal in domestic policy but safely orthodox in its diplomacy, Moscow has been rather lenient, allowing the Kadar government to incur substantial ruble deficits at least in its trade with COMECON. The Soviets have been much less accommodating toward Romania, the foreign policy maverick of the Warsaw Pact: ruble deficits in intra-COMECON trade have not been allowed, and the Bucharest regime has benefited very little from implicit subsidies in its bilateral trade with the Soviet Union.[11]

All these circumstances, once again, present the West with some intriguing policy questions. The main point is that, even if it is argued that expanded trade with Eastern Europe is on balance beneficial to the West, the argument cannot be founded on the premise that in developing economic relations the West will somehow be weaning an "economic prize" away from the Soviet Union. In actuality, a Cuba analogy might be offered in this context. It is generally accepted that whatever its other strategic benefits, Soviet support of the Cuban economy is an extremely onerous drain on Soviet resources, on the order of about $12 billion a year in explicit and implicit subsidies. From this perspective the premise could be developed that the West should encourage closer economic relations between the USSR and Eastern Europe because of the burdens this imposes on the USSR.

Even if one takes a somewhat less dramatic approach to the issues presented by the Soviet-East European economic relationship, difficult questions remain. The main one perhaps is how or to what degree the West can benefit from the changed circumstances of that relationship. Specifically, is it in the Western interest to take into account the decline in terms of trade between Eastern Europe and the Soviet Union as well as the increasing Soviet policy of differentiation in its dealings with the Eastern European countries—and by doing so encourage a greater loosening of European COMECON? Romania, for example, is obviously reluctant for general policy reasons to develop significantly higher levels of trade within COMECON to meet its economic difficulties. A substantial increase in imports from the West, however, would raise just the sort of credits issue that has been so sensitive in recent Romanian-Western economic interaction. Hungary itself, despite relatively favorable treatment by Moscow, confronted a deterioration in terms of trade with the Soviet Union on the order of about one-third between 1980 and 1985. Again, should the West try to fill the gap in this instance? It would be ironic if the Western countries, in their eagerness to exploit these opportunities, in effect partially replaced the Soviet Union as the guarantor of the economic systems of Eastern Europe.

Whatever answers may be appropriate to the above questions, it is well to summarize the fundamental changes in the Eastern European economic situation in the present decade that are bound heavily to influence Western policy calculations on trade with the East: a greatly reduced market for traditional Western hard-currency exports to Eastern Europe (most of the countries of the region have in fact had a surplus in their balance of payments with the OECD countries in recent years); the prospect of continued programs of economic austerity in Eastern Europe; a substantially altered economic relationship between the Eastern European states and the Soviet hegemon; and, finally, the unlikelihood for various reasons of a return to the generous credit policies of the 1970s. Under these circumstances, it would be highly beneficial if the United States and its European allies were to develop a coordinated and coherent joint policy on trade with Eastern Europe in order to deal efficiently with both the economic and political questions that arise. Unfortunately, the history of the last thirty-five years suggests that this may be extremely difficult to accomplish. An analysis of American and West European approaches to controls on transfer of strategic technology to the Communist bloc provides a rather vivid case in point.

THE UNITED STATES, WESTERN EUROPE, AND COCOM

Any consideration of the often sharply differing approaches of Western Europe and the United States to economic relations with Eastern Europe as well as the

Soviet Union has to begin with the observation that the economic importance of those relations is a great deal higher for Western Europe than for the United States. We have already referred briefly to some of the basic data. For instance, the total trade of the European Economic Community (EEC) with Eastern Europe and the Soviet Union, as a percentage of GNP, is about ten times that of the United States.[12] In 1981 there was a total trade turnover between the industrialized democracies (Western Europe, North America, and Japan) of $40.3 billion. The American share of this was only 7.7 percent. Of some significance to our subsequent discussion is the composition of this trade. American exports to the Soviet Union and Eastern Europe have historically been dominated by agricultural products. By contrast, almost 80 percent of West European exports to the Communist countries in 1980 were manufactures. It is hardly surprising, therefore, that in the sensitive area of high-technology transfers it is the West Europeans rather than the Americans who play the predominant role. American sales of technology to the Soviet Union and Eastern Europe peaked at around 8 percent of total exports in 1976 but declined steadily after that to only 2.7 percent in 1981. In that year, the total U.S. share of technology exports to the Communist world was only 3.6 percent of the total industrialized world exports of such items.[13]

The rather dramatic contrast in levels and types of trade outlined above are not just a function of objective factors, for example, geographical proximity, a history of much greater economic interaction extending back before World War II. They have also been significantly conditioned by fundamentally different premises about East-West trade. As a general matter, steadily expanding trade with Eastern Europe is regarded in West European capitals as a normal object of policy and is not a subject that arouses much domestic political debate. This attitude extends back in time even to the severest period of the Cold War in the late 1940s and early 1950s. At the same time as the United States was attempting to develop a coordinated punitive economic strategy toward Eastern Europe, the bulk of West European opinion demonstrated considerable reservations about the wisdom of such a policy. As noted, the countries of Western Europe had historically had a much greater economic interest in trading relations with the East. There was also a conviction that renewed trading links with Eastern Europe could help ease the serious "dollar gap" that existed at the time. At the general political level, the Europeans were doubtful that the embargo policy would effectively contribute to the Western power position. There was also concern that such a policy would consolidate Stalin's hold over Eastern Europe and thus impede progress toward an economically united postwar Europe. This argument was felt with particular force in the Federal Republic of Germany, where hopes for reunification were still high.[14]

One important aspect of West European attitudes toward trade with the Communist bloc in Europe has been a distinctly less alarmist attitude toward the perils of technology transfer, especially as it has concerned the Eastern European countries specifically. The assumption has been that the inefficient economies of the region generally have a very difficult time in developing an effective diffusion of the technology they receive. Moreover, the Soviet Union, it is argued, has its own vested interest in preventing its East European satellites from developing too sophisticated a technology base. These attitudes have meant that the West Europeans have often been reluctant to accept American guidance on specific technology export issues as they affect the non-Soviet members of COMECON in Europe.[15] Lending force to the notion that there is a particular Western European approach to trade with Eastern Europe that tends to unite all the countries of the area was the decision by the EEC in late 1974 to terminate the old bilateral trade agreements with individual COMECON countries and in its place institute a system of collective EEC arrangements with these countries negotiated by the Commission of the EEC.[16]

Enough has been said here already to indicate that the official American attitude toward trade with the Communist world has differed historically in rather fundamental ways from that adhered to by its allies in the West. The United States in fact has been the only OECD country that has defined "strategic goods" to be those with even indirect military implications, has seen the weakening of the Soviet economy as an appropriate goal of policy in itself, and has applied general foreign policy criteria in determining whether export licenses should be granted to private American firms for particular goods. One of the leading analysts of East-West trade, John P. Hardt, recently outlined the potential effect of these policies: "If the U.S. Government continues to diminish U.S. business opportunities in Eastern markets through its expressed policies, lack of official credit, etc., American firms might find themselves completely out of the Eastern market."[17] The same possibility has evidently occurred to those "American firms" themselves. The American business community, not noted for its general softness toward communism, has in the matter of trade taken a position close, if not identical, to that held by the West Europeans. Groups such as the National Association of Manufacturers and the United States Chamber of Commerce have argued strenuously against their own government's unique approach to trade policy with the socialist world. They have complained about the high business/economic costs associated with the prevailing system of controls as well as what is seen as their arbitrary and ineffective nature. It has been emphasized that foreign competitors are all too willing to fill the void left by a suspension or withdrawal of an American trading presence. Moreover, essentially political judgments on trade have often made it impossible for U.S. firms to fulfill already signed contracts, thus creating an impression of American firms being unreliable partners (the pipeline controversy as well as the 1980 grain embargo being cited as prime examples). The main thrust of the business community's recommendations is that Washington should put a halt to unilateral and especially retroactive political judgments on trade with the Communist world.[18]

The Differing Approaches: COCOM as the Focal Point

The principal forum in which the debate over Western trade policy with the Communist world has been waged has undoubtedly been the so-called Coordinating Committee (COCOM). Created on November 22, 1949, COCOM has for some thirty-five years been the main device by which the industrialized democracies have attempted to develop a coherent joint strategy on trade with the East. Its members include all the NATO countries (except Iceland) together with Japan. COCOM is not a treaty agreement but rather a "gentlemen's agreement," that is, it has no formal enforcement powers or sanctions at its disposal. The three basic tasks of COCOM have been to develop agreed-on lists of technologies/products not to be sold to the Communist countries, to hold consultations on possible exceptions to these lists, and to ensure as much as possible that COCOM regulations are adhered to. The lists referred to above deal with atomic energy, munitions and all military items, and industrial/commercial products, including potential "dual use" items (relevant to both civilian and military application).[19] A review of the evolution of the COCOM regime is rather instructive as to what it says about differing American and European approaches to the East-West trade issue.

The general pattern has been one in which the West European members of COCOM have striven to make the various lists of embargoed items as limited as possible, whereas the American side has continually argued for a more extensive definition of strategically relevant exports. The COCOM embargo lists reached their zenith in 1952-53 but have steadily fallen since then. Thus, the number of items included declined from some 270 in 1951 to only 149 by 1976.[20] Typical of the struggle between Washington and its European partners over the content of the COCOM lists was the European insistence in the late 1950s that the reduced range of items embargoed for sale to the European Communist countries should also be used in Western trade with the People's Republic of China. (A separate organization, CHINCOM, governed such trade.) After American refusal to deal with the so-called China differential, the European members of COCOM unilaterally adjusted their own CHINCOM lists.[21] It should be noted that each member of COCOM also maintains its own set of "national" lists in addition to the collective ones; the American lists are unique in being more restrictive than those of COCOM itself.

Three issues have arisen in the more recent evolution of COCOM that deserve particular attention. The first of these has revolved around the American concept of Militarily Critical Technologies (MCTs). The notion of MCTs dates back to the so-called Bucy Report in 1976, formally entitled "An Analysis of Export Control of U.S. Technology—A Department of Defense Perspective." The basic thesis of the Bucy study was that the Western powers had to redefine the whole notion of strategic technology. The report actually recommended an easing of controls on certain types of machinery, but at the same time offered an expansive new approach to the kind of items that should legitimately be proscribed for export to the Communist bloc. The emphasis was on the restriction of basic design and manufacturing knowledge, and on the intrinsic use of a product rather than on its supposed "intended" use. The assumption, moreover, was that it was possible precisely to identify those critical technologies basic to the national security. The Bucy Report was ultimately embodied in the 1979 U.S. Export Administration Act. The final terms of that act represented a compromise between the Defense Department, which wanted a primary role in defining MCTs, and other agencies such as the Commerce Department, which was concerned about undue restrictions on American export opportunities to the East. Defense was allowed to identify what it felt were critical items, but the final MCT list was to be arrived at in conjunction with Commerce.[22]

The Reagan Administration from its inception placed an especially pronounced emphasis on the need for stronger controls over transfer of high technology to the Communist countries. At the Ottawa summit of Western leaders in July 1981, the President urged that an intensive Western effort be undertaken to arrive at a joint technology-transfer policy. As a consequence, the first high-level COCOM meeting in some twenty-five years was held the following January. Criticism of the MCT concept, however, continued both in the United States and Western Europe. It was charged that the Reagan Administration was consistently enlarging the list of putatively critical materials and that the Defense Department, despite the terms of the Export Administration Act of 1979, was dominating the decision-making process on MCTs (a concern reinforced by the American suggestion to COCOM that a military subcommittee be established within the organization to ensure a proper military perspective). Most of the COCOM members themselves wanted to ban only that technology directly relevant to Soviet military potential.[23]

In partial response to the growing controversy, the President agreed to prune down what had become a very extensive list of key technologies "to only those items deemed truly militarily critical." The hope then was that COCOM would agree with this more focused approach. As the Administration put it, "a streamlined control list will considerably enhance the effectiveness of controls."[24] (Even after these concessions, however, the classified American MCT list still ran to 700 pages.) In announcing an end to the embargo of American-produced items for the Soviet gas pipeline in November 1982, President Reagan noted that NATO together with members of COCOM had agreed to undertake a general study of the strategic controls issue. One of the principal results of these deliberations was a COCOM decision in July 1984 to establish new rules for the export of computers, telephone switching and electronic equipment, and precision instruments to the Soviet Union and Eastern Europe. Controls on small computers and mainframe computers were relaxed, while new restrictions were applied to strategically significant technologies not previously covered, such as certain types of machine tools, space vehicles, dry docks, electronic grade silicon, semiconductor manufacturing equipment, and superalloy production technology. COCOM also agreed to cease until at least 1988 the export to COMECON of sophisticated telecommunications equipment.[25]

The evolution of the Reagan Administration's approach to the technology transfer issue—and to American trade with the Communist world generally—was capped by the President's signing into law on July 12, 1985, of the Export Administration Amendments (EAA) Act of 1985, which replaced the 1979 EAA. One of the principal controversies that had characterized the Administration's approach to the trade issue, as indeed that of past administrations, was the American government's determination to use general political criteria in determining export licenses, or even to honoring already signed contracts. The new legislation effectively confused this issue by saying that the President could break existing contracts only "if the strategic interests of the United States are threatened." This hardly seemed to represent any break from past practice, and the language of the act was even more obscure when it stated that the above "provision will allow U.S. exporters to be perceived as reliable suppliers, while at the same time maintaining adequate presidential authority to respond to those instances where the country's strategic interests are at risk."[26] At the same time, the Export Administration Amendments Act took steps to defuse some of the criticism of previous American policy that had been voiced. Overall processing time for export licenses to non-COCOM countries was shortened by one-third (from ninety to sixty days), the Commerce Department was required to take into account "foreign availability" when considering a license, and consultations with COCOM were mandated before the President might choose to apply political criteria to limit exports. The rather contradictory terms of the legislation stood in themselves as a testimony to the continued contradictions in overall American trading policy with the Communist world. Neither the terms of this particular act nor the limited COCOM agreements of July 1984 seemed calculated to lay to rest the perennial conflict between the United States and its European allies on a proper approach to technology transfer with Eastern Europe and the Soviet Union.

Concluding Controversies

One provision of the Export Administration Amendments Act dealt with an issue which in its own way has been almost as controversial as the American-European debate over technology transfer. To what extent is it appropriate, wise, or even possible for the United States to punish its European allies for not adhering to stated American policy? The controversy over this matter arose in an indirect manner when the Reagan Administration for a time attempted to force European subsidiaries of American firms to adhere to the boycott of technology sales for the Soviet gas pipeline. Far more sensitive to the Europeans, however, have been actual or suggested provisions within American law for applying sanctions to any European country that did not adhere to the United States' own trading policy with the Communist world. This issue extends back to the early congressional debate over the establishment of export controls in the late 1940s and early 1950s. The Congress generally supported a very tough line under which continued American aid to Western Europe would be predicated on European agreement to follow Washington's position on East-West trade. The Truman Administration argued for a somewhat more diplomatic stance toward Western Europe, and in practice failed to cut off any Marshall Plan aid to individual European countries despite apparent violations by some of U.S. export legislation. At the same time, West European governments were greatly concerned that this benign neglect might not always exist. Since American economic assistance to Western Europe around 1950 was several times larger than the total turnover of European trade with the Soviet Union and Eastern Europe, European leaders to a large extent went along with the American embargo and boycott policy. There was considerable resentment expressed, however, by both European politicians and European opinion generally, at what was seen as American strongarm tactics.[27]

Controversy over supposed "strongarm tactics" by the United States has continued down to the present day. The Export Administration Act of 1979 provided for possible import and export sanctions against foreign companies that violated American export policy. When the Senate was considering the Export Administration Amendments Act, there was also majority support at one point for a provision that would have banned imports from any nation violating U.S. legislation on controls over East-West trade. Sir Oliver Frank, British Ambassador in Washington, spoke forcefully for the European point of view when he wrote a letter to the Senate Banking Committee referring to the proposed stipulation. "In an alliance of democratic, sovereign nations there can be no question of one ally imposing its will on another." Frank stressed that "there has to be genuine consultation, compromise and give and take."[28] As it turned out, the offending provision was dropped from the final legislation, Secretary of State George Shultz being particularly opposed to the idea of imposing extraterritorial sanctions. Indeed, the act provided for an end to licensing requirements for export of low-technology items to COCOM members (which mainly involved computers and had itself been a matter of sensitivity, implying that COCOM members could not be "trusted" not to transfer such items to the Communist bloc). Even though an uneasy truce has thus been established on the issue of unilateral American coercive efforts to establish Western trade policy, the broader question remains: in attempting to "persuade" its European allies to accept American policy, does not the United States risk losing a good deal more in alliance cohesion than will be gained by limiting the sales of certain items?

A final issue that needs to be considered when evaluating overall Western policy toward trade with the East concerns the matter of "differentiation." In this instance, there is relatively less contention between the United States and its European allies. At the same time, the Europeans tend to see the American position on differentiation as an example of a lack of consistency, or at least intelligent calculation of policy, on East-West trade. The differentiation question involves the degree to which the United States specifically, and the West more generally, should make distinctions in its provisions for trade with individual Communist countries. In other words, should certain restrictions, especially on technology transfer, apply to some but not all of these countries? For purposes of the debate, the main focus is on the Soviet Union, the People's Republic of China, and, finally, various countries of Eastern Europe.

One of the main reasons the differentiation issue is of some importance is the "end-use" question. This mainly involves the Eastern European countries. Those who are concerned about an overly differentiated approach to trade that distinguishes between the Soviet Union and specific regimes in Eastern Europe stress the "conduit" factor. In this analysis, the regimes involved may benefit from more relaxed export regulations with respect to Western technology and in turn pass on the acquired items to the Soviet Union for military use. The reality behind these fears is not easy to judge. One analysis concludes that "few Western specialists on CMEA [COMECON] view any member as full, direct technology conduits to the U.S.S.R. from the West."[29] Even if such conduits did exist, it would not be easy to determine their existence. Importers of Western goods are required to sign end-use statements that the relevant items will not be transferred from civil to military purposes or consigned to a third country. A former Director of Strategic Technology and Munitions Control in the Defense Department has admitted, however, that such statements have limited effectiveness. "There is almost no chance of determining, once it has been exported to a Communist country, just how a technology will be used. ... Even if its diversion is discovered, it cannot be recalled, nor its value reduced."[30]

The Central Intelligence Agency has reported that the Soviet Union makes "extensive use of the East European intelligence services for their efforts in acquiring Western technology," even if this is not quite the same thing as acquiring the relevant technology through normal trading channels. What is of importance in this connection, however, is that the Soviet Union has openly and increasingly relied on the six non-Soviet members of COMECON for its own imports of various types of machinery. For instance, the extensive trade between West and East Germany has helped to modernize the DDR technological base and in turn has made that country a good deal more attractive as a machine supplier to the Soviet Union. The Soviet Union faces a dilemma of its own in this regard: whether to encourage more COMECON trade with the West in order for various members of that bloc to get the sort of technology that can be valuable to Moscow, or to press for greater COMECON integration and intra-bloc trade, mainly for political reasons.[31]

Given the ongoing debate about Eastern Europe as a conduit, it is of interest that the United States has for some time avowedly supported a position of differentiation in its economic dealings with the Communist countries. Thus, after the Soviet invasion of Afghanistan, President Carter submitted proposals for increasing the number of items embargoed for sale to the Soviet Union and for setting a quantitative limit on the value of contracts with the Soviets. These suggestions applied only to the Soviet Union, however, and not to Eastern Europe. Even the Reagan Administration, despite its general anti-Communist stance, has followed the same ostensible line. The Administration states that it is "prepared to offer relatively more favorable trading relations on the basis of mutual advantage to those nations which pursue relatively moderate domestic policies or which display a degree of independence in conduct of their foreign policy." As far as Eastern Europe is concerned, the unnamed countries are clearly Hungary, Romania, and Yugoslavia. In concert with the apparent ambiguity of its policy on other East-West trade issues, however, the Administration goes on to indicate that American export controls apply to the same items whether they are destined for the Soviet Union or Eastern Europe, "although a modest differentiation in licensing policy is justifiable because of varying foreign and domestic politics of the individual Warsaw Pact countries and possible because some items are unlikely to be diverted." Reagan officials do admit their concern that MCTs, if given to East European countries, may somehow be used by Moscow to gain a greater hold over Eastern Europe. There is also some care "taken to avoid diversions of Western technologies to the U.S.S.R., even though this is difficult to do." A reflection of the Reagan Administration's basically ambiguous policy on strategic controls may be seen in the fact that it did approve the sale by a private American company of a nuclear reactor to Yugoslavia as well as a reactor and associated fuel to Romania.[32]

As noted above, European opinion has regarded American policy on the differentiation question with some bemusement. There is a general consensus that it is in the political interest of the West to encourage Eastern Europe's autonomous tendencies by offering the potential of favorable trading arrangements to any or all in the region. The Europeans have argued this position for some thirty-five years, even during those periods in which Washington preferred to apply uniform policies to both Eastern Europe and the Soviet Union. At the same time, the European allies of the United States continue to regard Washington as still unduly obsessed with the relative military potential of various types of technology transfer, whether sold either to Eastern Europe *or* the Soviet Union. Finally, there is a belief that the United States is remarkably ready to effect an abrupt change in previous policy given a somewhat euphoric analysis of political developments. The People's Republic of China stands as a prime example.

The Reagan Administration has argued that a considerably more liberal export policy with Beijing is now appropriate because of fundamental changes in Chinese diplomacy—meaning that the PRC is now given more favorable treatment than either the Soviet Union or Eastern Europe. Among examples of technology that are now approved for sale to China but not to any of the European Communist countries are large computer networks for census purposes as well as oil exploration, telecommunications equipment, some types of technical data on aircraft production, and even pharmaceuticals.[33] It is not that European leaders are against the American opening to the PRC. It is merely that they question once again the seemingly arbitrary and above all relatively sudden shifts in Washington's attitude toward trade policy with the Communist world. Indeed, the Europeans would—and did—argue that the normalization of economic relations with Beijing should have come years before. This is not to say that the United States need necessarily accept *in toto* the Western European perspective on East-West trade. It is merely to state that the views of our most considerable and experienced allies might well be taken into serious consideration as this country attempts to develop a consistent stance on the practical interaction of political and economic factors in American economic policy toward the Communist world, and in particular toward the Communist regimes of Eastern Europe. In establishing such a policy, it may well be that the best can wind up being the enemy of the good.

NOTES

1. Josef Adamek, CENTRALLY PLANNED ECONOMIES, Economic Overview 1983, A Research Report from the Conference Board (Brussels: The Conference Board, 1983), 8-13.

2. Brookings Institution, ECONOMIC RELATIONS BETWEEN EAST AND WEST (Washington: Brookings Institution, 1978), 22-23.

3. David R. Francis, "East Europe Piles Up Debt with the West," CHRISTIAN SCIENCE MONITOR (July 16, 1976), 10.

4. Adamek, CENTRALLY PLANNED ECONOMIES, 19.

5. Ibid.

6. Organization for European Cooperation and Development, "Recent Trends in the International Financial Situation of Eastern Europe," FINANCIAL MARKET TRENDS (March 1985), 41-42.

7. U.S. Department of Commerce, "East Europe," BUSINESS AMERICA 8 (March 4, 1985), 20-26.

8. Jan Vanous, "Convertible Currency Indebtedness of the CMEA Countries: Its Implications and Outlook for 1983-1987," in EXTERNAL ECONOMIC RELATIONS OF CMEA COUNTRIES: THEIR SIGNIFICANCE AND IMPACT IN A GLOBAL PERSPECTIVE (Brussels: NATO Economics and Information Directorates, April, 1983), 243-273.

9. Andrezej Korbonski, "Detente, East-West Trade, and the Future of Economic Integration in Eastern Europe," WORLD POLITICS (April 1973), 586.

10. Vanous, "Convertible Currency Indebtedness," 243-44.

11. Laura D'Andrea Tyson, ECONOMIC ADJUSTMENT IN EASTERN EUROPE (Santa Monica, Calif.: Rand Corporation, September 1984), v-ix.

12. Commission on Security and Cooperation in Europe, THE HELSINKI PROCESS AND EAST-WEST RELATIONS: PROGRESS IN PERSPECTIVE (Washington: GPO, March 1985), 33.

13. U.S. Congress, Joint Economic Committee, EAST-WEST TECHNOLOGY TRANSFER: A CONGRESSIONAL DIALOG WITH THE REAGAN ADMINISTRATION, December 19, 1984, 98th Congress, 2d Session, 1-2, 9.

14. Gunnar Adler-Karlsson, WESTERN ECONOMIC WARFARE 1947-1967 (Stockholm: Almqvist and Wiksell, 1968), 5-6.

15. Angela Stent Yergin, EAST-WEST TECHNOLOGY TRANSFER, *The Washington Papers*, Vol. 8, no. 75 (Beverly Hills, Calif.: Sage Publications, 1980), 80.

16. PROGRESS IN PERSPECTIVE, 46-47.

17. EAST-WEST TECHNOLOGY TRANSFER, 101.

18. Richard Kaufman, "Changing U.S. Attitudes Toward East-West Relations," in EXTERNAL RELATIONS OF CMEA COUNTRIES, 62-64.

19. U.S. Department of State, Bureau of Public Affairs, "Controlling Transfer of Strategic Technology," GIST (Washington: GPO, April 1985).

20. Yergin, EAST-WEST TECHNOLOGY TRANSFER, 10.

21. Adler-Karlsson, WESTERN ECONOMIC WARFARE, 6-8.

22. For a discussion of the evolution of policy on MCTs, see J. Fred Bucy, "Technology Transfer and East-West Trade," INTERNATIONAL SECURITY (Winter 1980/81), 132-151.

23. EAST-WEST TECHNOLOGY TRANSFER, 94.

24. Ibid.

25. Angela Stent, "East-West Technology Transfer: The West's Search for Consensus," THE WORLD TODAY (November 1984), 459-460.

26. U.S. Department of Commerce, "Export Administration Amendments Act of 1985," BUSINESS AMERICA 8 (September 2, 1985), 2-5.

27. Adler-Karlsson, WESTERN ECONOMIC WARFARE, 5-6.

28. EAST-WEST TECHNOLOGY TRANSFER, 97.

29. Ibid., 83.

30. Gordon B. Smith, "The Politics of East-West Trade," in THE POLITICS OF EAST-WEST TRADE, ed. Gordon B. Smith (Boulder, Colo.: Westview Press, 1984), 8.

31. EAST-WEST TECHNOLOGY TRANSFER, 81.

32. Ibid., 13-25.

33. Ibid., 32-33.

Part III.

DOING GOOD AND DOING WELL: POWER AND PRINCIPLE IN AMERICAN POLICY TOWARD EASTERN EUROPE

13.
Ideals and Reality

Over the course of the last 200 years there have been two distinct themes in the American diplomatic experience, generally referred to as the idealist and realist impulses. At various times, first one and then the other appears to have assumed a particular predominance in American activity abroad. The classic statement of the realist approach still remains that which was offered by John Quincy Adams in 1823 in response to pressure on the United States to intervene to assist the Greeks in their war of independence against the Ottoman Turks. "Wherever the flag of freedom may be unfurled," Adams said, the heartfelt sentiments and sympathy of the American people would go out to those struggling for freedom. On the other hand, he argued, the United States should not and could not assume a direct responsibility in such struggles. In Adams' vivid phrase, America "goes not abroad in search of monsters to destroy."[1] The Adamsonian or realist approach to American foreign policy, then, posits that altruistic or moral concerns are essentially irrelevant to the real objectives of a sound national diplomacy, those objectives being the protection of one's own physical security and the political and economic well-being. In our external relations, the focus must ultimately be on power considerations and on the development of narrowly defined national self-interest.

Standing in contrast to the realist theory is what is generally referred to as the Wilsonian or idealist concept of American foreign policy. This asserts that our interests abroad include but are not limited to relative power advantage. Just as important—indeed at times more important—is the American struggle for certain basic principles in international life, such as self-determination, democracy, the rule of law, elementary human rights, and so forth. In asking for a declaration of war against Germany in April 1917, President Wilson announced that the United States was not going to war for any selfish purpose but rather in the service of a higher cause, which was to "make the world safe for democracy" and to bring an end at last to the very institution of war among states. To be sure, there was an interesting commingling of altruism and self-interest even in Wilson's seemingly unalloyed idealism. Not only was universal democracy and self-determination a good in itself, but it was also fundamental to a future stable international order, which was very much in America's own interest in both economic and security terms. Nevertheless, there was a marked contrast in the premises for foreign policy suggested by Adams on the one hand and Wilson on the other, and it may be argued that over the years the realist-idealist polarity has been central to the debate about the proper course of American foreign relations.[2]

If this has been true generally, it has been particularly evident in discussion about American policy toward Eastern Europe. A representative example of the weighing of pragmatic and altruistic goals in that policy could be found in the 1978 testimony of a former Deputy Assistant Secretary of State, William Luers, before the House International Relations Subcommittee on Europe and the Middle East. Luers stressed that Eastern Europe was important to the United States "for two fundamental reasons—security and humanitarian concerns."[3] In purely strategic terms, the United States had to continue to maintain a credible deterrent against possible military aggression by Warsaw Pact forces, which included both the Soviet Union and the majority of countries in Eastern Europe (Yugoslavia and Albania being the exceptions). From a somewhat different perspective, it was also in the American strategic interest to prevent an uncontrollable explosion within Eastern Europe that might well draw in both the Soviets and Americans in an escalating confrontation—for example, a disintegration of the Yugoslav state, or potential new mass revolts by one or more of the Eastern European peoples against Soviet domination on the order of Hungary in 1956. Even as he discussed the pragmatic security concerns of the United States vis-à-vis Eastern Europe, Secretary Luers also made reference to what he called our deep concern with the welfare of the Eastern European peoples as such, something that "matters deeply to all Americans."[4] The United States has a rather long tradition with respect to the struggle for freedom and human development in Eastern Europe, a history we will be referring to shortly.

In concluding our analysis of various problems in American foreign policy toward Eastern Europe, it seems appropriate to finish by weighing some of the issues that present themselves in the areas, respectively, of "power" and "principle" in American diplomacy. In other words, how can we evaluate the classic debate between idealism and realism as it affects this specific area of American international concern? First, we will consider American approaches to human rights questions in Eastern Europe and, following that, assess the region as a factor in overall American geopolitical and security concerns. The emphasis throughout this last part of our study will be on the basic conceptual issues that seem to be present in the interplay of power and principle in the American approach to Eastern Europe.

HUMANITARIAN CONCERNS IN PERSPECTIVE

We have already had occasion in earlier chapters of this book to refer to certain specific events that suggest a rather extensive historical precedent for an active American human rights interest in Eastern Europe. Reference has been made, for example, to the exuberant reception that an earlier Hungarian freedom fighter, Louis Kossuth, received in the United States following the failure of the Hungarian revolution of 1848. We have also discussed how the Wilson Administration eventually made self-determination in Eastern Europe an avowed part of its approach to a peace settlement (even if Wilson was initially disposed to allow the Austro-Hungarian Empire to remain in being after the war). The President's reference to an independent Poland in the Fourteen Points, his sympathetic reception of Thomas Masaryk and Wladyslaw Paderewski at the White House, even his little-known intervention on behalf of Albanian self-determination—all these seemed evidence of a general American concern for the fate of the Eastern European peoples.[5]

The right of Eastern Europeans to govern their own destiny also figured prominently in American policy at the end of World War II. A "Declaration on Liberated Europe" (DLE), for instance, was pressed on Stalin at the Yalta Conference, and called for free elections and genuine democratic processes in the formulation of the postwar Eastern European regimes. As it turned out, the DLE hardly had the effects the United States had hoped for, but it nevertheless stood as a symbol of American concern about the area.

Another manifestation of this concern in the early postwar period was the American insistence on a common human rights clause being inserted into each of the peace treaties concluded with the former Axis partners of Germany (Italy, Finland, Romania, Bulgaria, and Hungary). The respective countries were required under the terms of the treaties to "take all measures necessary to secure to all persons . . . without distinction as to race, sex, language or religion, the enjoyment of human rights and of the fundamental freedoms, including freedom of expression, of press and publication, of religious worship, of political opinion and of public meeting."[6] As with the Declaration on Liberated Europe, there was no mechanism established for interpreting and enforcing the terms of these human rights clauses, which led George Kennan, then head of the State Department's Policy Planning Council, to comment fatalistically that the Balkan treaties "contained numerous clauses which we know full well will never be implemented."[7] At best, they were seen as perhaps giving some support to the legal opposition in the various countries as well as providing a basis for American protests against subsequent repression of human rights in Romania, Bulgaria, and Hungary (a precedent for subsequent American use of the Helsinki accords). Such protests were in fact forthcoming but with little observable result.

The Carter Administration's stress on human rights as a key concern of contemporary American diplomacy was an even more recent manifestation of the Wilsonian tradition in the United States. To the extent that human rights was made a centerpiece of Carter's foreign policy, it also raised questions and doubts from those more comfortable with the realist approach to American international activity. Indeed, the idealist-realist debate was perhaps never joined quite so sharply as during the years of the Carter presidency. It is instructive to examine this debate, as well as that surrounding the Reagan Administration's position on human rights questions, as it bears on the area of Eastern Europe. It is particularly appropriate to analyze American human rights policy toward Eastern Europe as a distinct subject considering that the vast proportion of comment and analysis on Washington's human rights diplomacy toward the Communist world has focused on the Soviet Union. Policy toward Russia involves or impinges on policy toward the Eastern European states as well. Nevertheless, a number of quite distinct considerations and problems confront the United States in developing human rights policy toward Eastern Europe as opposed to the Soviet Union itself.

The fact is, of course, that the Soviet Union represents the principal rival of the United States on the international stage and is the only world power that disposes of sufficient military might to threaten American national security directly. Under these circumstances it is clear that Carter's emphasis on human rights in the Soviet Union, not to mention President Reagan's frequent references to human rights abuses in that country, was not just a function of our abstract commitment to improved conditions for the Soviet people, and more specifically for the Soviet dissident community. Instead, both have been very much a part of the general struggle that Moscow and Washington have waged since 1945. One may argue over whether human rights is a very efficient lever of pressure against the Soviet government, but it is important to recognize that at least in part it has been adopted as an "offensive" strategy that hopefully would result in tangible gains for America's own national interests and international position. As former Deputy Secretary of State Warren Christopher said, "A firm emphasis on human rights is not an alternative to 'realpolitik'. . . . It is, instead, a central part of a pragmatic, tough-minded policy. Our human rights policy serves not just the ideals but the interests of the United States."[8]

This particular approach to American human rights policy toward the Soviet Union has operated on the basis of at least three premises: (1) Since the founding of the Bolshevik system in 1917, Moscow has used ideological appeals as a basic tool of its foreign policy, and it is only appropriate—indeed, long overdue—for the Western powers to develop their own ideological counteroffensive. Patricia Derian, past State Department official in charge of human rights policy, reflected this argument when she lamented the fact that "for the last quarter of a century we have been on the ideological defensive. Our national pride and our credibility as a world power have suffered [as a result]."[9] (2) Because the Soviet system is particularly vulnerable on the human rights score, drawing attention to their sins of commission and omission in this area represents a valuable opening for an aggressive and self-confident Western diplomacy. (3) As George Marshall put it in a speech at the opening of the United Nations General Assembly in Paris in 1948, "Governments which systematically disregard the rights of their own people are not likely to respect the rights of other nations and other people, and are likely to seek their objectives by coercion and force in the international field."[10] From the latter perspective, encouraging or if possible compelling a regime to adopt more humane internal human rights practices may over the long run have indirect payoffs with respect to that regime's general style and content in foreign policy. Secretary of State George Shultz, on the tenth anniversary of the Helsinki Final Act, echoed Marshall's analysis when he asserted that "the interests of individual human beings are a fundamental part of security and stability in Europe. Greater security and a more stable peace among our nations depend on greater freedom for the people of Europe."[11]

In developing its human rights policy toward the countries of Eastern Europe, Washington has had to take into consideration a basic assumption of American policy toward the region since 1945, which is that the Eastern European countries historically have not been antagonists of the United States and have been since World War II only to the extent that their populations and resources were forcibly incorporated into the Soviet bloc system. The American attitude has been that without the Soviet presence in Eastern Europe, the countries of the area would favor and would pursue reasonably normal and even friendly relations with the United States. A major objective of our Eastern European policy then has been to work for the day when a genuine freedom of political choice could be restored to the nations of Eastern Europe. Under these circumstances, at least some of the rationale behind American human rights policy toward the Soviet Union has perhaps been of doubtful relevance to the overall American approach to Eastern Europe, and indeed might be considered counterproductive if pursued in the same way.

What, then, are the particular motivations or premises that may be said to have influenced American human rights policy toward the Eastern European region? Several elements may be identified, some of them potentially in conflict with one another. There is, first, the traditional American interest in the conditions of the Eastern European peoples themselves, an interest we have discussed earlier. Assistant Secretary of State Lawrence Eagleburger spoke for the Reagan Administration—and echoed similar statements emanating from that Administration's immediate predecessor—when he testified before Congress that a major American concern was "a deep, humanitarian interest in the welfare of the peoples of Eastern Europe, both because of their internationally recognized rights and because millions of Americans trace their heritage to the area."[12] In this sense contemporary attention to the human rights situation in Eastern Europe is only a linear descent of previous American expressions of concern about developments in the region of the sort produced in the middle of the last century, in 1918, in the immediate period after 1945, in 1956, and so forth. The presence of some 15 million Americans of Eastern European descent in this country, to which Eagleburger alluded, has provided a particularly powerful impetus to Washington to take what steps might be available to improve general social, economic, intellectual, and religious conditions for the peoples of Eastern Europe, a great many of whom may be represented by distant or near relatives in the United States. American human rights policy in Eastern Europe has also been a part of the general campaign which successive American administrations have waged since the 1960s to increase the Western presence and influence in the region. Human rights in this sense is only another aspect of the overall process of "bridge-building." As President Carter stated at Notre Dame in May 1977, "to ignore the trend" toward limiting the arbitrary power of governments over individuals, which he discerned as a worldwide phenomenon, "would be to lose influence and moral authority in the world. To lead it will be to regain the moral stature that we once had."[13]

Two other rationales have been posited for an active American human rights campaign in Eastern Europe, and their logic is substantially in contradiction. Some assert that to the degree the Eastern European states, with the encouragement and perhaps as a result of the pressure of the West, develop higher standards of human rights, this will have the net effect of loosening their association with the Soviet Union. The "loyalty" that, say, Poland or Hungary offers the Soviet Union is in part a result of objective power factors in the region, in particular the presence of Soviet troops in both countries. On the other hand, some of the links binding Moscow and the Eastern European regimes together are ones of perceived common interest—economic, political (maintenance of the Marxist-Leninist regimes' hold on power), military (mutual deterrence against a possible resurgence of German military adventurism, for instance), and so forth. To the extent that the Eastern European political elite, and even more the Eastern European peoples, see themselves as increasingly different from the Soviet Union as far as their basic interests are concerned, this may result in a greater turning toward the West as a more "natural" association for the Eastern European states. All this is based on the assumption that for the foreseeable future the Soviet Union will remain generally rigid and unyielding on basic human rights questions within their own system. Against such a background, a gradually improving and progressive stance on human rights in Eastern Europe would do much to emphasize the basic contradiction in Soviet and Eastern European attitudes and political values.

Others argue, however, that it is a dangerous illusion to think that the Soviets would sit idly by while their Eastern European partners in the Warsaw Pact and COMECON gradually move toward the West, or at least enter into a period of establishing much closer links with Western powers. The lessons of Hungary in 1956, Czechoslovakia in 1968, and (indirectly at least) Poland in 1981 are cited in this regard. The rationale for an active Western human rights policy toward Eastern Europe should be quite different from the one suggested above. The thesis is that the current Soviet hold over Eastern Europe is dangerously narrow, being based largely on sheer military predominance and actual or potential coercion. It is in the Western interest that the Soviet-East European relationship be put on a broader, or what Helmut Sonnenfeldt in a controversial analysis called an "organic," basis. What appears to be a rather startling theory is, however, explicable in terms of the continuing danger which further outbursts of popular discontent in Eastern Europe pose for Soviet-Western relations themselves, involving as they do the risk of a direct military confrontation. The continued denial of basic human rights by various Eastern European regimes provides substantial impetus to future upheavals such as the type that occurred in Hungary in 1956. To the extent that the West can pressure governments in Eastern Europe to be more relaxed on human rights questions—and, not incidentally, to persuade Moscow that this is necessary—the dangers of an uncontrollable escalation of popular resentment may be reduced. Progress on human rights matters in Eastern Europe, in sum, is ultimately in the interest of *all* the parties—the Soviet Union, the West (including the United States), the Eastern European regimes, and, of course, the Eastern European peoples themselves.

Whatever reason or rationale one may offer for the United States pursuing an active human rights policy in Eastern Europe, a number of ambiguities, complications, and even contradictions continue to confront Washington as it attempts to develop a coherent and consistent human rights stance toward the region. The first of these is the very diversity of human rights practices in the Eastern European countries. The differences are such that it may be idle to expect that an overall human rights policy can be set for Eastern Europe.

HUMAN RIGHTS IN EASTERN EUROPE: DIVERSITY WITHIN ORTHODOXY

In November 1983, the Senate Foreign Relations Committee held hearings in Chicago to hear testimony about the human rights situation in Eastern Europe and the Soviet Union. In addition to Administration spokesmen, the main participants were representatives of various ethnic organizations or academics with a particular ethnic connection with the area. Perusing the published record of these hearings, one comes away with two impressions: there continue to be (not surprisingly) repulsive violations of elementary human rights by the regimes in the Soviet Union and Eastern Europe, and the situation is as bleak today as it has been in the past. Without being unduly cynical, it appears that one major purpose of the hearings was to allow various individuals to vent their frustrations over the human rights position in Eastern Europe even if they couldn't offer any concrete suggestions as to how the United States might help to remedy this situation. Thus, one document included in the published testimony was from a group styling itself "The Union of the Kossovars Central Committee," which purported to demonstrate that Belgrade was practicing "genocide" against the large Albanian ethnic community in the autonomous region of Kosovo in Yugoslavia.[14] Washington's potential role in preventing such "genocide" was left unexamined.

A more balanced assessment of current human rights practices in Eastern Europe would suggest somewhat different conclusions than those that emerged in the Committee hearings. As a general matter (and with some notable exceptions), human rights policy in the area cannot be compared with the draconian standards that existed during an earlier era, especially the Stalinist period of the late 1940s and early 1950s. Take the specific matter of political dissent. Czechoslovakia was particularly notorious for the ferocity of its purge trials in the Stalinist era, which resulted in a number of death sentences against putative opponents of the regime. Prague by any measure has also been one of the most repressive regimes in Eastern Europe following its ill-fated and brief flirtation with genuine political liberalization in 1968. Yet even here the differences between the past and present cannot go unremarked. For the past decade the so-called Charter 77 movement (named after an initial petition of grievances to the government signed by various figures on January 1, 1977) has represented one of the major foci of internal political dissent in Czechoslovakia. The Prague authorities have reacted to Charter 77 with a series of political trials and various forms of harassment. Shortly after its formulation, however, Jiri Hanzelska, one of the most prominent Czech human rights activists, had to concede that some things do change, even in Czechoslovakia. Hanzelska, while alluding to the "unbelievable hysteria" of the Czech government following the publication of Charter 77, admitted that the harassment and repressive tactics of the government were "more 'refined' and 'sophisticated' than during the 'brutal' Stalin period."[15] As one comment had it at the time, in the past the regime would have cut off the heads of the dissidents; today they cut off their telephones. The authorities sometimes employ even more mundane methods. Thus, the publishers of Petlice Press, a *samizdat* operation that often prints politically sensitive material, is frequently harassed by having its supplies of paper and binding material seized.[16]

The trial of the so-called Belgrade Six is also a case in point here. In early November 1984, the Yugoslav government brought six dissident intellectuals into court on charges of organizing "an illegal hostile group" aimed at "the weakening and unconstitutional change of the socio-political system and the overthrow of the existing authorities." If convicted, the defendants faced prison terms ranging from five to fifteen years.[17] In reality, the main "offense" of the six was to participate in discussions and analysis concerning the future of the Yugoslav polity. As the proceedings continued, the trial became a considerable embarrassment to the Yugoslav regime. Even prosecution witnesses admitted that they knew of no attempt of the indicted to form any sort of group, hostile or otherwise. According to one account, the real purpose of the trial was to implement the views of hard-liners in the regime that given Yugoslavia's multiple problems, especially economic, it was necessary "to show the limits of debate and to reassert some authority."[18] If this was the purpose, the party conservatives must have been greatly disappointed by the outcome. (There were reports that other members of the party elite had been doubtful about the trial in the first place.) On

February 4, 1985, the trial ended with distinctly mild sentences being meted out to three of the defendants (ranging from one to two years), with one of the indicted being completely exonerated and two others being separated from the original six. The presiding judge, Zoran Stojkovic, in explaining the verdict, admitted that the accused had not incited others to undermine the state but expressed concern about their potential for "misleading" the nation's youth.[19]

The pattern being discussed here can also be seen in the instance of Hungary. Thus, the Kadar regime reacted to the issuance of a public statement by Hungarian dissidents in support of Charter 77 by suggesting that those involved might want to consider emigration. Gyorgy Krasso, a fifty-six-year-old economist noted for his active role in the 1956 Hungarian revolution and also for his activities in speaking, writing, and translating works on that period, was placed under police surveillance in late 1984, especially for his involvement with *samizdat* publications. In addition, he was warned against "using his telephone."[20] Krasso presumably had reason to reflect that under the AVO (Hungarian secret police) regime prior to 1956, his fate would have been somewhat more unambiguous. Hungary was also criticized for reneging on its promise to allow NGOs (Non-Governmental Organizations) full opportunity to hold public meetings during the CSCE-sponsored Budapest Cultural Forum in October-November 1985. Faced with these restrictions, the International Helsinki Federation adjourned to private homes and proceeded with their discussions without further interference from the regime.[21]

Even Romania, one of the most repressive regimes in Eastern Europe, allowed leading intellectual dissident Paul Goma to exit to Paris rather than to do his future writing in a Romanian prison. Moreover, in August 1985 Father Gheorghe Calciu-Dumitreasa, perhaps Romania's most prominent prisoner of conscience, was released from house arrest (he had been in prison since August 1984) and allowed to immigrate to the United States. This decision followed an extensive period of international criticism of Calciu's incarceration. He had spent a total of twenty-one years in Romanian prisons because of his activities supporting human rights and religious values.[22] The fact that Calciu (and Goma) remained alive was perhaps one of the more notable aspects of their trials and tribulations within the dogmatic politics of Nicolae Ceausescu's Romania.

None of the above is meant to excuse the continued authoritarianism of the Czech, Hungarian, and Romanian authorities, nor the very real violations of human rights on the part of other East European regimes. It is merely to state that in developing an effective and focused Western human rights policy toward Eastern Europe, attention has to be given to the rather different environment in which that policy must be defined and conducted. Any survey of that "environment" produces two general points for consideration. First, it is useful to make distinctions among the overall human rights records of East European countries. Thus, Yugoslavia can be considered to be the most open and unoppressive of the Marxist regimes in the area, although even in this case problems remain, especially in the category of religious and cultural freedom. Of the Warsaw Pact countries, Hungary is usually regarded as the most progressive in its human rights stance, the German Democratic Republic trails substantially behind, and Romania, Bulgaria, and Czechoslovakia are almost universally put in the least liberal category. (Albania, not a member of the Warsaw Treaty Organization, is virtually "written off" as insensitive to any of the basic human rights issues.)

This categorization of the Eastern European regimes, however, obscures the fact that considerable diversity of practice exists on certain specific matters. Even when considering the most "repressive" East European countries, for example, one finds that in various areas regime performance is more forthcoming than would be expected. In contrast, the more "liberal" regimes often stand accused of being unusually obdurate on one issue or another. Poland is a good example of this mixed picture. The general impression conveyed in the Western press is of a government that, following the imposition of martial law in December 1981, has installed (or reinstalled) a system that is a police state in all but name. Yet the State Department, in one of its recent reviews on implementation of the Helsinki Final Act, concedes that "despite the deterioration in the human rights situation in the reporting period [Poland continues] to offer its citizens a degree of personal freedom unusual in a Warsaw Pact country. Debate is allowed in the media on a wide range of subjects, although not on issues of fundamental importance to the government."[23] Consider also the trial of four members of the Polish security service (SB) on charges of murdering Catholic political activist Father Jerzy Popiuluszko, which eventually resulted in convictions against each of the four. As the State Department noted, "The trial was unique in that security officers were put on public trial for illegal actions against a member of the opposition."[24] Again, it is well not to be too sanguine about what this implies about the Jaruzelski regime's commitment to personal rights—the trial was converted toward its end into a propaganda festival for the government denouncing Solidarity, and there remains the fact that at least sixteen Solidarity activists were brutalized by the SB in the year preceding the trial. The point remains, however, that even in the case of Poland, it is important to make distinctions about the actual circumstances of the current human rights situation.

A complicating factor in the Eastern European human rights situation which has considerable significance for American policy is that for the most part current human rights protests are not oriented toward the replacement of the prevailing Communist regimes, but rather toward their humanization. As one study puts it, "The dissenters in these countries are not expecting the overthrow of the Communist rule, but call for its reform in the treatment of human rights, and the fulfillment of guarantees written into the Communist Constitutions, the United Nations Covenants and the Helsinki Final Act."[25] The Charter 77 movement in Czechoslovakia is a case in point. In February 1980 it stressed that it had "no intention of changing the existing social system" and that it wanted only "to consolidate Czechoslovak statehood by pressing for the observance of laws guaranteed to its citizens by the Constitution of the Republic and supplemented by international pacts on human and political rights."[26] This is an important point, for many Americans continue to assume that protest against a given Eastern European regime at least implies a desire for a dramatic political restructuring. Although such may have been true in the late 1940s, when the communization of the Eastern European countries was still in its relative formative stages, it is not the case today, at least for most of those involved in human rights protest movements. The implications of this fact for American policy were sketched out by a Czech émigré who was himself heavily involved in the Charter 77 movement. "There is an evident need," he said, "to define areas in which [Western] criticism of human rights performance is fully compatible with respect for existing social and political systems." If the West insists on fundamental political changes in Eastern Europe as a basis for its human rights stance, the analysis concluded, this would risk making the Helsinki Final Act either irrelevant or impractical as a basis for policy.[27]

In practice, it seems rather difficult to "define those areas" where one can criticize human rights abuses in Eastern Europe and at the same time show "respect for the existing social and political systems" that after all give rise to those abuses. Nevertheless, it has been necessary for the West generally, and the United States more specifically, to decide on the matter of emphases, that is, which types of human rights issues in Eastern Europe should receive primary attention. There has also been the challenge of deciding on policy instruments for addressing these particular issues. In practice, of course, the availability or potential effectiveness of various "instruments" has to play a role in judgments as to which human rights objectives this country should devote its energies.

NOTES

1. An excellent analysis of Adams' attitude toward the Greek issue is contained in Norman Graebner's "John Quincy Adams: Empiricism and Empire," in MAKERS OF AMERICAN DIPLOMACY, eds. Frank J. Merli and Theodore A. Wilson (New York: Charles Scribner's Sons, 1974), 128-130.

2. A classic treatment of the realist-idealist controversy remains Robert Osgood's IDEALS AND SELF-INTEREST IN AMERICA'S FOREIGN RELATIONS (Chicago: University of Chicago Press, 1953).

3. U.S. Congress, House of Representatives, International Relations Committee, Subcommittee on Europe and the Middle East, "Statement by William H. Luers, Deputy Assistant Secretary of State for European Affairs," September 7, 1978 (Washington: GPO, 1978), 27.

4. Ibid.

5. Victor Mamatey's THE UNITED STATES AND EAST CENTRAL EUROPE (Princeton: Princeton University Press, 1957) is an instructive survey of the background here.

6. Amelia C. Leiss, ed., EUROPEAN PEACE TREATIES AFTER WORLD WAR II (Boston: World Peace Foundation, 1954), 163-341.

7. Cited in Geir Lundestad, THE AMERICAN NON-POLICY TOWARD EASTERN EUROPE, 1943-1947 (Oslo: Universitetsforlaget, 1978), 342.

8. U.S. Department of State, Bureau of Public Affairs, "Human Rights and the National Interest," Statement by Deputy Assistant Secretary of State Warren Cristopher, August 4, 1980. Current Policy No. 206 (Washington: GPO, 1980), 2.

9. Ibid., "U.S. Commitment to Human Rights," Statement by Assistant Secretary of State Patricia Derian, June 13, 1980. Current Policy No. 198 (Washington: GPO, 1980), 3.

10. Walter Laqueur, "The Issue of Human Rights," COMMENTARY (May 1977), 33.

11. Secretary of State George Shultz, "Ten Years After Helsinki," DEPARTMENT OF STATE BULLETIN 85 (October 1985), 30.

12. U.S. Department of State, Bureau of Public Affairs, "U.S. Policy Toward the U.S.S.R., Eastern Europe and Yugoslavia," Testimony by Assistant Secretary Lawrence Eagleburger before the Subcommittee on Europe and the Middle East of the House Foreign Affairs Committee, June 10, 1981 (Washington: GPO, 1981), 4.

13. Ibid., "Humane Purposes in Foreign Policy," President Carter at the Commencement Exercises of the University of Notre Dame, May 1977 (Washington: GPO, 1977).

14. U.S. Senate, Committee on Foreign Relations, THE PROMOTION AND PROTECTION OF HUMAN RIGHTS IN EASTERN EUROPE AND THE SOVIET UNION, Hearings, November 9, 1983, 98th Congress, 1st Session.

15. U.S. Congress, House of Representatives, Committee on the Judiciary, HUMAN RIGHTS AND U.S. CONSULAR ACTIVITIES IN EASTERN EUROPE (Washington: GPO, 1977), 41.

16. David Andelman, "The Road to Madrid," FOREIGN POLICY (Summer 1980), 162.

17. U.S. Commission on Security and Cooperation in Europe, CSCE DIGEST, January 25, 1985 (Washington: GPO, 1985).

18. THE WASHINGTON POST, December 11, 1984, A21.

19. U.S. Commission on Security and Cooperation in Europe, CSCE DIGEST, March 1, 1985 (Washington: GPO, 1985), 3-4.

20. Ibid., December 20, 1984 (Washington: GPO, 1984), 8-9.

21. Ibid., December, 1985-January, 1986 (Washington: GPO, 1986), 1. I am grateful to Leo Gruliow, one of the members of the American delegation at Budapest and past editor of the Current Digest of the Soviet Press, for his analysis of the proceedings at the Cultural Forum.

22. U.S. Commission on Security and Cooperation in Europe, CSCE DIGEST, October 1985 (Washington: GPO, 1985), 1.

23. U.S. Department of State, Bureau of Public Affairs, IMPLEMENTATION OF THE HELSINKI FINAL ACT, Eighteenth Semiannual Report, October 1, 1984-April 1, 1985 (Washington: GPO, 1985), 2.

24. Ibid., 11.

25. Tufton Beamish and Guy Hadley, THE KREMLIN'S DILEMMA: THE STRUGGLE FOR HUMAN RIGHTS IN EASTERN EUROPE (San Rafael, Calif.: Presidio Press, 1979), 12.

26. THE TIMES (London), February 5, 1980, 6F.

27. Vratislav Pechota, "East European Perceptions of the Helsinki Final Act and the Role of Citizen Initiatives," VANDERBILT JOURNAL OF TRANS-NATIONAL LAW 13 (Spring-Summer 1980), 475.

14.
Goals and Means in
American Human Rights Policy

We have suggested that, in developing a reasoned human rights policy toward Eastern Europe, the United States has had to make judgments as to which categories or types of human rights it wants to emphasize. Principle VII and Basket Three of the Helsinki Final Act provide one reference point for considering different areas of human rights adherence in Eastern Europe. Principle VII concentrates on "fundamental freedoms," including freedom of thought, conscience, religion, or belief. Basket Three, formally entitled "Cooperation in Humanitarian and Other Fields," concerns itself primarily with the free movement of individuals, information, and ideas.[1]

In a well-known speech on Law Day at the University of Georgia in April 1977, Secretary of State Cyrus Vance offered his own categorization of basic groups of human rights: the right to be free from governmental violations of the integrity of the person; the right to the fulfillment of such vital needs as food, shelter, health care, and education; and the right to enjoy civil and political liberties.[2] This categorization reflected some of the main emphases at Helsinki, but it also involved a somewhat different structuring of human rights issues as well as a stress on certain matters left more or less implicit in the Final Act. In our subsequent discussion we might use Vance's typology as a basis for assessing the main goals of American human rights policy in Eastern Europe. In theory, all three groups of rights deserve equal attention and support, but in practice certain emphases and discriminations in American policy can be observed.

THE OBJECTIVES OF AMERICAN HUMAN RIGHTS POLICY

Even the most captious critics of the political situation in Eastern Europe today would, for example, generally concede that as far as "vital needs" are concerned, the current regimes are at least making a committed and serious effort. Their record in fact deserves some respect on this score, at least when compared to the performance of the regimes of Eastern Europe prior to World War II. The testimony of a prominent Czech émigré associated with the Charter 77 movement is relevant in this regard. "It would be an easy and essentially incorrect generalization to suggest that the countries of the East Europe region fail to live up to international standards in every respect," he comments. "There are clearly areas where their human rights record is commendable, for instance where economic, social, and cultural policies guarantee education, free medical care, and complete health and social insurance for every citizen."[3]

The United States, while not necessarily denying these socioeconomic achievements, generally has spent relatively little time either expressing its approval of such gains or suggesting specific ways in which further progress is appropriate.[4] The American attention in the human rights areas has instead emphasized, first of all, certain aspects of category one, "the integrity of the person," particularly protection against arbitrary arrest or imprisonment, denial of fair public trial, and invasion of the home. An official State Department protest concerning the Czech regime's treatment of various participants in the Charter 77 movement, issued at about the time of Vance's speech, made particular reference to these items.[5] The United States also made the release of Father Gheorghe Calciu-Dumitreasa from prison in Romania a major focus of its relations with the Bucharest regime. After his release in August 1984, the State Department continued to protest his conditions of house arrest, and American representations to Romania were evidently an important factor in Father Calciu's eventually being allowed to emigrate to the United States in the Fall of 1985. More recently, the American government has pressed the Hungarian regime concerning the police surveillance imposed on dissident Gyorgy Krasso for his supposed anti-regime activities. The case of Miklos Duray has been a principal one in relations between Washington and Prague as well. Duray was an important spokesman for Hungarian minority rights in Czechoslovakia, and after his arrest in May 1984, he was confined to prison without prospects of immediate trial.[6] Needless to say, the Jaruzelski regime's treatment of Solidarity and other activists after the declaration of martial law in December 1981 has also been a main focus of American human rights policy. President Reagan made a point of addressing Polish violations of their Helsinki commitments on the occasion of the fifth anniversary of the Gdansk agreement legalizing Solidarity in 1980. "We here in the United States have also heard Solidarity's message and respond to it with all our hearts," the President said. "We call upon the Polish Government to do likewise. This is not a subversive organization. It asks only that basic human rights be observed."[7]

Equally as important to American human rights policy in Eastern Europe as the integrity of the person, in some ways perhaps even more central, has been an emphasis on category three rights, "the enjoyment of civil and political liberties." Vance specified these as being freedom of thought, speech, assembly, press, and religion as well as freedom of movement both within and outside the country, and finally, freedom to take part in government. The last concern has been a particular focus of the Reagan Administration (together with the associated freedoms of thought, speech, etc.), as evidenced by the so-called democratization campaign. In a speech before the British Parliament on June 8, 1982, the President called for the fostering of the "infrastructure of democracy—the system of a free press, unions, political parties, universities—which allow a people to choose their own way, to develop their own culture, to reconcile their own differences through peaceful means." Reagan referred specifically to the United Nations' Universal Declaration of Human Rights, "which among other things guarantees free elections."[8]

The implicit if clear target of this rhetoric was the Communist world, and more specifically the Soviet Union and Eastern Europe. If there were any doubts as to the target, they were dispelled later that Fall when the State Department arranged a conference on the Democratization of Communist Countries. Secretary of State George Shultz, in his keynote address, was careful to say that the United States was not calling for a policy of military liberation of Eastern Europe. "In the final analysis, internal forces must be the major factor for democratization of Communist states. We do not seek to foment unrest or undermine Communist regimes. Yet we will not ignore the individuals and groups in Communist countries who seek peaceful change. . . . We must aid their struggle for freedom." Shultz specifically referred to private organizations as well as government-financed institutions such as Radio Free Europe as useful methods for influencing the political transformation of Eastern Europe.[9] The following Spring saw the development of the so-called Project Democracy designed to implement some of President Reagan's ideas concerning support for democratic institutions. More significantly, a National Endowment for Democracy (NED) was funded by Congress in November 1983 to oversee the general democratization campaign. NED works through various private organizations (such as the two national political parties) and focuses not just on the Soviet Union/Eastern Europe but also on the Third World. The creation of NED, in any case, was testament to the Administration's particular emphases within the broad spectrum of human rights.[10]

Two developments in Eastern Europe since the Helsinki Final Act have attracted the special attention of the United States with regard to the subject of civil and political liberties. One of these has concerned the fate of the so-called Helsinki monitors, private and unofficial groups created in the Soviet Union and much of Eastern Europe after 1975 to oversee their own government's adherence to the provisions of the Final Act. The target regimes have generally dealt very harshly with these Helsinki monitors, especially in the Soviet Union and Czechoslovakia, and many of the original monitoring groups have virtually disappeared. Washington has continually protested this form of repression, and Max Kampelman made a particular issue of the fate of the Helsinki monitors at the CSCE Review Conference in Madrid. He reported with approval that whereas at the Belgrade review meeting only two countries (the United States and the Netherlands) even made reference to the plight of the Helsinki monitors, at Madrid fully fourteen states gave their attention to the issue. Substantially because of American pressure and encouragement, the concluding document at Madrid contained a renewed pledge that the CSCE participating governments "would encourage genuine efforts to implement the Final Act" and would take the necessary action to insure the freedom "of the individual to know and act upon his rights and duties in the field of human rights and fundamental freedoms."[11]

A second development of particular interest to the United States in the early 1980s has been the establishment of unofficial organizations in several of the East European countries concerned with problems of peace and disarmament. These are not to be confused with the state-sponsored "peace councils" that are a standard feature of the political scene in the region and undertake carefully orchestrated mass demonstrations for peace on designated occasions. Perhaps the most prominent of these independent movements for disarmament has been in the German Democratic Republic, where the groups involved, such as Women for Peace, work in close consultation with the Lutheran Church, which gives them some measure of protection from police harassment. In Hungary, an organization called the Peace Group for Dialog was founded in 1982, and in Poland a new group styled the Committee for Social Resistance (KOS) has also entered the field. The Charter 77 movement in Czechoslovakia recently began to take a special interest in problems of disarmament and tension-reduction. From the American point of view, the emergence of these groups raises at least a modest prospect of genuine public pressures on the relevant regimes for more forthcoming stances on arms control and security questions, such as the matter of intermediate nuclear forces in Europe. (The development of several of the peace groups was given a particular spur by the introduction of new Soviet nuclear missiles into Czechoslovakia and the DDR in response to NATO's proceeding with deployment of the Pershing II and cruise missiles in Western Europe.) Most of the groups mentioned here have preferred not to be regarded as "dissidents" and have pointedly criticized both NATO and the Warsaw Treaty Organization for their military policies.[12] Despite these attempts at appearing "objective," however, the relevant peace organizations, like the Helsinki monitors, have been subject to varying degrees of regime repression. The United States at the Madrid review conference made a particular point of denouncing such repression, referring particularly to such episodes as a police assault on 300 peace demonstrators in Prague in June 1983 and the East German government's threat to expel students in peace groups from schools or to fire involved workers from their jobs.[13]

Aside from American interest in the "right to take part in government" in Eastern Europe, two other items in Vance's category three have received special attention: religious freedom and the right to emigrate. A congressional fact-finding mission to Eastern Europe in 1977, for example, spent a good deal of its time questioning local officials and religious figures about the state of religious practice in their countries. Particular attention was given to the situation of the Jewish community in Romania and Hungary. The evidence was that the small Jewish population was given some latitude in maintaining the faith and in sponsoring religious education.[14] Ms. Geza Seifert, secretary-general of the Board of Hungarian Jews, indicated in a later interview that Budapest was home to almost 100,000 Jews, and that the Hungarian regime practiced basically a policy of conciliation, with one result being that only about ten Hungarian Jews each year applied for permission to emigrate to Israel. "Anti-Semitism exists here," she concluded, "but compared to the past, we enjoy a very, very happy situation."[15] Perhaps it was because the Jewish community in these two countries is so small today, given the catastrophic effects of the Holocaust on their numbers, that the respective governments feel they can exercise some generosity. A subsequent congressional delegation followed up on the situation of the Romanian Jews, meeting in the course of their visit with the Chief Rabbi, Moses Rosen, who stressed that "there is no longer a Jewish problem in Romania." Rabbi Rosen noted that some 350,000 Jews had been allowed to emigrate from the country since 1945. The American conclusion in this case was that the remaining 30,000 Jews in Romania had "achieved considerable cooperation from the Romanian Government in developing Jewish life and culture."[16]

Two other issues that have informed American concerns about religious liberty in Eastern Europe have involved the relationship between the regime and the major religious denominations as well as governmental tolerance of minority sects. Even amidst a steady barrage of criticism of the Jaruzelski regime, for example, the State Department admits that the "Polish Government allows significant religious freedom," both for the Catholic Church and for the small Protestant denominations in the country.[17] Hungarian treatment of its Catholic majority also receives praise, as does the relatively benign stance the Bucharest regime takes toward the Romanian Orthodox Church (based, to be sure, on the long-established passivity of the Church in political matters). On the other hand, considerable criticism has been leveled at the Czech government for its continued harassment of the Catholic Church in its own country, which the regime evidently feels is a potential source of political dissension on the model of the Polish church. Catholic priests and lay believers have been subjected to house searches, harassment, arrests, and imprisonment. Secretary of State Shultz, in his speech in Helsinki on July 30, 1985, commemorating the tenth anniversary of the Final Act, specifically denounced the recent arrest of seven Czech priests and nuns for "obstructing state supervision over churches and religious orders."[18]

As far as minority sects are concerned, one of the principal human rights issues complicating relations between Washington and Bucharest has been Bucharest's policy, carried out through the Department of Cults, of constraining the religious activities of groups such as the Pentecostals, Seventh Day Adventists, and especially the small Baptist community (whose numbers have tripled to around 300,000 over the last twenty years). In contrast to its attitude toward the fourteen major recognized religious communities, the Ceausescu regime evidently has misgivings about the implications of free worship for Protestant fundamentalist sects. One particular issue has been the Romanian opposition to past or planned Baptist churches. As a consequence of representations from Washington, the Romanian government has agreed to provide for future construction of Baptist religious facilities as well as an expanded licensing for Baptist ministers to preach their faith.[19] Bucharest's invitation to the American evangelist Billy Graham to conduct a six-city, twelve-day preaching tour in the Fall of 1985 was also seen as another reaction to U.S. concern about the religious situation in Romania.[20]

Aside from the question of religious freedom, the United States has also put considerable pressure on various Eastern European regimes with respect to their policies on emigration. We have already referred to the Jackson-Vanik Amendment's role in this regard. A particular emphasis as far as emigration is concerned has been the matter of family reunification, that is, allowing relevant individuals emigrant visas so that they may rejoin their kin in the West. It is interesting to note that, even while protesting alleged "interference" in their internal affairs as a consequence of the American human rights campaign, the Eastern European governments have been relatively receptive to family reunification pleas. This was, of course, an important element in Basket Three of the Helsinki Final Act, and since once again the numbers are not large, the regimes involved have evidently felt they could acquire some badly needed human rights "credit" by displaying some liberality on the matter. Even the most repressive East European governments have taken steps in this direction. Thus, the Czech regime, under Resolution No. 58, promulgated in March 1977, established a plan for normalizing the legal status of Czechs who had left the country following the Soviet invasion of August 1968. The evidence was that the decree would greatly facilitate the emigration of additional Czech nationals for purposes of family reunification.[21] The State Department admitted in a recent assessment that the subsequent Czech performance on family reunification was generally good.

Even Poland and Bulgaria come in for some praise for their relative openness to family reunification claims. (Bulgaria has promised to resolve sixteen out of the eighteen divided family cases the American Embassy in Sofia has presented to them.) A survey of the current outstanding family reunification cases in Romania, Poland, Hungary, Czechoslovakia, and Bulgaria suggests that these total only about 1,100, with Poland and Romania accounting for the overwhelming majority.[22] None of this addresses, of course, the right of East European nationals to travel for purposes other than family reunification, and of the countries mentioned above only Hungary has a reasonably open policy in this respect, with Poland more stringent and Bulgaria, Czechoslovakia, and Romania regarding family reunification as the only generally legitimate reason to give exit visas. Nevertheless, the comparatively forthcoming position of the East European regimes on family reunification stands as at least a modestly encouraging aspect—to which U.S. pressure legitimately can be seen as contributing—of an otherwise somber human rights picture.

THE INSTRUMENTS OF AMERICAN HUMAN RIGHTS POLICY

Establishing the main goals of American human rights policy toward Eastern Europe is one issue; selecting the most efficient means for achieving these goals is another. In our earlier discussion we reviewed the use of trade and credits as a lever or "quid pro quo" to secure various concessions from the East European regimes, including concessions on human rights issues. In addition to the Jackson-Vanik Amendment, a typical attempt to use economic policy to further humanitarian concerns was President Carter's pledge of $200 million in credits to the Polish government at the end of 1977 to purchase American grain in return for a promise from Gierek, the Polish leader, that he would look into the granting of emigration permits to some 250 Polish nationals who had applied in vain for permission to join their families in the United States. Earlier that year it was reported that the Hungarian regime had reached a general understanding with the United States that accepted the importance of human rights as a factor in American trade policy toward Hungary. Budapest was evidently willing to accept this connection in return for congressional agreement to limit the restrictions that still applied to American trade with Hungary. (As noted, the Kadar regime did receive MFN status at the beginning of 1978.)[23] There is no need to repeat our basic conclusions concerning the quid pro quo approach to American trade and credits policy, except to say that in the instance of specifically focused human rights concerns there may be greater prospect of success than when the tradeoffs involve basic foreign or domestic political issues.

A second technique for furthering American human rights goals in Eastern Europe is to make known the details of the evolving human rights situation in the area to as wide an audience of Eastern Europeans as possible. A prime tactic of, say, the Czechoslovak government in reacting to dissent is to attempt to isolate it, both within Czechoslovakia and within Eastern Europe generally (that is, prevent its existence from being known outside Czechoslovakia itself). There is evidence that the "quarantine" strategy is in reality a coordinated strategy by Moscow and other Warsaw Pact countries to prevent "infection" or "spillover" from individual protest movements within these countries. Thus, an attempt by Polish and Czech groups in 1978 to establish contacts with one another and a joint plan of action ended in the arrest of the main initiator from Charter 77. This has not halted further attempts by East European dissidents to develop a coordinated strategy for reform and democratization. In November 1979, for example, Andrei Sakharov and other prominent members of the Soviet human rights movement called on Charter 77 and the Polish Self-Defense Committee (KOR) "to come forward with a joint statement by human rights defenders in Poland, Czechoslovakia and the USSR," a proposal that was warmly greeted by the Polish and Czech groups.[24] In early 1984, a statement datelined Prague and Warsaw once again expressed the determination of Charter 77 signatories, individuals from KOR, and Solidarity underground activists to establish a joint program for securing the implementation of human rights and freedom in their respective countries.[25]

If it is accepted that in numbers there is strength, and more specifically that a coordination of analysis and strategy among various national dissident groups presents East European authorities with more substantial problems of repression, then a prime American contribution to the human rights struggle in Eastern Europe may well be the "information offensive" represented basically by Radio Free Europe (RFE) and to a lesser extent the Voice of America (VOA). Perhaps the basic service which the radios can provide is to make individual dissidents aware of the variety and nature of other forms of protest in Eastern Europe. We will focus here basically on RFE, which specifically targets the countries of Poland, Hungary, Czechoslovakia, Romania, and Hungary, and the bulk of whose programming is devoted to developments within these countries or to matters of direct concern to them. The Voice of America, the official broadcasting service of the United States Information Agency, is concerned primarily with presenting reports on American social, cultural, economic, and political affairs as well as general world developments, and broadcasts worldwide, not just in Eastern Europe. This is not to say that there may not be some indirect effect in the region of information about "human rights practices" in this country, and it should be noted that VOA, unlike Radio Free Europe, is basically free of jamming and does reach a rather wide audience, estimated to range from 43 percent of the Polish adult population to about 35 percent in Czechoslovakia, 25 percent in Hungary, and even 22 percent in Bulgaria.[26]

RFE was founded in 1950, and for years it was a thinly disguised secret that the Central Intelligence Agency was its actual source of support. In 1971 the Congress decided to sever all ties between the radio and the CIA, and RFE currently operates under an independent Board for International Broadcasting (BIB) established in 1973 and funded directly by Congress. Based on its own research, RFE is easily the most popular Western radio network in Eastern Europe. A BIB study found that in an average week the percentage of the population tuning in to RFE at least once was some 61 percent in Poland, 55 percent in Hungary and Romania, 34 percent in Bulgaria, and 26 percent in Czechoslovakia.[27] These figures are obviously affected by the degree of jamming which the East European regimes employ to prevent RFE signals from reaching their populations. Hungary and (curiously) Romania have not engaged in extensive jamming for some twenty years. By contrast, about 80 percent of RFE Polish programming is subject to jamming, and in Prague and other major Czech cities there is also heavy jamming, although it is often possible to receive RFE transmissions in the rural areas.[28]

The Helsinki Final Act gave explicit encouragement to the dissemination of information broadcast by radio—"the participating states note the expansion in [such dissemination] and express the hope for a continuation of this process"— but, not surprisingly, various East European regimes have been somewhat unenthusiastic about full implementation of this notion. Their standard criticism of

RFE's activities is that they constitute an "unacceptable" interference into the domestic affairs of the target countries and that the broadcasts are designed to create instability and unrest throughout Eastern Europe.

Since its inception Radio Free Europe has been subject to the accusation—and not just from aggrieved politicians in Eastern Europe—that it presents a distinctly skewed version of political, social, and economic realities in Eastern Europe and is nothing more than a barely concealed propaganda enterprise. A more specific criticism mentioned above has been that RFE at times has rather irresponsibly contributed to revolutionary ferment in Eastern Europe and even implied American military support for East European "freedom fighters." Those convinced of the validity of this charge point in particular to the fact that RFE does employ a large number of East European émigrés on its staff, who could hardly be considered to have an impartial view of conditions in the old homeland. RFE's performance at the time of the Hungarian events in 1956 is, of course, a standard reference point in the critics' evaluation. An interesting attempt to meet this criticism, particularly the charge that RFE transmissions were inevitably biased and hostile to the East European regimes, was an offer in 1978 by the then-Chairman of BIB, John Gronouski, to provide airtime on RFE for East European regime spokespersons to present their complaints and rebuttals.[29] Nothing came of this novel proposal, but the basic controversy over the content of RFE programming continued as it had in the past.

The evidence on this score does not seem to support at least the more extreme accusations. In the case of Hungary in 1956, for example, the CIA official in charge of Radio Free Europe at the time argues rather convincingly that with the exception of one unauthorized and rather ambiguous broadcast, RFE did not provide any unwarranted encouragement to Hungarians thinking of liberation.[30] Subsequent investigations in 1957 by the West German government, the Council of Europe, and even the United Nations also arrived at essentially the same conclusion (although there was some reference to possibly misleading "impressions" RFE programming may have presented).[31]

Especially since its severance from CIA control in 1971, moreover, RFE has generally put great emphasis on objective reporting and has thus evidently consolidated its role as a source of information for Eastern Europeans, particularly on human rights issues. Veterans of RFE recall, for example, that in the early 1970s they were under especially strict guidelines from Administration authorities not to engage in arbitrary denunciations of East European political figures. A comment by the head of the Hungarian service of the RFE at the time was particularly revealing. "We in RFE are not asking the Communists to give up Communism," he said. "I am not the Voice of Free Hungary or the Hungarian conscience. We don't broadcast the views of Hungarian émigré politicians because they live in the past. We have to be realistic. We would like a beautiful Communism, or as Khrushchev said, a goulash Communism."[32] This statement, incidently, aroused considerable wrath among elements of the Hungarian-American community in the United States, who have continued to feel that the Hungarian service of RFE has been *too* "objective" and detached in its broadcasts to Hungary.

The issue of the content and focus of RFE programming, however, has been raised anew since the beginning of the Reagan Administration. As a general matter, the President and his chief foreign policy advisers have been persuaded, perhaps more than those in earlier administrations were, of the potential impact of Western broadcasts on the Communist world. The establishment of Radio Martí targeted toward Cuba was only one reflection of this predisposition. As far as RFE is concerned, the Administration has supported rather substantial increases in its budget but perhaps more significantly has argued for a more "activist" programming policy that would stress democratic values in contrast to those held by the Communist regimes. An internal memo circulated to the language desks at RFE headquarters at Munich caught the tone of the Administration's new approach. "Our goal should be to weaken the Communist camp, not by stirring up revolts, but by giving the people alternative values that they can use in bringing about peaceful change. . . . At present all we are doing is informing, but what is the point of continually providing information without goals?"[33] Secretary of State George Shultz summarized the role of RFE to be that of serving "as the communist world's surrogate free press."[34] Obviously, there are dangers in making RFE seem to be merely the dogmatic advocate of American political philosophy. Indeed, the effectiveness of Radio Free Europe to date, especially in the human rights areas, has been precisely the impression it has conveyed to East Europeans that it is not insisting on the inevitable superiority of American definitions of human rights standards. At the same time, the Reagan Administration's concept of the potential role of RFE, if properly controlled and defined, has something to recommend it. Information after all *is* power, and the disparate human rights groups in Eastern Europe, if provided with appropriate information on the activities of like-minded activists in other East European countries, presumably can employ this newfound "power" to some advantage.

Another potential technique for implementing American human rights policy in Eastern Europe is the continued development of educational and cultural exchange. The theory here is that with increasing East European exposure to Western scholars, artists, films, books, newspapers, and general cultural activity, it will become more and more difficult for the Eastern European regimes to insist on the old rigid conformity and sterile intellectual standards. In this regard, when an American advisory commission on educational and cultural affairs visited various East European capitals shortly after the Helsinki Final Act was completed, they found a perhaps surprising degree of enthusiasm among East European officials for following through on the Basket Three provisions of Helsinki concerning movement of ideas and information. The American commission discovered that these officials were very well informed on the cultural and educational exchange aspects of Basket Three, agreed that the full implementation of these provisions would lead to improved American-East European relations, and even admitted that the presence, for example, of American professors and students in Eastern Europe did lead to an increase in "mutual understanding."[35]

A model for such exchanges was the one signed with the Hungarian government in April 1977. The agreement obligated the respective governments to "encourage the further development of interest in the cultural heritage and a wider knowledge of the cultural achievements of the other country." Even before this agreement was reached, Hungary was notable in the number of American films it provided for the domestic audience. One estimate was that some 12 million Hungarians out of a total audience of 73 million had seen at least one American film. Ironically, the Hungarians have claimed that they have displayed far more American material in Hungary than the United States has done in America (a consistent complaint of virtually all East European cultural authorities).[36] Although the disparity can be accounted for in part by the vastly different output of, say, the American and Hungarian film industries, it does appear that greater attention to reciprocity may be in order. The Hungarians have also established a privately funded Chair in American Studies at Budapest's Elte University, and now require that third-year English students at the University of Pecs spend a year abroad, preferably in the United States, where the Hungarian authorities are seeking partner institutions as part of this curriculum.

Elsewhere in Eastern Europe, the United States has bilateral "umbrella agreements" with Bulgaria and Romania that provide guidelines for official cultural and academic exchanges and for officially sanctioned private exchanges.[37] Bulgarian authorities have for the first time expressed interest in sending their own graduate students to the United States, although the Romanian authorities have not generally utilized their quotas for research scholars in the United States. American cultural exchanges with Czechoslovakia, Poland, and the German Democratic Republic currently go forward in some areas even without formal bilateral agreements. One particular American initiative is the so-called AmPart (American Participant) program, in which the United States Information Agency (USIA) sponsors American lecturers to speak before various audiences in Eastern Europe. For example, Alan Platt, Director of European Arms Control Issues at the Rand Corporation, visited Prague under USIA auspices in November 1984, and his schedule included a presentation at the Czech Institute for International Relations. The privately sponsored International Research and Exchanges Board (IREX) also oversees exchanges of scholars with some Eastern European countries. Finally, the Fulbright program sent some eight American lecturers and researchers to Romania, Poland, Hungary, and Bulgaria in 1984.[38] All this may be considered somewhat modest in its potential impact, but it does remain that following the Helsinki Final Act the general picture has been one of a steadily expanding cultural and educational exchange between the United States and Eastern European countries.

In discussing the means by which the United States can hope to achieve its human rights objectives in Eastern Europe, we have thus far not referred to the traditional modes of diplomacy and negotiation. We will discuss below the use of multilateral diplomacy, as represented particularly by the Belgrade and Madrid Review Conferences of the Helsinki Final Act, as examples of the American use of this policy tool vis-à-vis human rights in Eastern Europe. For present purposes it is useful to refer to a particular diplomatic phenomenon that emerged following the Final Act, which was the series of bilateral discussions that developed between the United States and individual East European countries on the CSCE, particularly with respect to Principle VII and Basket Three. Thus, in the period after the Belgrade Review Conference American delegations composed of both State Department officials and members of Congress met with official groups from Hungary, Romania, East Germany, Poland, and Bulgaria.[39]

Especially interesting have been the two Romanian-American Human Rights Roundtables held in 1980 and 1984. The American delegation in the 1984 meeting was composed of individuals from the departments of State, Commerce, and Labor as well as the USIA; in addition, staff members from the Congressional Commission on Security and Cooperation in Europe played a prominent part. The Romanian group was headed by a Deputy Minister of the Romanian Foreign Ministry.[40] Accounts of this meeting suggested that the usual "frank exchange of views" took place, but this somewhat banal phrase perhaps does not do justice to the potential achievements of such meetings. The evidence suggests that the Romanian-American encounters, as well as those with other East European countries, have resulted in tangible progress on certain human rights issues, for example, specific family reunification questions. The more fundamental point, however, is that such meetings allow the Eastern European governments involved to discuss human rights questions with the United States in an environment free of the sort of polemics between Washington and Moscow that were such a feature of, say, the Belgrade CSCE review conference. Obviously, the East Europeans feel that this atmosphere limits their flexibility on human rights matters.

Private American groups involved in monitoring the Helsinki accords have also attempted to establish either bilateral or multilateral links with their counterparts in Eastern Europe. Thus, members of the New York Helsinki Watch Committee have informed monitoring groups in Poland and Czechoslovakia of their own activities and, in an extension of this activity, met with representatives of KOR in Poland and Charter 77 in Czechoslovakia.[41] These contacts don't have the potentially immediate policy implications of, say, the Romanian-American Human Rights Roundtable, but they nevertheless stand as a useful adjunct to the rather promising pattern whereby American representatives are able to deal directly with their East European counterparts on human rights questions rather than always having to involve Moscow in the dialogue.

NOTES

1. The full text of the Helsinki Final Act may be found in DEPARTMENT OF STATE BULLETIN 73 (September 1, 1975).

2. U.S. Department of State, Bureau of Public Affairs, "Human Rights Policy. Secretary Cyrus R. Vance on Law Day before the University of Georgia Law School." (Washington: GPO, 1977), 1.

3. Vratislav Pechota, "East European Perceptions of the Helsinki Final Act and the Role of Citizen Initiatives," VANDERBILT JOURNAL OF TRANSNATIONAL LAW 13 (Spring-Summer 1980), 476.

4. For example, Ambassador Griffin Bell, in his opening address to the CSCE review conference in Madrid on November 13, 1980, merely referred to the fact that "there has been encouraging progress in some countries toward creating more responsive and diverse social and economic systems." See DEPARTMENT OF STATE BULLETIN 79 (January 1981), 19.

5. Tufton Beamish and Guy Hadley, THE KREMLIN'S DILEMMA: THE STRUGGLE FOR HUMAN RIGHTS IN EASTERN EUROPE (San Rafael, Calif.: Presidio Press, 1979), 84-86.

6. U.S. Department of State, Bureau of Public Affairs, IMPLEMENTATION OF THE HELSINKI FINAL ACT, Eighteenth Semiannual Report, October 1, 1984-April 1, 1985 (Washington: GPO, 1985), 9-14.

7. DEPARTMENT OF STATE BULLETIN 85 (November 1985), 60.

8. U.S. Department of State, Bureau of Public Affairs, CURRENT POLICY No. 399 (Washington: GPO, 1982).

9. James L. Tyson, INTERNATIONAL BROADCASTING AND NATIONAL SECURITY (New York: Ramapo Press, 1983), 116.

10. DEPARTMENT OF STATE BULLETIN 83 (March 1983), 79. The NED has had a rather tumultuous subsequent history, with charges being made that it has been used for narrow partisan political purposes. See "Crusaders Fall Out," THE ECONOMIST (June 16, 1984), 25.

11. Ambassador Max Kampelman, "The Madrid CSCE Follow-Up Meeting: An Assessment." Statement in Madrid on July 15, 1983.

12. U.S. Commission on Security and Cooperation in Europe, THE SITUATION OF ANDREI SAKHAROV AND UNOFFICIAL PEACE GROUPS IN THE U.S.S.R. AND EASTERN EUROPE, Hearings, May 22, 1984. 98th Congress, 2d Session, 41-43.

13. Statement by Ambassador Max Kampelman, Head, U.S. Delegation to the Conference on Security and Cooperation in Europe, Madrid, July 18, 1983.2

14. U.S. Congress, House of Representatives, Committee on the Judiciary, HUMAN RIGHTS AND U.S. CONSULAR ACTIVITIES IN EASTERN EUROPE (Washington: GPO, 1977), 34-38.

15. William Erickson, "Jews in Hungary Thrive Under Nation's Conciliatory Laws," CHRISTIAN SCIENCE MONITOR (November 1, 1985).

16. U.S. Senate, Committee on Foreign Relations, HUMAN RIGHTS ISSUES IN UNITED STATES RELATIONS WITH ROMANIA AND CZECHOSLOVAKIA (Washington: GPO, April 1983), 14.

17. IMPLEMENTATION OF THE HELSINKI FINAL ACT, 11.

18. Secretary of State George Shultz, "Ten Years After Helsinki." DEPARTMENT OF STATE BULLETIN 85 (October 1985), 32.

19. Deputy Assistant Secretary of State Gary Matthews, "Human Rights in Romania," DEPARTMENT OF STATE BULLETIN 85 (August 1985), 60.

20. Eric Bourne, "Romanians Flock to See Billy Graham," CHRISTIAN SCIENCE MONITOR (November 5, 1985), 5.

21. HUMAN RIGHTS AND U.S. CONSULAR ACTIVITIES IN EASTERN EUROPE, 17.

22. IMPLEMENTATION OF THE HELSINKI FINAL ACT, 23.

23. Beamish and Hadley, THE KREMLIN'S DILEMMA, 70, 113.

24. Pechota, "East European Perceptions," 488.

25. U.S. Commission on Security and Cooperation in Europe, CSCE DIGEST, March 30, 1984 (Washington: GPO, 1984).

26. NEW YORK TIMES (November 28, 1983), 4.

27. U.S. Board for International Broadcasting, Radio Free Europe/Radio Liberty, "Listening to Western Radio in East Europe, 1981-Early 1982" (Washington: GPO, 1982).

28. IMPLEMENTATION OF THE HELSINKI FINAL ACT, 33-35.

29. U.S. Board for International Broadcasting, FOURTH ANNUAL REPORT 1978 (Washington: GPO, 1978), 3-4.

30. The official referred to is Cord Meyer. See his FACING REALITY (New York: Harper and Row, 1980), 123-130.

31. David Wise and Thomas B. Ross, THE INVISIBLE GOVERNMENT (New York: Random House, 1964), 324-327.

32. Henry Kamm, "Radio Free Europe, The In Sound from Outside," NEW YORK TIMES MAGAZINE (September 26, 1972), 37.

33. Tyson, INTERNATIONAL BROADCASTING AND NATIONAL SECURITY, 98.

34. Ibid., 118.

35. U.S. Advisory Commission on International Educational and Cultural Affairs, THE EFFECTS OF THE CONFERENCE ON SECURITY AND COOPERATION IN EUROPE ON THE CULTURAL RELATIONS OF THE UNITED STATES AND EASTERN EUROPE, A Special Report to Congress, April 1976 (Washington: GPO, 1976).

36. HUMAN RIGHTS AND U.S. CONSULAR ACTIVITIES IN EASTERN EUROPE, 26.

37. U.S. Commission on Security and Cooperation in Europe, THE HELSINKI PROCESS AND EAST-WEST RELATIONS: PROGRESS IN PERSPECTIVE (Washington: GPO, March 1985), 180-181.

38. IMPLEMENTATION OF THE HELSINKI FINAL ACT, 38-39.

39. THE HELSINKI PROCESS AND EAST-WEST RELATIONS, 9.

40. U.S. Commission on Security and Cooperation in Europe, CSCE DIGEST, March 9, 1984.

41. Virginia Leary, "The Right of the Individual to Know and Act upon His Rights and Duties: Monitoring Groups and the Helsinki Final Act," VANDER-BILT JOURNAL OF TRANSNATIONAL LAW 13 (Spring-Summer 1980), 387.

15.
Ambiguities and Good Intentions

The respective demands of American self-interest and American idealism have at times contended in Eastern Europe just as they have in other areas of the world where a given administration has attempted to apply human rights policy within the broader context of American strategic interests. We have already referred to the fact that Romania received MFN status three years before it was conveyed to the Hungarians, even though almost all objective observers would concede that the Hungarian record on freedom of emigration was distinctly superior to that of the Romanians. One can appreciate the sometimes difficult choices that confront the United States in blending humanitarian and pragmatic concerns in Eastern Europe. Nevertheless, there has been a pattern of perhaps excessive selectivity in American policy toward the East European regimes with regard to human rights.

In view of Romania's geopolitical importance and the value to the West of its relatively independent foreign policy, for example, it may have made sense to downplay the actual Romanian stance on emigration. It is hard to explain why President Carter in April 1978 felt it necessary to go beyond such diplomatic discretions by informing President Ceausescu that "our goals are also the same, to have a just system of economics and politics, to let the people of the world share in growth, in peace, in personal freedom."[1] Ceausescu's putative commitment to "personal freedom" presumably came as something of a surprise to his own citizens. Carter's statement came during a period in which the Bucharest regime was cracking down heavily on its Hungarian minority, had begun to imprison various priests and religious figures, and was protesting publicly against the necessity of giving even pro forma assurances of free emigration in return for MFN privileges.[2] During his earlier visit to Poland in December 1977, the President also seemed to be unnecessarily effusive in blurring basic differences in human rights standards, saying that "our concept of human rights is preserved in Poland." Carter did criticize the Polish authorities' refusal to allow a handful of dissident journalists to attend his press conference in Warsaw, but the overall impression left was that the Gierek regime and Washington had an identity of views on human rights practices, which was hardly reflective of Warsaw's general record at the time.[3]

The pattern of American selectivity in criticizing human rights violations in Eastern Europe was particularly evident in the two review conferences at Belgrade and Madrid of the Helsinki Final Act. Thus, the primary target of American denunciations were the German Democratic Republic, Czechoslovakia, and, of course, the Soviet Union. Poland (at least prior to December 1981), Hungary, and even Romania were subject to much milder remonstrations.[4] Secretary of State Shultz's closing speech at the Madrid Conference referred to those "heroes who will not let us forget." The heroes he mentioned were "Polish workers [martial law now having been invoked], Czech intellectuals, East German clergy and peace demonstrators, and Soviet dissidents of all faiths and from all walks of life."[5] Yugoslavia was virtually exempted from mention at either Belgrade or Madrid, and this provides perhaps one of the most interesting examples of what we have termed "excessive selectivity."

As noted previously, Yugoslavia does have a relatively good record on observing human rights standards, yet the country cannot be considered a model of pluralistic democracy either. There is continued harassment of political dissidents, with an estimated 200 political prisoners currently incarcerated (and a pattern of increased intolerance of dissent over the last several years), charges that the Yugoslav security service (SDS) has engaged in attempted assassinations of hostile émigrés, and evidence of excessively harsh treatment of the large Albanian ethnic population in the autonomous region of Kosovo.[6] Despite all this, the Commission on Security and Cooperation in Europe, not to mention the State Department, seldom refers to possible human rights violations in Yugoslavia.

The experiences of Ambassador Laurence Silberman in Belgrade in 1975-76 were unusually vivid testimony to the attitude of benign neglect that Washington has generally taken toward Yugoslav human rights practices. Silberman was not a career diplomat, and he took a most undiplomatic stance during his tenure in Belgrade in denouncing what he saw as the failings of the Tito regime. He was particularly exercised by the case of one Laszlo Toth, an American of Yugoslav origin, who during a visit to Yugoslavia was arrested and eventually sentenced to a prison term for alleged espionage. When Toth was finally released, after a year of increasingly acrimonious exchanges between Silberman and the Yugoslav authorities concerning the case, he commented publicly that Toth was "no more a spy of any kind than my Aunt Matilda or my ten-year old daughter."[7] President Tito denounced Silberman for "giving lessons about our internal and foreign policy and interfering in our affairs."[8] The Eastern European section at the State Department recommended that Silberman be formally censured for his comments, and on November 17, 1976, President Ford accepted his resignation with some evident relief.[9] One may question whether Silberman's tactics did not eventually become counterproductive in dealing with the Yugoslav regime on human rights and other matters, yet his unhappy demise as Ambassador was an event that prompted some legitimate reflection concerning Washington's policy toward Yugoslavia. Belgrade has consistently denounced what it feels is an "undue" emphasis by the Western countries on the human rights aspects of the Helsinki process, just as other, relatively less moderate, East European regimes have done. One Yugoslav jurist noted with approval that his country had been "reluctant to join the impatient ones" at Helsinki and later Belgrade, and, in perhaps unconscious irony, stressed that Yugoslavia had "maintained its specific approach to human rights in the international as well as the national sphere."[10]

PHYSICIAN, HEAL THYSELF

Any society that makes human rights a prime focus of its foreign policy also has to contend with the problem of whether its own practices make it well placed to press for a better human rights performance in other nations. A prime criticism of American human rights policy offered by some is that the United States needs to pay greater attention to its own human rights inadequacies before or at the same time as it pressures others to improve. An organization founded in 1978 to reflect such concerns was the Washington Helsinki Watch Committee, a coalition of approximately twenty civil rights, civil liberties, and poverty organizations. The focus of this group is entirely on American compliance with Helsinki rather than on the performance of other nations. The committee has focused attention on a number of putative violations of the Final Act by the United States, including police abuse of blacks, Hispanics, and American Indians, continued governmental insensitivity to poverty and economic deprivation, lack of attention to women's rights, and even denial of self-determination for Micronesia.[11]

The Commission on Security and Cooperation in Europe (CSCE), the principal congressional watchdog group set up to monitor compliance with the Helsinki Final Act, announced in 1979 that it would itself undertake a study of this country's adherence to the obligations of Helsinki. The subsequent document, entitled "Fulfilling Our Promises," concluded that "overall U.S. performance [of its Helsinki obligations] is very good. More importantly, the efforts undertaken by the U.S. Government and private groups since the Final Act was signed in 1975 reveal a consistent striving for improvement." At the same time, the CSCE admitted that the American implementation record was not perfect and that "there are areas where additional improvement is needed to bring the U.S. closer to full compliance with its obligations under the Final Act."[12] There are at a minimum three issues that can legitimately be raised with regard to the bona fides of the United States in criticizing the human rights practices of others.

First, there is the matter of American immigration and visa policy. It is rather ironic that, although free emigration from the Eastern European countries has been a prime goal of American human rights policy there, our own laws often make it difficult for those who do emigrate to gain access to the United States.

Thus, one provision of the 1952 U.S. Immigration and Nationality Act denies members of proscribed organizations, including the Communist party, entry into the United States without a special waiver. Similar provisions in the 1952 legislation deny entry to individuals who more generally may constitute a "detriment" to American national security interests. A waiver to these provisions may be obtained if the individual involved can demonstrate that he or she was an "involuntary" member of the party or else can now be considered a defector. In practice, waivers have now become the rule rather than the exception, at least for those applying for nonimmigrant visas. The so-called McGovern Amendment to the Foreign Relations Authorization Act of 1978, which was offered specifically to bring the United States into greater compliance with Helsinki, further placed the burden on the government to show why entry of a particular person should not be allowed. Nevertheless, the continuing existence of the 1952 legislation, with its sometimes cumbersome, if not degrading, waiver procedures, has led the Commission on Security and Cooperation in Europe to observe that the law hardly "makes sense today, given the United States' international and national commitments to the free movement of people."[13]

A related issue here is the current allocation procedures for nonpreference visas for individuals from Eastern European countries. In the aftermath of the Helsinki Final Act, the United States placed particular emphasis, as noted, on family reunification issues. Yet in the instance of Romania, to cite only one example, there were some seventy-five cases in 1977 involving primarily family reunification in which the relevant individuals had received exit visas from the Romanian government but could not gain entry in a timely fashion to the United States because of prevailing immigration law. The situation has worsened since that time. Prior to 1980, many Romanians who received permission to leave the country but were not eligible for direct entry into the United States availed themselves of the Third Country Processing (TCP) program. Under this arrangement, the people involved traveled to Rome on Italian transit visas and were subsequently granted settlement in the United States through private voluntary agencies. As a result of the Refugee Act of 1980, however, the options available through the TCP program were substantially eliminated. (The act was passed largely as a protest against the TCP's "end-run" around normal immigration restrictions.) Increasing limitations were placed on the total number of TCP applicants from all countries, and by 1982 the American Embassy in Bucharest had stopped accepting applications by Romanians for TCP status. Ironically, at the same time the Ceausescu regime continued to issue exit visas for those wishing to avail themselves of this program, with the result that thousands of Romanian nationals were technically eligible to leave their country, yet could not obtain documents for entry into Italy (and even less for entry directly into the United States).[14] As Joshua Eilberg, one of the principal congressional experts on American immigration practices once commented, "It is indeed ironical that the U.S. Government makes every effort to encourage the Government of Romania to remove emigration barriers, but at the same time our current procedures and practices preclude us from accommodating those who have been permitted to leave that country."[15]

A second point of controversy in the American human rights position concerns this country's failure to ratify several major United Nations-sponsored conventions dealing with humanitarian issues. Included here are (until recently) the Convention on Genocide, as well as the International Convention on the Elimination of All Forms of Racial Discrimination, the International Covenant on Civil and Political Rights, and the International Covenant on Economic, Social and Cultural Rights. As the Commission on Security and Cooperation in Europe states, "The sincerity and credibility of the United States in the field of human rights are seriously impaired by the fact that we have not ratified the Covenants."[16] The basic arguments against ratification have historically been twofold: that the treaties in some areas constitute an unwarranted interference in the domestic sovereignty of the United States, and that—ironically—several of the covenants don't go far enough and indeed may allow repressive governments to legitimize their own anti-human rights practices. If the United States regards itself as having a substantial role in the furtherance of international human rights, however, in this case particularly in Eastern Europe (where the conventions in question have received almost universal ratification), American failure to act can only be regarded as an ongoing "achilles heel" in the United States' position.

The Eastern bloc countries have not been reluctant to refer to this flaw in the American moral armor. In November 1979 the Soviet daily *Pravda* charged that "of the 40 existing international agreements on human rights, the United States of America has ratified only 10." It was made clear that this omission would be a prime defense tactic against the expected American charges of Soviet human rights violations at the upcoming Madrid Review Conference of the Final Act.[17] Not surprisingly, Bulgaria, Czechoslovakia, and East Germany did introduce a proposed recommendation at Madrid that all states should accede to the international human rights covenants.[18] The Delegation of Poland at the later meeting of human rights experts in Ottawa in 1985 also offered a resolution that all Helsinki signatories who had not ratified the relevant UN Conventions should do so promptly.[19] Perhaps in belated recognition of the fact that American nonratification of various human rights treaties was a serious drawback to the American role in the Helsinki process, the Senate on February 19, 1986, finally did ratify the Convention on Genocide.

Finally, there is the continued presence in the United States of alleged war criminals involved in pro-Nazi activity during World War II in Eastern Europe. Until recently, such individuals received comparatively little attention from American authorities, and their presence here was a continuing source of friction between Washington and various East European governments. In 1979 the Justice Department did establish an Office of Special Investigations (OSI) to pursue the issue, and the OSI has undertaken deportation proceedings against various individuals. One of the most prominent cases involved one Andrija Artukovic, a former minister of the interior in the short-lived Croatian regime from 1941 to 1945. Artukovic was charged with the mass slaughter and torture of Serbs, Jews, and Gypsies during his time in office. He had lived in Southern California since his admission to the United States in 1948. For years the Yugoslav authorities had sought to have Artukovic extradited to stand trial in Yugoslavia for his crimes, and under pressure from Belgrade the OSI did institute action against him. There was heated objection to this decision from many quarters, especially from émigré circles, on the basis that Artukovic could not expect to receive a "fair" trial in Yugoslavia. The expression of such opinions, together with the fact that the proceedings against Artukovic seemed to drag out endlessly, provided ample ammunition to spokespersons in Yugoslavia and elsewhere in Eastern Europe about the alleged inconsistency and even hypocrisy in the supposed American commitment to human rights.

Artukovic was eventually extradited to Yugoslavia in February 1986, but a number of other cases remain, such as that of Bishop Valerian Trifa, charged with fascist sympathies in Romania before and during World War II and more specifically with complicity in various anti-Jewish atrocities. Trifa has lived comfortably in Grass Lake, Michigan, following his admission to this country in 1948, and his political philosophy is summarized in his statement that "the interest in the Holocaust will backfire," that is, revive anti-Semitic sentiment in the United States. Trifa is on record as saying that his extreme anti-Jewish articles published in Romanian newspapers many years back were justifiable because "they were true."[20] It might be noted that Trifa was granted an extensive interview on Radio Free Europe on May 1, 1979, in order to expound on his views concerning Romanian politics, an event that led to a subsequent congressional investigation.

None of this is to say that the United States has had a policy of welcoming and protecting individuals in the postwar era who were avowedly fascist. Rather, the policy, especially in the immediate years after the war, was to accept people who were fierce in their anti-Communist protestations and who could conceivably provide useful intelligence on the regimes and societies they formerly served. Nevertheless, the continued existence of such persons in this country has compromised the credibility of American concerns about the current human rights situation in Eastern Europe.

THE UNITED STATES AND THE HELSINKI PROCESS

The above are specific problem areas in American human rights policy. A more general criticism that some have leveled at this policy as it involves Eastern Europe may be summarized as follows. Since the signing of the Helsinki accords in 1975, the United States has made much of its concern with human rights in the region, and particularly in the Belgrade and Madrid review conferences, as well as a 1985 meeting in Ottawa of human rights experts, it has pursued a strong policy of public denunciation of human rights abuses in the Soviet Union and Eastern

Europe. Yet an examination of the origins of the human rights clauses in the Helsinki Final Act reveals that the United States was a reluctant partner to those provisions. Moreover, the subsequent confrontational stance that this country has adopted at various meetings to review the Final Act has had more to do with the United States' wanting to polish its public image, and perhaps to assuaging certain domestic political constituencies as well, than with a concern for real progress on the human rights front in Eastern Europe.

We will deal with the second part of this indictment shortly. As far as the original American role in the CSCE is concerned, there seems little doubt that the United States did not play the major role in securing the inclusion of Principle VII and the various items in Basket III in the Final Act. At the time the Ford Administration pointed to these sections of the Helsinki accords as representing a significant success for American human rights policy. In reality, it was the efforts of certain West European participants in the negotiations, particularly the Scandinavians, Austrians, Swiss, and representatives from the Benelux countries, that were decisive. One European commentator has described Secretary of State Henry Kissinger as being "contemptuous" of the whole enterprise of the CSCE in its early stages and of never showing "any signs of seeing intrinsic value in the conference itself and of [seeming] wholly uninterested in negotiations on human rights, human contacts and other humanitarian proposals."[21] This may appear a little strong, but a reading of Kissinger's memoirs does reveal very little enthusiasm concerning the potentialities of Helsinki. He dismissed most of the issues being discussed as part of the CSCE process as being "too abstruse—they were mostly pedantic drafting problems in a collective document—to lend themselves to top-level solutions, though they were discussed inconclusively at considerable length."[22]

From this perspective the United States was more led than leading on the human rights questions involved at Helsinki, basically because our attention was on the security and trade and technology provisions of Helsinki as ingredients in an expanded détente with the Soviet Union. (Of the literally thousands of proposals offered during the negotiations leading up to the Final Act, the United States was specifically responsible for only two.)[23] Focus on the human rights situation in Eastern Europe, and more particularly in the Soviet Union, was not likely to encourage the Soviet leaders to view such an expansion as an unmixed blessing.[24] Moreover, there is evidence that this relative disdain for Principle VII and Basket III continued for some time even after the Helsinki Final Act had been signed in 1975, at least within the domain of the State Department and other branches of the Executive foreign policy establishment in Washington. When the Congress established the Commission on Security and Cooperation in Europe in June 1976, for example, to monitor compliance with the Helsinki Final Act, especially the human rights provisions, the reaction from State was distinctly cool. The first chairman of the new commission, Representative Dante Fascell (D-Fla.), recalls that "the State Department was fearful that such a body might prove counterproductive to traditional modes of 'quiet diplomacy'." Additional concern was expressed, according to Fascell, that the "extraordinary interest in CSCE by non-governmental units," for example, the East European ethnic lobby, would prove difficult to manage as well.[25] President Ford, in signing the legislation creating the commission on June 3, 1976, stressed that the three executive branch participants in the group would be only observers, not full members. He also commented that any executive branch participation in the commission raised questions about the constitutional separation of powers.[26]

Even after the Carter Administration took power, and despite the new President's expressed interest in human rights issues, the same pattern seemed to continue within the State Department. Thus, prior to leaving for the Belgrade Review Conference of the CSCE, one of the members of the American delegation—an academic rather than a government official—would later recollect rather tartly that he observed no great intensity of feeling on the part of the State Department itself as far as raising human rights questions at Belgrade was concerned. It is of some interest that the only really coherent position papers available to him prior to Belgrade were those provided by the Congressional Commission. At the State Department, his experience was that there was no real established and thought-out position on the stance the United States ought to adopt on human rights during the upcoming conference.[27]

This is not to say that the United States was forever precluded from adopting a genuinely active and concerned role vis-à-vis human rights in Eastern Europe simply because it was somewhat desultory in its original expressions of interest on the subject when the Helsinki Final Act was being negotiated. It is merely to state that a certain degree of caution seems advisable when, as subsequently happened, Washington is prone to lecture its Western European partners on their own lack of zeal for the human rights cause. The basic shift in at least Washington's public stance toward the human rights provisions of Helsinki is a subject in itself, and constitutes the second part of the "indictment" referred to above. This shift in approach also raised some rather basic general questions about the utility of different policy options in securing progress in the human rights field in Eastern Europe.

We have pointed out that the State Department, whether under President Gerald Ford or Jimmy Carter, was somewhat dubious about converting the human rights provisions of the Helsinki Final Act into a major focus of American foreign policy. At the very least, the predisposition was to rely on traditional norms of quiet diplomacy to deal with those issues arising from Principle VII and Basket Three. As the United States began to make preparations for the Belgrade Review Conference, however, this stance came to be increasingly questioned. Senator Clifford Case (R.-N.J.) sounded the basic theme when he commented that he was worried about the composition and assumptions of the American delegation to Belgrade. "I have not frankly seen yet the kind of spirit that intends to have the knock-down, drag-out real confrontation that I think is called for at this stage."[28] As it happened, White House National Security Adviser Zbigniew Brzezinski was also pondering the same question. As early as April 1977, he had been urging the State Department to consider a "confrontationist" approach to the Helsinki Review Conference. The department, he said, was "horrified even by the thought." When a final decision came on the structure of the American delegation, Brzezinski succeeded in his "inner hope" of "stiffening the backs" of American policymakers by blocking the appointment of what he called "a relatively unknown State Department nominee" to head the delegation (Deputy Secretary of State Warren Christopher). In his place, the Carter Administration designated Arthur Goldberg, a former Secretary of Labor, Supreme Court Justice, and Ambassador to the United Nations, to be the main American spokesman at Belgrade. Brzezinski later commented that "his [Goldberg's] leadership gave the United States the visibility and impact we desired."[29]

Goldberg's performance at Belgrade did indeed create a considerable amount of "visibility" for this country on human rights questions. There is an extensive debate, however, over the actual "impact" of this new posture on improving the human rights situation in Eastern Europe. Critical to the Goldberg approach at Belgrade was his tendency during both the plenary and closed sessions to stress Basket III implementation while giving a good deal less attention to the provisions of Helsinki relating to such matters as European security or technological and scientific exchanges. Equally important were the extensive press briefings that the American delegation provided on the human rights discussions originating again in both plenary and supposedly closed sessions. In apparent disregard of a prior agreement among the Western delegations, Goldberg's press officers also provided specific names of individuals in the Soviet Union and Eastern Europe whom he had referred to in general terms in the plenary sessions.[30]

These tactics evidently were a source of considerable discomfort to most of the other West European attendants at Belgrade. As a general matter, the West Europeans doubted the efficacy of making accusations against specific countries or with reference to specific individuals (although they did make a point of the violation of Principle VII represented by the trials of Czech Charter 77 activists as well as the East German government's stance on emigration to the FRG).[31] The American habit of giving primary attention to the plight of Soviet dissidents also came under criticism, for the West European view of the Helsinki process placed substantial emphasis on CSCE as a device for bringing together the two halves of Europe rather than berating Moscow. Another source of tension in the respective American and European approaches to Helsinki was the Europeans' interest in developing additional specific commitments from the Eastern bloc on matters such as visa issuance procedures and better working conditions for scholars, businessmen, and journalists. The United States, by contrast, preferred to focus on the issue of whether the socialist countries were living up to the commitments already made in 1975 in the Final Act.[32] A particularly frustrated group of participants at Belgrade were the so-called N and N delegations (neutral and nonaligned states such as Switzerland, Sweden, Austria, and Yugoslavia), who had aspirations to serve as mediators and facilitators between the two superpowers and their close allies. In the event, all the efforts of the neutrals to take the lead in drafting a final document for the Review Conference came to nought. The requirement that this document receive unanimous approval from all in attendance played a not inconsiderable role in the outcome. Belgrade in any case concluded with merely an anodyne statement of a few pages noting that "representatives of the participating States held a thorough exchange of views," which supposedly constituted in itself "a valuable contribution towards the achievement of the aims set by the CSCE."[33]

Those who were critical of the general American approach to Belgrade were only somewhat less captious in their analysis of the American performance at the Madrid Review Conference, which convened two years later. Three similarities in particular were identified. First the American delegation was not headed by a professional diplomat but by individuals with no formal diplomatic background (initially former Attorney-General Griffin Bell and later political activist Max Kampelman). Second, both Bell and Kampelman spent a considerable portion of their time in specific and public denunciation of the Soviet Union and at least some of the East European regimes for their human rights performance, to the possible detriment of consideration of other aspects of the Final Act. Then there was the composition of the American delegation, quite aside from its principal spokesperson. Both at Belgrade and Madrid the United States was virtually unique in including a variety of nondiplomatic personnel in its delegation. Thus, at Madrid a total of 128 members were officially listed in the American group (compared to 28 for the Soviet Union, 20 for West Germany, and 16 for the United Kingdom). Twenty-one of these were members of Congress (eight congressional wives were also part of the list), and there were thirty "public members" representing a variety of ethnic, labor, religious, and civic interest groups.[34] The charge was made that the notably amorphous character of the American delegation, which seemed intent above all on touching every political base in the United States, was in itself evidence that Washington regarded the Madrid conference as an exercise in public relations more than serious negotiation.

In assessing the often heated debate over American tactics at Belgrade and Madrid, we need to focus on a fundamental issue that this debate ultimately raises. Simply stated, the question is this: by applying pressure, especially public pressure, with respect to human rights in Eastern Europe, does the United States help or hinder the work and general situation of human rights activists in Eastern Europe itself? More generally, by making a public issue of human rights violations, are we contributing to the welfare and greater freedom of the peoples of Eastern Europe?

Critics of recent American performance in the context of CSCE Review Conferences would argue that the United States not only did not help to further human rights in Eastern Europe but actually succeeded in undermining the cause of human rights. As one member of the American delegation at Belgrade rather colorfully put it, "The Chesire cat smiles on the faces of Soviet delegates at the end of the Belgrade Conference had to be seen to be believed. They had succeeded beyond their wildest dreams."³⁵ The argument here was that American "confrontationist" tactics had made it virtually certain that there would be no concluding document that referred to the specific human rights issue within the CSCE review process. Another member of the American group at Belgrade has asserted that East European human rights activists were themselves discomforted by the American stance, in part because it caused the Soviets to be even less tolerant of dissent in Eastern Europe and in part because the United States was obviously being inconsistent in condemning, say, Soviet abuses of Principle VII and Basket Three while remaining silent on equal outrages by American allies such as South Korea or the Philippines (the latter, to be sure, not part of the CSCE regime).³⁶ Those who indict American conduct at Belgrade and Madrid argue that the United States was, in reality, not very concerned about the "effectiveness" of different approaches to human rights questions. Instead, both the Carter and Reagan administrations adopted a position at the two conferences that was designed to appeal to domestic political constituencies, to reinforce the image of both Presidents as firm defenders of human rights, and to use CSCE as a weapon against the Soviet Union without much regard for the effect of such a strategy in Eastern Europe.

If we consider the above issue (i.e., a "public" versus "private" strategy on human rights) in general terms, quite aside from any specific verdict on the American performance at Belgrade and Madrid, the evidence is inevitably somewhat mixed. An authoritarian regime, if embarrassed by open criticism of its practices, may often react by even greater repression, if only to demonstrate that it remains master in its own house. In addition, if the regime can establish in the minds of the mass of its population a putative direct link between local dissidents and outside support, it may succeed in discrediting this dissent as not being "genuinely" patriotic and devoted to the interests of the nation. Voices everywhere that call into question the competency and even more the bona fides of the leaders of the state are subject to a prevailing instinct among the general populace that to do so is somehow to cast aspersions on the nation itself. This phenomenon has operated not just in authoritarian systems, but often in the West as well—witness the reception given to most anti-Vietnam War protesters in the United States in the early years of that struggle.

In the case of the Soviet Union, the regime does seem to have had some success in portraying, say, Alexander Solzhenitsyn or Andrei Sakharov as being "renegades" of Soviet society, irreparably hostile to the achievements of the Soviet people, perhaps even simply tools of the West.³⁷ There is also some evidence that, in the case of the Charter 77 movement in Czechoslovakia, the widespread outcry in the West at the government's crackdown on the people involved moved the Prague regime to be even more repressive. There is additional evidence that for whatever reason the government was able to isolate the Charter 77 signers rather effectively from the mass of the Czech population.[38] Whether this was because of an upsurge of pro-government "patriotic" support may be questioned, of course; it may have had even more to do with a prevailing apathy that Charter 77 could change things significantly, as well as a reluctance to involve oneself with a movement that was bound to bring significant personal penalties.

On the other hand, there is also some interesting evidence that, properly organized and conducted, overt Western human rights pressure can contribute measurably to improved conditions in Eastern Europe. The Final Act of the Helsinki Conference, for example, was widely publicized and distributed in the area. (The official Soviet government paper *Izvestiya* itself printed in full the text of the Final Act.) As one analysis put it, this fact "reinforced the claims of the dissenters that they were not engaged in any criminal or politically subversive activities, but had legitimate grounds for condemning violations of human rights which their own Communist authorities had acknowledged under the U.N. Covenants and confirmed at Helsinki."[39] Reference to the Final Act brings us back to the question of the Belgrade and Madrid Review Conferences, and of the pointers they provide as to the utility of different Western and more particularly American approaches in assisting the cause of human rights in Eastern Europe.

The formal outcomes of Belgrade and Madrid were noticeably different. Thus, the Madrid Conference, in contrast to the Belgrade Conference, did eventually result in a concluding document of some thirty-eight pages that covered almost every aspect of East-West relations and that paid particular attention to human rights questions, in some cases adding new language to that originally contained in the Final Act. There were specific references to the right of free religious practice, to the necessity of improved measures for family reunification, to the equable treatment of national minorities, to the legitimate role of the so-called Helsinki monitors in Eastern Europe, and to the right of free labor union activity. The document even contains a specific reference to Solidarity. Moreover, the Madrid concluding document also provided for a follow-up meeting of human rights "experts" in Ottawa in the Spring of 1985.[40] All this stood in some contrast to the tepid statement that emerged out of the Belgrade negotiations.

How do we account for the differences in the two outcomes? Evidently, the Western and American delegations at Madrid were prepared to trade-off certain concessions to the Soviet Union and some of the Eastern Europe countries in return for a final document containing, *inter alia*, references to human rights. The tradeoff referred to was the Soviet interest in a future conference on Disarmament in Europe and Confidence and Security-Building Measures. Both of these were logically linked to the original Soviet concerns at Helsinki, that is, Basket One dealing with European security questions. Agreement was established for a conference dealing with these matters (the CDE), which began in Stockholm in late 1984. Thus, one lesson here seems to be that, even if the United States pursues a largely "confrontationist" strategy in discussing human rights, if it is prepared pragmatically to deal with other aspects of the CSCE of particular interest to the socialist bloc, at least modest progress can be made on Principle VII and Basket Three issues.

As far as Belgrade is concerned, the verdict on the American strategy would seem unavoidably to be less charitable. At least at the level of formal agreement, it is difficult to assert that Belgrade accomplished very much, and indeed the argument that it was a counterproductive exercise has some viability. Not surprisingly, Ambassador Goldberg felt otherwise. In a curt rejoinder to one of his critics, he indicated that "while we showed good manners at Belgrade, we were not shy nor should we have been."[41] Goldberg did avoid most evidence of being "shy" at Belgrade, but again the results of his assertiveness would appear problematic (although one prominent Yugoslav dissident criticized the American delegation for downplaying human rights at the conference and said that this represented a surrender to the "realists" within the American government).[42] The outcome of the Ottawa meeting of human rights experts could perhaps be considered in the same light as Belgrade. In this case as well, it proved impossible to agree on any substantive final document, and the reactions to this failure echoed those following the earlier 1977 review conference, some arguing that the breakdown at Ottawa showed the futility of continued American participation in the Helsinki process, whereas others once again questioned the "abrasive" approach of the American delegation.

Yet there may be something else here that needs mentioning as well. One can legitimately criticize American conduct at Belgrade, Madrid, and Ottawa and yet at the same time conclude that whatever the American tactics employed, the very act of holding conferences such as these (other ones being a meeting on human contacts in Berne, Switzerland, in April 1986 and another general CSCE review conference in Vienna at the end of 1986) is its own justification. One spokesman for the Czech-American community has argued strenuously that the Helsinki accords are "the basis on which the human rights activists in all of Eastern Europe stand. If this is withdrawn or weakened, then I guess their position would be weakened very much."[43] For example, in anticipation of Belgrade several East European countries modified some of their human rights practices lest they come under embarrassing scrutiny at the conference. Some political prisoners were amnestied (particularly in Poland and Romania); a number of long-standing family reunification cases were settled; emigration statistics rose; more binational marriages were allowed; and there was even some modest appearance of Western journals and newspapers in certain East European capitals.[44] An authority on the Helsinki process summarizes the evidence: attention to the "human rights provisions of the Helsinki Final Act have exerted a significant liberalizing impact upon a number of East European countries, a crucial fact that appears to have gone unnoticed in the West."[45]

An American journalist covering the Belgrade meetings recalled how diplomats from the non-Soviet Warsaw Pact countries would emphasize—out of earshot of their Soviet "colleagues"–how important continued emphasis on the Final Act was to their country's political future. He even reported the rather wistful comment by East Europeans to the effect that if the Final Act had been in effect, the Soviets would never have dared invade Czechoslovakia.[46] The same phenomenon was evident at the 1985 meeting of human rights experts in Ottawa. One State Department official stressed that the "East European countries . . . are more ashamed of the honest opinion of mankind" and consequently "will respond more to CSCE pressures."[47] The head of the American delegation at Ottawa, Ambassador Richard Schifter, indicated that in private negotiations, but even on public occasions, his East European counterparts were willing to adopt human rights stances at some variance from those of Moscow. He commented that the Hungarians generally said little to support Soviet bloc positions, "the Czechs would only look out for themselves," the Romanians "were totally on their own," and even the Bulgarians "looked after themselves and nobody else." Ambassador Schifter concluded that the East European regimes were quite interested in better relations with the West, and that they recognized that "improvement in their human rights performance could play a significant role in improving their standing in the West."[48]

The argument that if the Helsinki Final Act had been in place in 1968 it might have prevented the Soviet invasion of Czechoslovakia seems to be a somewhat utopian interpretation of the potential of the Helsinki process. At the same time there is something to be said for relying on the opinions of East Europeans themselves as a source of guidance to those in the West debating the "wisdom" or "efficiency" of applying pressure, especially public pressure, on human rights issues. Perhaps the ultimate expression of what Western concern can mean to the struggle for human rights in Eastern Europe came, rather significantly, from Jan Patocka, one of the original signers of Charter 77. Shortly before his death, brought on in part by police interrogation following his arrest on March 13, 1977, Patocka indirectly addressed the question of the Western role in the Eastern European human rights campaign. His comments are particularly striking because, as already noted, it might be argued that the Charter 77 movement suffered from too much outside attention. Patocka disagreed.

Many people ask whether Charter 77 will not lead to increased "vigilance," which in turn will have adverse effects on all citizens. Let us be frank about this. In the past, no conformity has yet led to any improvement in the situation, only a worsening. The greater the fear and servility, the more brazen the authorities have become. There is no way to make them relax the pressure other than by showing them that injustice and discrimination are not ignored. What is needed is for people to behave at all times with dignity, not to allow themselves to be frightened and intimidated, and to speak the truth–behavior which is impressive just because it is in such contrast with the way the authorities carry on."[49]

Patocka was speaking in part to his own Czech compatriots. He was also evidently issuing a call to the Western democracies as well. If we truly cherish those humane values that make up the core of that democratic tradition, and if we desire and need to remain true to ourselves, then we cannot ignore the sort of appeal Patocka issued. The traditional phrase still has it right: all that is needed for evil to triumph is for good men to remain silent.

NOTES

1. Cited in Jeane P. Kirkpatrick, "Establishing a Viable Human Rights Policy," WORLD AFFAIRS 143 (Spring 1981), 326.

2. David Andelman, "The Road to Madrid," FOREIGN POLICY (Summer 1980), 166.

3. Ernest Lefever, "The Trivialization of Human Rights," POLICY REVIEW (Fall-Winter 1978), 20.

4. H. Gordon Skilling, "CSCE in Madrid," PROBLEMS OF COMMUNISM (July-August 1981), 10.

5. U.S. Commission on Security and Cooperation in Europe, THE MADRID CSCE REVIEW MEETING (Washington: GPO, November 1983), 61.

6. Amnesty International, AMNESTY INTERNATIONAL REPORT 1985 (London: Amnesty International Publications, 1985), 299-302; Adriad DeWind, "Yugoslav Repression," NEW YORK TIMES (July 16, 1984).

7. Cited in Andrew Borowiec, YUGOSLAVIA AFTER TITO (New York: Praeger, 1977), 72.

8. Ibid., 73.

9. Ambassador Silberman gives his own version of his tense relations with the Tito regime—and with his nominal superiors in the State Department as well —in "Yugoslavia's 'Old' Communism," FOREIGN POLICY (Spring 1977), 3-27.

10. Vojin Dimitrijevic, "The Place of Helsinki on the Long Road to Human Rights," VANDERBILT JOURNAL OF INTERNATIONAL LAW 13 (Spring-Summer 1980), 261, 263.

11. Virginia Leary, "The Right of the Individual to Know and Act upon His Rights and Duties: Monitoring Groups and the Helsinki Final Act," VANDER-BILT JOURNAL OF INTERNATIONAL LAW 13 (Spring-Summer 1980), 385-386.

12. U.S. Commission on Security and Cooperation in Europe, FULFILLING OUR PROMISES: THE UNITED STATES AND THE HELSINKI FINAL ACT (Washington: GPO, November 1979), 311.

13. Ibid., 256-270.

14. U.S. Senate, Committee on Foreign Relations, HUMAN RIGHTS ISSUES IN UNITED STATES RELATIONS WITH ROMANIA AND CZECHOSLOVAKIA (Washington: GPO, April 1983), 9-10.

15. U.S. Congress, House of Representatives, Committee on the Judiciary, HUMAN RIGHTS AND U.S. CONSULAR ACTIVITIES IN EASTERN EUROPE (Washington: GPO, 1977), 25.

16. FULFILLING OUR PROMISES, 168.

17. William Korey, "Sins of Omission," FOREIGN POLICY (Summer 1980), 172.

18. Skilling, "CSCE in Madrid," 13.

19. U.S. Commission on Security and Cooperation in Europe, CSCE DIGEST, June 10, 1985 (Washington: GPO, 1985).

20. Alan A. Ryan, Jr., QUIET NEIGHBORS (New York: Harcourt Brace Jovanovich, 1984), 245. This is one of the best studies of the issue of alleged war criminals resident in the United States.

21. Richard Davy, "The United States," in BELGRADE AND BEYOND: THE CSCE PROCESS IN PERSPECTIVE, eds. Karl Birnbaum and Nils Andren (Rockville, Md.: Sijthoff and Noordhoff, 1980), 4.

22. Henry Kissinger, YEARS OF UPHEAVAL (Boston: Little, Brown and Co.: 1982), 1165.

23. William Korey, HUMAN RIGHTS AND THE HELSINKI ACCORDS (New York: Foreign Policy Association, 1983), 25.

24. A very good survey of the background and negotiating strategy that led to the Helsinki Final Act is John Maresca's TO HELSINKI: THE CONFERENCE ON SECURITY AND COOPERATION IN EUROPE 1973-1975 (Durham, N.C.: Duke University Press, 1985).

25. Dante Fascell, "The Helsinki Accords: A Case Study," ANNALS OF THE AMERICAN ACADEMY OF POLITICAL AND SOCIAL SCIENCE 442 (March 1979), 75.

26. Korey, HUMAN RIGHTS AND THE HELSINKI ACCORDS, 29.

27. These points are part of a private memorandum provided for the author's benefit by one of the American participants at the Belgrade Conference.

28. U.S. Commission on Security and Cooperation in Europe, BASKET III: IMPLEMENTATION OF THE HELSINKI ACCORDS, Hearings, June 3, 1977 and June 6, 1977: "U.S. Policy and the Belgrade Conference," Vol. 4, 95th Congress, 1st Session, 96.

29. Zbigniew Brzezinski, POWER AND PRINCIPLE (New York: Farrar, Straus and Giroux, 1983), 300.

30. Davy, "The United States," 9.

31. THE MADRID CSCE REVIEW MEETING, 130.

32. Dante B. Fascell, "Did Human Rights Survive Belgrade?" FOREIGN POLICY (Summer 1978), 113.

33. U.S. House of Representatives, Committee on International Relations, THE BELGRADE FOLLOWUP MEETING TO THE CONFERENCE ON SECURITY AND COOPERATION IN EUROPE: A REPORT AND APPRAISAL (Washington: GPO, May 17, 1978), 74.

34. Harold Molineu, "Hanging on to Helsinki," Paper prepared for the annual meeting of the International Studies Association, March 1984, 12.

35. Carroll Sherer, "Breakdown at Belgrade," THE WASHINGTON QUARTERLY 1 (Autumn 1978), 85.

36. Albert W. Sherer, Jr., "Goldberg's Variations," FOREIGN POLICY (Summer 1980), 163.

37. For a discussion of this point, see Robert G. Kaiser, RUSSIA (New York: Washington Square Press, 1984), especially ch. 11.

38. Thomas E. Heneghan, "Human Rights in Eastern Europe," WORLD TODAY (March 1977), 90.

39. Tufton Beamish and Guy Hadley, THE KREMLIN'S DILEMMA: THE STRUGGLE FOR HUMAN RIGHTS IN EASTERN EUROPE (San Rafael, Calif.: Presidio Press, 1979), 35.

40. THE MADRID CSCE REVIEW MEETING, 11-13.

41. Arthur Goldberg, "Letter," FOREIGN POLICY (Fall 1980), 190.

42. Mihajlo Mihajlov, "Human Rights: A Means or an End? THE NEW LEADER (November 3, 1980), 6-8.

43. U.S. Senate, Committee on Foreign Relations, THE PROMOTION AND PROTECTION OF HUMAN RIGHTS IN EASTERN EUROPE AND THE SOVIET UNION, Hearings, November 9, 1983, 98th Congress, 1st Session, 48.

44. THE BELGRADE FOLLOWUP MEETING TO THE CONFERENCE ON SECURITY AND COOPERATION IN EUROPE, 7-8; Fascell, "Did Human Rights Survive Belgrade?", 116.

45. Korey, HUMAN RIGHTS AND THE HELSINKI ACCORDS, 56.

46. Don Cook, "Belgrade: Spinning a European Web," THE ATLANTIC (November 1977), 15.

47. U.S. Commission on Security and Cooperation in Europe, IMPLEMENTATION OF THE HELSINKI ACCORDS. THE OTTAWA HUMAN RIGHTS EXPERTS MEETING AND THE FUTURE OF THE HELSINKI PROCESS. Hearings, June 25, 1985, 99th Congress, 1st Session, 34.

48. Ibid., 8, 47.

49. Beamish and Hadley, THE KREMLIN'S DILEMMA, 95.32.

16.
The Strategic Calculus

In concluding this study of problems in the American-East European relationship, it is appropriate to focus on the importance of East Central Europe to the strategic/geopolitical position of the United States, which remains critical not only to American but also to all foreign policymaking. The emphasis in these final chapters will be not so much on a detailed recitation of specific events in American policy toward Eastern Europe as on the development of a conceptual framework within which one can identify and assess American options in dealing with this region of the world. The following analysis thus represents a "summing up" of the challenges and dilemmas in American foreign policy toward Eastern Europe.

In purely strategic terms, it may be argued that Eastern Europe ranks below other regions of the world, for example, the Middle East, Western Europe, or Latin America, in its importance to the United States. At least this has been the position adopted by American administrations since 1945, in practice if not in rhetoric. It can also be argued, however, that Eastern Europe as a strategic factor has been underrated by both practitioners and students of American foreign policy. Two pragmatic security concerns in particular engage, or ought to engage, American concern about the future of East Central Europe. The first of these relates to the capabilities that various East European countries add to the aggressive potential of the Warsaw Pact. Thus, the non-Soviet members of the Warsaw Treaty Organization (WTO) in 1985 disposed of over 1.1 million troops, some 2,300 combat aircraft, and close to 15,000 tanks, to cite only three measures of military power.[1] This is not the place to consider the virtually endless debate as to whether the Soviet-dominated WTO is basically a device for assuring a defensive buffer against future invasions of the Soviet Union or is instead a tool designed to give Moscow an opportunity for additional military adventurism in Europe. Nor do we address here the question of the comparative "reliability" of various East European contingents within the WTO.[2] Suffice it to say that should the

174

Soviets decide on a military move against Western Europe, their putative ability to call on the resources of the majority of the East European states (excepting Albania and Yugoslavia) in such an endeavor is a matter that must give the United States considerable pause, especially since the defense of Western Europe has generally been regarded as a core element in the overall American security position.

It is also well to consider the burden of history. Both world wars had their immediate origin in Eastern Europe, and it is not too much to say that even today it is only the Middle East that seems to outrank Eastern Europe as a potential flash point leading to a general international conflagration. Any one of the crises that occurred in the region in 1953, 1956, 1968, and 1981, to name only the most dramatic occasions, could easily have escalated given miscalculation on the part of either East or West. Hence, the prospect that yet another and perhaps final global confrontation could emerge out of Eastern Europe does not seem fanciful. Even if it is argued, then, that American involvement in Eastern Europe is less directly relevant to the American national interest than commitments in other areas, the inherent combustibility of the region virtually dictates that American security will be influenced by developments there.

At the same time as Eastern Europe remains relevant to larger American interests, certain delicate features of the American-East European relationship make the region a particular challenge to the execution of a sound American policy. Indeed, it might be argued that Eastern Europe presents one of the United States' most difficult problems in diplomacy today. The first important variable in the American-East European relationship is that Eastern Europe has long been regarded by the Soviet Union as the *ne plus ultra* of its own security position. In other critical world regions referred to above, the United States may legitimately be regarded as having either a superior security concern of its own (Latin America, Western Europe) or at least shares such a concern in equal measure with its Soviet adversary (the Middle East). The same does not apply in the case of Eastern Europe. The Soviet Union's willingness to undertake major military interventions in the area in 1956 and 1968 in order to retain its dominant influence provides vivid testimony to this reality. Clearly, then, any consideration of American policy options has to take into serious consideration the Soviets' extreme sensitivity to political developments in Eastern Europe.

The second important variable is the inherent fragility of the Eastern European political landscape. In part, this results from the unnatural process by which the regimes of the area originally came to power and are sustained in power. Societies with a history of intense nationalism are bound to resent the imposition of political order from the outside. Such feelings have been reinforced in the instance of Eastern Europe by the traditional anti-Russian (not just anti-Soviet) sentiments which are so prevalent in countries like Poland, Hungary, and Romania.

East European nationalism has another, and potentially highly destabilizing, quality as well. If Soviet control were to be removed from Eastern Europe tomorrow, future developments in the region would not likely proceed in tranquil fashion. On the contrary, considerable turmoil and even violence would probably characterize relationships among the East European regimes. Focusing solely on East European resentment of the Soviet hegemon obscures the fact that in Hungary the Transylvanian question (involving a large Hungarian minority living under Romanian rule) continues to be a major issue of politics, or that Yugoslavia and Bulgaria have not laid to rest their bitter dispute over the future of Macedonia. Even within individual East European countries, one often finds such a mosaic of differing ethnic and religious groupings that sustaining an orderly polity in any "post-liberation" period would be rather problematic. The point here is that the United States has to tread with some care in any attempt to manipulate the Eastern European political scene in the cause of advancing American interests. The end result of such attempts could well be even more tragic than the current situation.

There is, of course, the root question of how much ability the United States has to "manipulate" Eastern Europe, which brings us to the final factor that impacts on the development of American policy toward the region. In other areas of the world, the United States disposes of some important capabilities, political, economic, and military, for the achievement of defined goals. As we have attempted to demonstrate in the second part of this book, Washington's degree of economic leverage in Eastern Europe is distinctly limited. Moreover, American inaction at the time of the Hungarian and Czechoslovak crises—not to mention the American decision not to use force to deter Stalin's takeover of Eastern Europe after World War II—suggests that the military option can be virtually ruled out as a potential tool of American policy in the area. This leaves, of course, the traditional recourse to diplomacy as well as what we have called the "information offensive" (symbolized by Radio Free Europe) as alternative methods of achieving American ends in Eastern Europe. It might be argued that these are fairly thin grounds on which to base any hopes for American success in gaining these ends. In considering the American-East European relationship, we are confronted with something of a paradox, which is unique in current American foreign policy: objectively, it can be demonstrated that Eastern Europe is important to the American national interest, yet we have relatively limited tools to shape an active policy that is commensurate with that importance.

In order to provide a framework for the consideration of American security policy toward Eastern Europe, the remaining discussion will be divided into two parts. First, we will attempt to identify the United States' basic overall strategic options in dealing with East Central Europe, and will offer a tentative assessment of each of these approaches. Second, we will analyze certain specific policy quandaries that confront the United States in its relations with Eastern Europe and how these necessarily will affect any option or combination of options that this country may select in future dealings with the region.

POLICY CHOICES

The United States could take any of four basic approaches in structuring its overall policy toward Eastern Europe. For purposes of the present discussion, each of these will be considered as being self-contained and standing apart from the others, even though several of them are not necessarily mutually exclusive and some combination of elements from each of them is conceivable.

Disengagement

In this scenario, the United States accepts the fact of Soviet hegemony over Eastern Europe, as well as the limits on American leverage in the area, and adopts a general policy of "benign neglect" in its dealings with the East European regimes. The intellectual rationale for such an approach might well be based on President Roosevelt's own attitude toward the future of East Central Europe as expressed to Archbishop Francis Spellman in September 1943. "There would be no point in opposing Stalin's territorial demands," Spellman reported the President as saying, "because the Russian leader had the power to take these areas, regardless of what Britain and the United States did." Roosevelt's conclusion was that the East Europeans "would simply have to get used to Russian domination."[3] Some consideration was also given within the Truman Administration in the late 1940s to withdrawing American recognition and diplomatic personnel from all the Communist-dominated Eastern European states as well as putting an end to overt American protests against political repression in the region (the assumption being that such protests only invited continued rebuffs). Both suggestions were eventually rejected as being unnecessary or counterproductive.[4]

As expressed above, the disengagement option might appear to combine in equal measure a naive isolationism and a moral pusillanimity. Two arguments that might be adduced in its favor, however, may perhaps give it somewhat more respectability. One of them ironically concerns the fortunes of the East European peoples themselves. On the assumption that the Soviet Union has the military power ultimately to impose its political will on Eastern Europe, and on the further assumption that the Soviets are, as noted, extremely sensitive to any signs of their losing control over the region, it may well be in the interest of the East Europeans for the Soviets to feel a general confidence about the stability of Eastern Europe. In these circumstances, a measure of domestic autonomy and even liberal reform may be far more acceptable to Moscow than the feeling that its East European empire is being threatened by external forces.

The second argument might be called a joint moral/pragmatic consideration at the level of international relations generally. If one assumes that the American relationship with the Soviet Union is the key fulcrum of the current world situation, and that a military confrontation between the two superpowers would spell disaster for all (Americans, Russians, *and* Eastern Europeans), perhaps it makes sense to exclude Eastern Europe as a potential source of confrontation between Moscow and Washington. From a somewhat narrower American national interest perspective, it may be argued that either tacit or explicit Soviet cooperation is necessary to secure tangible American objectives in a variety of world areas, for example, the Middle East, or on a number of functional issues, such as arms control. Does it make sense to "link" developments in Eastern Europe to Soviet-American negotiation on these matters?

In evaluating the disengagement option, it is necessary to concede that it does raise some serious broader questions of policy. For example, there is considerable evidence that the East European regimes themselves feel greater latitude, at least on domestic matters, during periods of relative détente between the Soviet Union and the United States. No less an authority than Henry Kissinger argued along these lines in responding to criticisms of supposed American concessions at Helsinki in 1975. "It has been generally accepted," Kissinger said, "that the freedom of maneuver of the various countries [in Eastern Europe] is enhanced in a period of relaxation of tension, and it is precisely those countries most concerned with their autonomy that have also been the greatest advocates of a relaxation of tensions."[5] Kissinger was undoubtedly convinced of this proposition in part because of his own personal contacts with East European leaders, such as Gierek of Poland. He describes the Polish leader as being unequivocally committed to détente on the assumption that "Poland's autonomy could thrive best under conditions of relaxation of tensions."[6] Some ten years later, there was a palpable relief in most East European capitals at the convening of the Reagan-Gorbachev summit conference, as well as a hope that the summit might presage an improved East-West climate that would redound to the benefit of the regimes in Eastern Europe.[7] Soviet spokespersons at the Ottawa human rights meeting in Spring 1985 themselves suggested that increased détente would lead to greater respect for human rights, whereas increased international tension led to a clampdown on human rights (obviously in the Soviet Union but presumably in Eastern Europe as well).[8]

From the above perspective, if American benign neglect of Eastern Europe helps to contribute to détente, paradoxically such neglect may work in the East Europeans' favor, not to mention that of the international community more generally. On balance, however, an overt American program of "disengagement" from the affairs of Eastern Europe does not seem credible in either moral or practical terms. As discussed in Part I of this book, the fate of the region continues to be an emotional and pressing issue for many Americans of East European ethnic heritage. In a democratic and pluralistic society, it is difficult to assert that the aspirations of these millions should be set aside in the interests of "broader" policy concerns. Even if a given American administration should desire to do so, there is overwhelming evidence that the domestic political costs of adopting such a policy have been consistently seen as prohibitive.

Two other pragmatic objections to disengagement exist. We have already referred to the United States' concrete security interests. Because the American national interest can be significantly affected by developments in the region, it seems contradictory to assert that the United States should basically ignore whatever leverage it does possess to influence these developments in a positive way. Moreover, the military-industrial potential of Eastern Europe does provide a significant increment to the overall Soviet power position. It may be that this increment will remain fairly constant over the foreseeable future, but it seems excessively passive or deterministic to accept that Moscow will necessarily always be able to command the resources of its East European empire. To the extent that a long-term movement in the global balance of power favorable to the West is desirable for both political and ethical reasons, it makes little sense to concede the Soviet Union a permanent source of strength in the power competition. In sum, disengagement may have a few alluring bits of logic to it, but it does not seem to merit serious consideration as an actual American policy option with respect to Eastern Europe.

Liberation

One obvious way in which a shift in the world power balance favorable to the West could occur would be if the West were to succeed in severing Soviet control over Eastern Europe and restoring full sovereignty in both domestic and foreign policy to these states. Assuming that genuinely independent governments in Eastern Europe would not likely commit their military and industrial strength to Soviet purposes (Bulgaria perhaps being the only potential exception), there would be a substantial net diminution in the Soviet power capability. In the most optimistic scenarios, the newly liberated Eastern Europe would switch alliances and add its resources to those of the NATO countries. Even if the East European states should opt for neutrality, however, the effects on the overall Soviet strategic position would still be dramatic. Moreover, surely as important as the geopolitical effects of the liberation of Eastern Europe would be the fact that the peoples of the region would finally be in control of their own destiny and could pursue policies, especially in domestic affairs, that would reflect popular demands for democracy and economic progress unfettered by Marxist-Leninist dogma.

For some forty years now specialists in foreign policy have regarded an overt Western policy of seeking the "liberation" of Eastern Europe as the province of dreamers and even more of irresponsible or unreconstructed Cold Warriors. One standard item in the criticism of the diplomacy of John Foster Dulles, for example, was his supposed commitment not just to containing Soviet power but to its "roll-back," especially in Eastern Europe. Much sardonic comment has been offered concerning the Dulles-sponsored plank in the 1952 Republican party platform which denounced "the negative, futile and immoral policy of 'containment' which abandons countless human beings to a despotism and godless terrorism."[9]

The choice of language in this instance did seem to be a trifle flamboyant, yet considered strictly in its own terms the liberation strategy is the one American approach to Eastern Europe that has perhaps the least moral ambiguity and in a curious sense is also the most logical in geopolitical terms.

We have already referred to the geopolitical advantages that are posited by the concept of liberation and that are far more problematic in other potential options for American policy toward East Central Europe. With regard to the moral content of liberation strategy, it must be conceded that Western attempts to liberate Eastern Europe would not face the cultural and political ambiguity that have existed in other, especially American, crusades to "save" a nation or nations from an "alien" ideology. The example of Vietnam inevitably comes to mind. It is questionable at best whether the U.S. attempt to create and defend a "free" Vietnam in its own image ever took into consideration the vastly different (or at least non-Western) milieu in which this effort operated. Such a consideration would hardly obtain in the case of Eastern Europe. An interesting survey of East European opinion in the middle-1970s, for example, revealed that 68 percent of the respondents preferred freely elected democratic regimes, 87 percent would have liked their countries to join the Common Market, and 83 percent desired participation in a politically united Europe.[10] The point is that, again with the possible exception of Bulgaria (or Albania), the countries of East Central Europe have historically felt themselves an integral part of the Western cultural tradition. Indeed, a prime source of tension in the Soviet-East European relationship is the conviction among the East Europeans that the Soviets have artificially broken the historic bonds between Western and Eastern European societies.

A second moral aspect in the concept of liberation is the fact that the Marxist-Leninist regimes in Eastern Europe were originally the result almost entirely of the brute force of Soviet military pressure. Even today these regimes are sustained substantially by the continued threat of Soviet military intervention. Again, the comparison with Vietnam is instructive: the ultimate North Vietnamese/Viet Cong success there was partly a function of military coercion, but the Communist triumph also depended to a considerable degree on the voluntary allegiance of many South Vietnamese to the combined program of nationalism and societal reform that the Communists promised (and that the Saigon regime could not offer in an equally credible way). Thus, it might well be asked (and was asked), precisely whom was the American Army "liberating" the South Vietnamese people from? This question would not be very difficult to answer in the context of a Western effort at liberating Eastern Europe.

Despite the compelling arguments that may be offered in defense of a liberation strategy for Eastern Europe, it is a commonplace that such a strategy has received little serious consideration by successive American administrations. To be more precise, it has received little consideration to the extent that it implied the use of force to achieve liberation. This, of course, is the key variable in true liberation theory. The use of economics, propaganda, or diplomacy in an effort to wean

Eastern Europe away from the Soviet Union does not constitute a liberation strategy, although they might well be part of such a strategy; the potential application of military force is what distinguishes liberation theory from other superficially similar approaches to Eastern Europe. The American government's basic position on such an option was established in a major policy study completed in December 1949. NSC 58/2, formally entitled "United States Policy Toward the Soviet Satellite States in Eastern Europe," did argue that the fundamental American goal "must be the elimination of Soviet control from these countries and the reduction of Soviet influence to something like normal dimensions." At the same time, resort to war to achieve this objective "should be rejected as a practical alternative," in part, the study said, because it was not "organically feasible" for the United States to initiate such a conflict, although an American military move into Eastern Europe was not ruled out if war was initiated by the Soviet side.[11]

The most that the United States has been prepared to do in the way of coercive measures to "liberate" Eastern Europe have been essentially low-level paramilitary covert operations under the auspices of the Central Intelligence Agency. For example, from 1950 to 1952 the United States airdropped various agents and military equipment to anti-Communist opposition groups in Poland (a particularly futile exercise since the relevant groups were later discovered to be under the control of Polish security forces). A somewhat sensational study of the American intelligence community also claims that the CIA sent agents into Hungary in 1956 (and contemplated doing so in Czechoslovakia and Romania) to assist in the destabilization of these regimes.[12] A better documented British and American attempt was also made in the early 1950s to subvert the regime of Enver Hoxha in Albania by landing anti-Communist Albanian émigré elements in that country. This, too, came to nought, in part because, as already noted, British double agent Kim Philby informed his Soviet controllers of the Albanian scheme.

The more typical American stance, however, has been to reaffirm both privately and publicly, especially during times of crisis in Eastern Europe, that the United States had no thought of using force to overturn political arrangements in the region. Thus, even as Dulles made references to the Republican party's commitment to "liberation" in the 1952 presidential campaign, Eisenhower himself studiously avoided references to a liberation strategy, particularly as it implied the use of military measures. In actuality, one of the principal "means" by which the Eisenhower Administration attempted to implement "liberation" was by sending balloons filled with anti-Communist propaganda wafting through the air space of various Eastern European countries ("Operation Prospero").[13]

A survey of Washington's conduct during the periodic outbursts of rebellion in Eastern Europe is particularly instructive, for it was precisely these types of upheavals that might have been expected to rouse whatever liberation sentiment existed. In the face of anti-regime protests in East Germany in 1953, the Eisenhower Administration was only prepared to take a fairly permissive attitude toward the efforts of the U.S.-sponsored "Radio in the American Sector" (RIAS), based in West Berlin, to broadcast details of the turmoil as well as some encouragement to the mass of the East German citizenry. Supplementing this was a Senate resolution praising the "heroic resistance" of the East Germans and suggesting that "this sacrifice for freedom will aid the cause of freedom in all Communist enslaved nations."[14] The American response to the more substantial Hungarian uprising of 1956 was essentially the same. One high American official explained American inaction in the face of Soviet repression of Hungarian freedom fighters by saying that "much as we would have liked to help Hungary, we had to decide that interference there might have precipitated a third world war involving hundreds of millions of people and the whole of civilization."[15] President Eisenhower made clear at the time and later that he never seriously considered American military action to assist the Hungarians.

The pattern of American restraint in the face of turmoil in Eastern Europe was also visible during the Czechoslovak affair in 1968 and the Polish events of 1980-81. President Johnson, in referring to the tension between Dubček and the Soviet leadership, characterized his policy by saying that "we could only try to avoid any action that would further inflame the situation. We hoped that increasing world criticism, combined with the confidence a great power like the Soviet Union should have, would convince Moscow not to crush the modest liberalism among the Czechs."[16] Through both his public and private statements, Secretary of State Dean Rusk also seemed bent on assuring the Soviet Union in advance that the United States would take no action should the Soviets move militarily against Czechoslovakia, assuming their "confidence" as a great power proved insufficient to tolerate the Czech heresy.[17]

Finally, both the Carter and Reagan administrations were careful to rule out any prospect of American military support for Solidarity in the event of Soviet intervention to crush the Polish trade union movement. In September 1980, after the AFL-CIO had decided to provide direct financial assistance to Solidarity, President Carter called in the Soviet Ambassador to stress that his Administration had nothing to do with the AFL-CIO action.[18] Although the President did warn the Soviets of adverse consequences in East-West relations if Moscow invaded Poland—on one occasion in early December 1980 going so far as to use the hot line to send a message to Brezhnev carrying this warning—there is no evidence of any coercive threat in any of these communications.[19] The Reagan Administration basically followed Carter's lead in this regard. A few months before the Jaruzelski regime's declaration of martial law in December 1981, Under Secretary of State Lawrence Eagleburger assured Congress that the United States would "continue to refrain from words or actions which would complicate the resolution of Poland's problems by the Poles themselves."[20] Left unsaid was the fact that even if Poland's problems weren't "solved" by "the Poles themselves," the United States did not contemplate a military response to support the Polish people. Secretary of State Alexander Haig characterized one aspect of Administration policy as being to avoid "excessive provocation to the Soviets." Haig said that the consensus was "to offer humanitarian aid to the Polish people, but not even hint that the United States would under any circumstances go beyond that."[21]

None of this, of course, should have come as a surprise given the basic premises of American policy toward Eastern Europe, particularly as it evolved during the 1960s and 1970s. Thus, one of the central ingredients in President Johnson's concept of "building bridges" between the United States and Eastern Europe was an acceptance of the integrity of the postwar European borders. In a speech on October 7, 1966, Johnson stressed the necessity of recognizing the current territorial facts of life in Central Europe, and he admitted that he had the Oder-Neisse line between Poland and Germany especially in mind. As he put it, he wanted both the Polish and Soviet governments "to know that we would never resort to force to alter the Oder-Neisse line or any other generally accepted territorial border. That was the meaning of the carefully chosen words I used in New York, and I was sure that every European from the Atlantic to Moscow understood them."[22]

In case there were any Europeans who didn't understand the American position, the circumstances surrounding the American adherence to the Helsinki Final Act in 1975 should have provided conclusive evidence. We have discussed the Conference on Security and Cooperation in Europe from the human rights perspective, but for present purposes what is central is that in that agreement the United States formally accepted the nonalteration of the postwar European borders—and more broadly postwar European political arrangements—by force. This was done on the theory that such a "concession" would contribute in its own way to discrete American security objectives in Europe. As Kissinger adviser Helmut Sonnenfeldt later put it, "We sold it [the CSCE] for the German-Soviet treaty, we sold it for the Berlin agreement, and we sold it again for the opening of the MBFR [Mutual and Balanced Force Reduction talks]."[23]

In evaluating the intrinsic merits of "liberation" as an overall American strategy toward Eastern Europe, as well as the consistent rejection of the liberation option by various administrations, three observations seem appropriate. We have already observed that there is a certain inner logic, even an inherent appeal, to liberation theory, whether one focuses on its moral or pragmatic aspects. At the same time, a balanced assessment would dictate that the liberation strategy has been and is as flawed as its intellectual opposite, the concept of "disengagement," although for different reasons. Consider, in the first place, the conventional wisdom that an attempted American military intervention in Eastern Europe would invite a fatal Soviet-American confrontation. Just because a piece of wisdom is "conventional" does not always mean that it is for that reason incorrect, and in this instance there is very strong reason to suppose that it in fact is correct. Eastern

Europe is the core of the Soviet security system, at least as Moscow itself perceives it, and the notion that the United States could by force attempt unilaterally to shatter what the Soviet Union has established over forty years without drastic consequences strains credulity.

In the immediate postwar years there was a theoretical possibility that if the West moved military forces into the region Stalin might have felt constrained to retreat rather than face what he saw as a much stronger enemy. Recent analyses suggest that the Soviet "juggernaut" in Europe after World War II existed largely in the minds of Western commentators and that Stalin was acutely conscious of his own military weakness.[24] Even if this "window of opportunity" did exist at one time, however, it had closed by the early 1950s. With the military balance of today, the notion that a Western liberation option still remains in Eastern Europe does not bear up under empirical examination. To paraphrase a famous comment from the Vietnam War, the "liberation option" today evidently comes down to our having to destroy Eastern Europe in order to save it.

There are two other fundamental objections to liberation theory. Ironically, the initial "liberation" of an oppressed people can in some sense be the easiest part of liberation strategy. Far more difficult, especially for a notoriously fickle democratic foreign policy, is the long-term commitment of political and military resources to sustain the fruits of liberation. In the case of Eastern Europe, this suggests that even if by some miracle Soviet power could be pushed back to the Soviet frontier itself, the inherent geopolitical realities of the region—that is, the presence of a Soviet superpower on the borders of a much weaker collection of states—would demand a substantial and continuing Western presence in order to counterbalance this reality. A relevant precedent for the dilemmas inherent here is the series of Western interventions into Russia following the Bolshevik Revolution in 1917. To the extent that these interventions were designed to "liberate" the Russian people from the burden of Leninism, a fair criticism of them is that the powers involved (Great Britain, France, Japan, the United States) were not prepared to maintain a significant presence in Russia for some years in order to sustain the initial victory. Without such a presence, it was reasonable to assume that the organizational abilities of the Bolsheviks would likely gain them power. A somewhat different question was whether the Western powers ever understood the Russian scene well enough to control political developments there.[25] The reality is that there is a certain element of irresponsibility, even moral blindness, in any liberation strategy that does not take into full account the enormous obligations that such a strategy imposes.

Finally, there is the basic question of whether American public opinion at any time would have supported a policy of active liberation of Eastern Europe. As noted earlier, even among Americans of East European ethnic extraction there has been far less support for an overt liberation strategy than is often supposed. If this is true of Americans with at least some direct connection to Eastern Europe, without doubt opposition to an aggressive liberation policy toward East

Central Europe has been widely felt as well among the American people as a whole. A democratic leadership cannot take a country into a major military commitment without at least passive support from the populace, and in the majority of situations there is a need for even more—for a fully convinced and supportive society. There is virtually no historical evidence that such an environment ever existed for the American pursuit of a liberation strategy in Eastern Europe. This is perhaps scant consolation for those in Eastern Europe who have suffered and continue to suffer under repressive regimes aided and abetted by Soviet power, but as the cliché has it, politics is the art of the possible. Few would argue that in these terms the liberation option was ever really possible.

Destabilization

The United States could theoretically adopt a third option as the foundation for its overall approach to Eastern Europe, and it is well to give it at least brief mention, even though it has much less of a pedigree or conceptual unity than liberation or even disengagement theory. The "destabilization" approach would take as a starting point one central assumption: despite occasional putative displays of "independence" on the part of the East European states, basically the United States has dealt and continues to deal with a unified Warsaw Pact, at least as far as the security threat to the West is concerned. From this assumption flows the basic policy conclusion that the Soviet Union and its Eastern European Warsaw Pact allies should be treated essentially as one hostile force. In this formulation, it is illusory to offer favored treatment in, say, the area of trade to those Eastern European countries that are supposedly more "moderate" in their political stance. Such moderation is seen as a cleverly contrived mask disguising the aggressive instincts of all members of WTO.

A representative sample of this sort of thinking sometimes emerges with respect to the ostensible maverick of the WTO, Romania. One analysis thus argues that Romania can be considered to be as opposed to Western interests as any of the more "orthodox" WTO members, and that its supposed independent course obscures the fact that it basically follows the Soviet line on European security questions.[26] Even Yugoslavia, which is not a member of the Warsaw Pact, has at times been included in the notion of a hostile Soviet-East European bloc. The precedent for what might seem a rather surprising conclusion was a study published several years after Tito's break with Moscow which argued that Yugoslavia was a "Trojan Horse" in the European arena. This analysis concluded that the supposed "break" between Tito and Stalin had been agreed on in advance by the two leaders in order that Yugoslavia might receive massive aid from the West and thus strengthen the overall socialist camp in Europe.[27] It would be going too far to suggest that Ambassador Silberman's previously discussed attitude toward the Belgrade regime was this contentious, but there were at least echos of the earlier Trojan Horse formulation in his own theory concerning Yugoslav "independence."[28] Finally, Alexander Haig recalls the demands of some of his colleagues in the National Security Council for a more "red-blooded" approach to the Polish crisis. They were, said Haig, "prepared to look beyond Poland, as if it were not in itself an issue of war and peace, and regard it as an opportunity to inflict mortal political, economic, and propaganda damage on the U.S.S.R.."[29]

In examining the essence of the "destabilization" approach to American relations with Eastern Europe, it is useful to consider how it differs from both disengagement and liberation theory. As far as disengagement is concerned, the main distinction centers around the idea of an "offensive" or "forward" strategy for the United States. Adherents of destabilization decidedly do not believe that the United States should accept Soviet domination over Eastern Europe as a given of American foreign policy. On the contrary, they believe that the United States should aggressively confront the Eastern European subsystem of the Soviet empire, in particular because this subsystem may well constitute an Achilles heel of the overall Soviet power position. At the same time, those arguing for a destabilization approach to Eastern Europe do not generally entertain any immediate notions of "liberating" Eastern Europe from Soviet control. For one thing, they are dubious that this can be achieved in any conceivable analytical time frame. From another perspective there is some reason to hope that full liberation does not take place. This apparently paradoxical position requires further elaboration, particularly as it applies to the more recent approaches taken by this school of thought.

The concept of destabilization has led to two quite different policy emphases historically. One of these we have already discussed: the Western strategy in the late 1940s and early 1950s of applying economic sanctions equally to the Soviet Union and its Eastern European satellites. The underlying premise here was that what weakened Eastern Europe by definition also weakened the overall Soviet aggressive capability. Critical to this approach was the belief that Eastern Europe represented a reservoir of strength for the Soviet Union and that the Soviets benefited greatly from a crass exploitation of the resources of the Eastern European states. To the extent that these resources were crippled by a punitive Western economic policy, Moscow would have far less to draw on in developing its own military-industrial potential.

Over approximately the last two decades, however, adherents of the destabilization option have factored into their calculations the theory that Eastern Europe has become as much a liability as an asset in many ways to the Soviet leaders, especially in economic terms.[30] The new strategy indicated, then, was to accelerate the burden which Eastern Europe represented to the Soviet Union. Ironically, the logic of such a strategy was based on the very fact that Eastern Europe was seen as critical by Moscow, and thus the Soviet leadership presumably would be prepared to accept whatever costs were required to maintain hegemony in the region. In a sense, the idea here was to turn Moscow's own strategy on its head. The Soviets supposedly had long pursued a policy of committing relatively limited resources into areas of prime American concern, for example, Central America or Southeast Asia, exploiting regional instabilities in the expectation that the United

States would feel compelled to respond—and at a greatly disproportionate cost to what Moscow was expending. Eastern Europe seemed to represent an area in which the costs-benefits equation could be reversed.

How to increase the Soviet "burden" in Eastern Europe? One obvious option was to encourage continued political instability in the region through devices such as Radio Free Europe or even covert paramilitary operations (cf. the landing of agents in Albania). At a minimum, instability would absorb the decision-making energies of the Soviet leadership, and at a maximum it would require actual Soviet military intervention, with all the attendant costs in world public opinion and strain on Soviet force structures. Some analogy to the Afghanistan situation may be relevant here. The argument has been advanced that from a purely pragmatic point of view it is in the interest of the West to have the Soviets so heavily engaged in that country, and not incidentally for the West to aid the continued Afghan resistance, since this reduces Moscow's potential for major initiatives elsewhere. A somewhat less cynical or brutal scenario may lie in the economic sphere. As noted earlier, some opinion was expressed at the time of the declaration of martial law in Poland in 1981 that the West should declare Poland officially in default on its debts and thus force Moscow to assume the onus of managing and subsidizing the Polish economy, presumably a considerable drain on limited Soviet resources (a strategy that one high official described as "bringing her [the Soviet Union] to her knees").[31] More generally, adherents of the destabilization strategy have asserted that Western willingness to continue normal trading relationships with the Eastern European countries absolves Moscow of the necessity of "saving" its Eastern European allies from the consequences of their own Soviet-imposed and irrational economic mechanisms. It goes without saying that destabilization spokespersons have not expressed any enthusiasm about the underlying system of tradeoffs implicit in the Helsinki accords. Quite to the contrary, they were quite exercised about the West's willingness to accept a relatively low-cost (to the Soviets) hegemony over Eastern Europe in return for supposed Soviet "concessions" on other matters.

As with disengagement and liberation theory, some elements of the destabilization argument cannot be dismissed out of hand. Perhaps the most compelling item in this approach is the undeniable fact that since 1945 the West has been forced into—or has chosen—a reactive mode when dealing with the Soviet challenge. Given the generally aggressive posture of Soviet policy over the last forty years, it is intuitively satisfying to consider a strategy that might put Moscow as much on the defensive as the West has frequently been. On the other hand, the concept of destabilization shares with the two other strategies another feature: when its full implications are considered, certain evident fallacies in logic and practicality seem to render it moot as a potential option for Western or American policy.

Three flaws in particular present themselves. We criticized liberation theory as presenting an unacceptable risk of escalation or confrontation in Soviet relations with the West. The modalities of destabilization are not quite as adventurous perhaps as those suggested by full-blown liberation adherents—for example, direct use of military force to free Eastern Europe—but this seems to be a matter more of degree rather than of kind. Under the strategy of destabilization, the West would pursue an avowed goal of economic and political dislocation in Eastern Europe in order to commit Soviet power and resources to continued efforts at "normalization" of the East European scene. With such Western provocation, it is hard to imagine that over time Moscow would be willing to adopt a totally reactive posture of its own. On the contrary, it would likely attempt to reduce the pressure in Eastern Europe by itself launching "destabilization" efforts, say, in West Berlin or the Middle East, to a far greater degree than in the past. The consequences of such moves might well involve a major military showdown between East and West. There is also the lesson of the policy of economic sanctions adopted by the Western powers in the 1950s. Destabilization would involve—indeed would count on—pushing Eastern Europe ever more tightly into the Soviet embrace. On the assumption that a superpower like the Soviet Union would ultimately be able to absorb the costs of empire, the West would once again be writing off a major military-industrial card in the world power struggle. A prominent European leader summarized the issues here as follows: "Destabilizing the Soviet bloc would lead to outright East-West confrontation. It would [also] arouse a nationalistic rallying in the Soviet Union and shove Romania, Hungary, and the others closer to the Soviets."[32]

Finally, we have had occasion to refer to the moral implications of liberation and disengagement theory. What strikes one about the destabilization approach is that it is content to use the East European countries and societies basically as pawns in the broader East-West struggle. One standard criticism of the American policy of "differentiation" in its dealings with Eastern Europe—a policy to be analyzed shortly—is that Washington is unduly prone to favor East European regimes on the basis of their apparent defiance of Moscow. In a somewhat different way, destabilization theorists are guilty of the same conceit, except that in their case they take as a given that the East Europeans are inevitably subject to the Soviet Union. Thus, they don't hold out even the possibility that an individual Eastern Europe regime may be treated with favorable consideration if ostensibly promising steps are taken in domestic or foreign policy. At least it may be said of the liberation theorists that they are after all concerned about the freedom and self-determination of the Eastern European countries. Even the adherents of disengagement sometimes argue that such freedom may be increased if the West ceases to make an issue of Eastern Europe. In contrast the essence of the destabilization approach seems to present an unrelievedly bleak prospect for the countries of East Central Europe.

We have considered, and have dismissed, three particular options for American policy toward Eastern Europe. Perhaps *faute de meilleur*, we now address yet another such option, and in this instance the structure of the discussion inevitably is somewhat different, since this final choice is not just theoretical but has been at the core of American policy toward East Central Europe for some time now.

NOTES

1. International Institute for Strategic Studies, THE MILITARY BALANCE 1985-1986 (London: IISS, 1985), 31-36, 62, 67.

2. A very good collection of articles on the reliability question is SOVIET ALLIES: THE WARSAW PACT AND THE ISSUE OF RELIABILITY, ed. Daniel N. Nelson (Boulder, Colo.: Westview Press, 1984).

3. John Lewis Gaddis, THE UNITED STATES AND THE ORIGINS OF THE COLD WAR, 1941-1947 (New York: Columbia University Press, 1972), 90.

4. U.S. Department of State, FOREIGN RELATIONS OF THE UNITED STATES 1948, Volume 4: Eastern Europe and the Soviet Union (Washington: GPO, 1974), 312.

5. DEPARTMENT OF STATE BULLETIN (November 3, 1975), 641-642.

6. Henry Kissinger, WHITE HOUSE YEARS (Boston: Little, Brown and Co., 1979), 1268.

7. Eric Bourne, "E. Europe Watches for Post-Summit Signals," CHRISTIAN SCIENCE MONITOR (December 12, 1985), 15.

8. U.S. Commission on Security and Cooperation in Europe, CSCE DIGEST, June 10, 1985 (Washington: GPO, 1985), 7. The U.S. delegation rejected such a linkage, saying that it held observance of human rights "hostage" to the general political environment. This position was not entirely consistent with other statements by American officials on the same topic both before and after Ottawa.

9. A good example of the prevailing attitude toward Dulles' diplomacy, especially as it involved "liberation," can be found in John Lewis Gaddis, STRATEGIES OF CONTAINMENT (New York: Oxford University Press, 1982), especially ch. 5.

10. Bennett Kovrig, "The United States: 'Peaceful Engagement' Revisited," in THE INTERNATIONAL POLITICS OF EASTERN EUROPE, ed. Charles Gati (New York: Praeger Publishers, 1976), 142.

11. U.S. Department of State, FOREIGN RELATIONS OF THE UNITED STATES 1949, Vol. 5: Eastern Europe; The Soviet Union (Washington: GPO, 1976), 44.

12. Harry Rositzke, THE CIA'S SECRET OPERATIONS (New York: Readers Digest Press, 1977), 169-171; William Corson, THE ARMIES OF IGNORANCE: THE RISE OF THE AMERICAN INTELLIGENCE EMPIRE (New York: Dial Press, 1977), 366-372.

13. David Wise and Thomas B. Ross, THE INVISIBLE GOVERNMENT (New York: Random House, 1964), 322.

14. Bennett Kovrig, THE MYTH OF LIBERATION (Baltimore: Johns Hopkins University Press, 1973), 133-137.

15. Ibid., 193.

16. Lyndon Baines Johnson, THE VANTAGE POINT (New York: Holt, Rinehart and Winston, 1971), 496-497.

17. Jiri Valenta, SOVIET INTERVENTION IN CZECHOSLOVAKIA 1968 (Baltimore: Johns Hopkins University Press, 1979), 131-133.

18. Zbigniew Brzezinski, POWER AND PRINCIPLE (New York: Farrar, Straus and Giroux, 1983), 464.

19. Jimmy Carter, KEEPING FAITH (Toronto: Bantam Books, 1982), 584-585.

20. U.S. Department of State, Bureau of Public Affairs, "U.S. Policy Toward the U.S.S.R., Eastern Europe and Yugoslavia," Statement by Assistant Secretary of State for European Affairs Lawrence Eagleburger before the Subcommittee on Europe and the Middle East of the House Foreign Affairs Committee, June 10, 1981 (Washington: GPO, 1981), 4.

21. Alexander M. Haig, Jr., CAVEAT (New York: Macmillan Co., 1984), 250.

22. Johnson, THE VANTAGE POINT, 475.

23. TIME (August 4, 1975), 22. The State Department, in somewhat more judicious language, admitted the truth of Sonnenfeldt's statement. "Before agreeing to the convening of the CSCE, the United States and its NATO allies insisted on the opening of exploratory talks to deal with MBFR in central Europe." "Conference on Security and Cooperation in Europe," DEPARTMENT OF STATE BULLETIN (September 26, 1977), 407.

24. See, for example, Matthew A. Evangelista, "Stalin's Postwar Army Reappraised," INTERNATIONAL SECURITY (Winter 1982-83).

25. George Kennan's THE DECISION TO INTERVENE (New York: Atheneum, 1967) is the best single-volume treatment of Western policy in Russia following the revolution.

26. R. D. Kaplan, "Rumanian Gymnastics," THE NEW REPUBLIC (December 17, 1984). Kaplan summarizes his view of Bucharest's foreign policy: "Far from a bold maverick, Ceausescu . . . is a bird singing loudly in a cage," 12.

27. Slobodan M. Draskovich, TITO, MOSCOW'S TROJAN HORSE (Chicago: Henry Regnery Co., 1957).

28. Thus, Ambassador Silberman denounced the "facile and fatuous description of Yugoslavia as a friendly country. It is not. It is predominantly an adversary." Silberman did admit, however, that there was a limited concurrence of interest between the United States and Yugoslavia. Laurence Silberman, "Yugoslavia's 'Old' Communism," FOREIGN POLICY (Spring 1977), 24.

29. Haig, CAVEAT, 240.

30. An early discussion of this theory was Paul Marer's "Has Eastern Europe Become a Liability to the Soviet Union? The Economic Aspect," in THE INTERNATIONAL POLITICS OF EASTERN EUROPE, ed. Charles Gati (New York: Praeger, 1976).

31. Haig, CAVEAT, 240.

32. Harry B. Ellis, "Should US, Allies Use Poland to Destabilize Soviet Bloc?" CHRISTIAN SCIENCE MONITOR (February 16, 1982), 6.

17.
The Parameters of
Normalization

It will be recalled that in the landmark NSC 58/2 study in 1949 of American relations with Eastern Europe, a prime American goal was considered to be the "reduction of Soviet influence [in Eastern Europe] to something like normal dimensions."[1] I would suggest that what one might call the "normalization" option stands as a fourth basic choice for an overall American strategy toward Eastern Europe. A review of the historical record indicates that the United States has in fact selected this option for its East European policy, at least over the last two decades.

It is important to recognize that "normalization" in the sense that we are using it here is a rather different concept from that which obtained in the NSC 58/2 analysis. Thus, the phrase referring to "normal" relations between the Soviet Union and Eastern Europe in that study was preceded in the same sentence by reference to "the elimination of Soviet control from these countries." The implication was that the overall goal of American policy was to convert the Soviet-East European relationship into something resembling that obtaining between fully sovereign countries. More recent normalization theory has not been so ambitious. The essential thrust of contemporary normalization efforts has been to wean away some or all of the Eastern European states from a virtually total reliance on Moscow for guidance on foreign and domestic policy. Two characteristics of such an approach need to be highlighted at this point. The process of "normalization" is expected to be an extremely gradual one, and it necessarily has to be based on nonviolent policy alternatives (such as trade, cultural exchange, and diplomatic negotiation), which is what separates the normalization option from liberation theory. A second characteristic of the normalization option—which also distinguishes this approach from the ideology of liberation—is that it does not anticipate, at least within the foreseeable future, a systemic elimination of a major Soviet role in Eastern Europe. The idea instead is gradually to reduce this role to a level that would be more palatable to the West, not to mention the East

European countries themselves. Thus, the strategy of normalization is fundamentally an incrementalist model of policymaking, which takes as a given the basic validity of past goals and policy instruments and by a series of gradual steps attempts to expand on these.[2]

A central issue that has always influenced the debate over the particulars of normalization has been whether the strategy should focus mainly on the sheer diminution of Soviet influence from the target countries, or whether there should also be an associated effort to alter over time the commitment of the relevant regimes to standard Marxist-Leninist dogma. In other words, are we basically interested in creating independent regimes in Eastern Europe, regardless of whether or not they are Communist, or is the goal a broader one: to change the internal ideology of these states as well? Adherents of the normalization option have generally concentrated on the former rather than the latter, and for two reasons.

First, an overt program of attempting to transform the Marxist polities of Eastern Europe has been seen as precisely the sort of policy calculated to induce a violent reaction from Moscow. The assumption here is that the Soviet Union may be willing to accept a gradual lessening of its controls in Eastern Europe provided that the affected regimes maintain a "safety net" of continued commitment to Marxism. ("Safety net" is used here in the sense that a Marxist Poland or Hungary would, in the Soviet view, be unlikely to adopt openly hostile policies toward the preeminent socialist state.) Second, doubt has been expressed about the degree to which Eastern European societies could be expected to move toward pluralistic democracy even in the absence of Soviet coercion. Much is made of the fact that, with the exception of Czechoslovakia, there is no real democratic tradition in Eastern Europe that could be restored or revived. In a curious sense, the Marxist authoritarian regimes there may be seen as a variant on the traditional authoritarian political systems of Eastern Europe.

Based on these premises, normalization strategy focuses on the creation or encouragement of what NSC 58/2 termed "schismatic communist regimes" or, more vividly, "heretical communism." The precedent for this approach was the American position on the first "heretical Communist" in the socialist world, Marshall Tito of Yugoslavia. The Truman Administration made little attempt to disguise the continued dictatorial nature of the Yugoslav regime, which they felt precluded genuinely warm American-Yugoslav relations. At the same time, the Administration was convinced that the Belgrade–Moscow fissure was a genuine one. An analysis by the State Department's Policy Planning Council that was approved by Secretary of State George Marshall set out a sophisticated strategy for dealing with Tito, which was to pursue a middle course of not being too openly approving of the Yugoslavs (thus providing Stalin with a lever to embarrass Belgrade), but at the same time not turning a cold shoulder to the Yugoslav regime either (which would discourage other potential rebels in Eastern Europe). The basic policy was to offer Tito prudent assistance, especially in the economic sphere, to help him maintain his "heresy," which was seen as important to the

American national interest.[3] Washington's willingness at the time to ignore the lack of democracy in Yugoslavia in order to secure larger geopolitical interests has been the bedrock of American policy toward Belgrade ever since, spanning eight American administrations. Repeated references to the essential premise of American-Yugoslav relations have been offered in almost identical language. Thus, the State Department in 1964 reaffirmed that "United States policy toward Yugoslavia has sought to offer Yugoslavia an alternative to dependence on the Soviet bloc and to make it possible for Yugoslavia to establish its independence firmly and irrevocably."[4] In June 1981 Lawrence Eagleburger spoke for the Reagan Administration by saying that "we firmly support Yugoslavia's independence, political unity, and territorial integrity." Eagleburger's argument once again was that an independent Yugoslavia "capable of resisting external pressures is a factor for stability and peace in the Balkans, the Mediterranean, and Europe as a whole."[5]

VARIETIES OF DIFFERENTIATION

In discussing issues bearing on American trade with Eastern Europe, we have had occasion to refer to the "differentiation" question. This involved the degree to which the United States was prepared to make distinctions among various Communist systems as far as American policy toward credits and most-favored-nation status was concerned. In this instance, the focus was on distinctions between the People's Republic of China, the Soviet Union, and Eastern Europe generally. The question of "differentiation," however, has a somewhat different and more specific application in the context of our discussion of normalization strategy.

From what has already been said, it is evident that differentiation is at the heart of the concept of normalization. That is, the United States under this option does make a clear distinction between the Soviet Union and the East European states in various areas of policy, and in so doing hopes gradually to erode the tight bonds joining Moscow and its East European dependencies. A dramatic illustration of the differentiation concept in operation was contained in a speech by a State Department official shortly after the Soviet invasion of Afghanistan. Deputy Assistant Secretary Robert Barry went out of his way to emphasize that the United States did not hold the East Europeans responsible for the Soviet aggression against Kabul. He said that they were apparently not even "consulted about it in advance" and that privately American officials continued to hear convincing expressions of East European disapproval of the Soviet action. Barry's conclusion was that it made little sense to apply sanctions against the East European regimes similar to those directed at the Soviet Union, "as this would give them no incentive to conduct policies reflecting their own national interests. Indeed, in the wake of Afghanistan we should—and will—try harder to maintain and build on the progress we have made with the countries of the region."[6]

As the normalization strategy has evolved, a considerable debate has arisen among those supportive of normalization on how the notion of differentiation should be applied in practice. This debate perhaps constitutes the chief theoretical issue dividing those otherwise joined on the general wisdom of pursuing normalization. Two particular matters comprise the core of the discussion.

First, there is the argument over whether the United States should stress what might be called "full" as opposed to "partial" differentiation. Full differentiation suggests that this country ought to attempt normalization with all the East European states without exception and with roughly equivalent zeal (e.g., by granting MFN privileges to each of the relevant regimes). "Partial" differentiation, on the other hand, while not rejecting hopes that normalization may one day come to embrace Eastern Europe as a whole, argues that what has been called "prioritization" should inform American policy. In this scenario, the United States divides the East European states into two categories: those for whom normalization is an immediate prospect or even reality, and those who for a variety of reasons are less promising candidates for normalization. The idea here is that the United States has limited resources and energies to expend on its East European policy, and it ought to focus these on the most "promising" group of regimes in the area. Those convinced of the wisdom of prioritization unanimously cite Hungary and Romania as prime targets of American policy, whereas Czechoslovakia and Bulgaria are consigned to the "on hold" category. A key premise of the "partial differentiation" argument is that given political realities in the United States, it would be self-defeating to try to convince Congress and the American people to treat all East European governments the same. Such an effort might erode the fragile consensus that exists for even the limited openings that have been achieved to selected Eastern European countries.

A second ingredient in the debate over differentiation concerns the degree to which the United States should "reward" congenial political behavior by certain Eastern European regimes, or whether this country ought to take the initiative itself in normalization on the assumption that political benefits will follow. The argument here is over a reactive as opposed to an active American policy in Eastern Europe, the issue being whether the East European regimes should demonstrate their bona fides before or after favorable treatment by the United States. Reference to those bona fides raises a final element in the discussion on differentiation: should the primary emphasis be on domestic or foreign policy, or perhaps some combination of the two? It is important to reemphasize here that as far as domestic policy is concerned none of the advocates of normalization are expecting that the East European governments will abandon Marxism. The issue is a different one—to wit, the willingness of the regimes in the region to modify some of the more rigid or authoritarian aspects of Marxist political practice, that is, to move toward what Alexsander Dubček termed "socialism with a human face." In the foreign policy arena, of course, the prime criterion is the degree to which the East European regimes are prepared to adopt positions at least somewhat distinct from those pursued by the Soviet Union.

It is instructive to observe the evolution of the debate over differentiation as it has been reflected in the actual policy positions of recent American administrations. The normalization strategy generally may be said to have originated in President Johnson's "bridge-building" speech of May 23, 1964. As the President put it, "Today we work to carry on the vision of the Marshall Plan." The significance of the reference was apparent, since a prime goal of the Marshall Plan was to contribute to economic and, by implication, political integration among all the countries of Europe. (Czechoslovakia and Poland initially did signal their desire to participate in the Marshall Plan.) Johnson parenthetically indicated that he felt able to propose the building of bridges to Eastern Europe in part because the previous month the United States Chamber of Commerce had denounced the "irrationality" of past American policy toward the region. Johnson felt that this helped to quiet the "thunder on the right" that had always arisen whenever talk of normalization had emerged in past years.[7] At the same time, the Johnson Administration avoided stating whether the new policy would stress what we have called full or partial differentiation.

This issue was addressed directly by Johnson's successor. The Nixon Administration as a general matter committed itself to following the broad lines of policy toward Eastern Europe established by President Johnson. Thus, in President Nixon's foreign policy report to Congress in 1970, he stated that his Administration was "prepared to enter into negotiations with the nations of Eastern Europe, looking to a gradual normalization of relations. We will adjust ourselves to whatever pace and extent of normalization these countries are willing to sustain."[8] Evidence of the President's attitude toward possible openings in Eastern Europe could be seen in official trips he made during his first term to Warsaw, Belgrade, and Bucharest. As Kissinger said with reference to these visits, "The symbolism was inescapable. The United States would pay special attention to those Eastern European countries pursuing an autonomous foreign policy."[9]

As President Nixon's version of normalization evolved, however, it was evident that it was based on two principles. First, there was a clear decision in favor of prioritization. Moreover, it was agreed that the United States should insist on prior demonstrations of independence by East European regimes before the United States entered into cultural, commercial, and scientific agreements. The criteria established in this regard were the degree of internal Leninism or loyalty to Soviet foreign policy interests. The result of these deliberations divided Eastern Europe into two categories. Bulgaria, for example, was placed at the bottom of the "list" of potential partners in normalization with the United States; no agreements would be established with Sofia unless the same arrangements had already been undertaken with Romania or Czechoslovakia (which in turn ranked lower than, say, Poland).[10]

In April 1977 officials of the Carter Administration met to consider PRM-9, an interagency study outlining possible new directions in American policy toward Eastern Europe. Four broad options were discussed: (1) To differentiate more sharply among the East European regimes based on their relative independence of Moscow; (2) to stress the degree of internal liberalization as the basis for an increased differentiation; (3) to limit American ties with all the East European governments; and (4) to expand ties with all these governments ("full differentiation"). Carter's National Security Adviser Zbigniew Brzezinski argued strongly for option "2," for he felt it was the best way to encourage polycentrism in Eastern Europe. As is typical in these situations, the eventual policy decision was to combine something of the old and something of the new. Presidential Directive 21 (PD-21), which Carter signed on September 13, 1977, ostensibly rejected a rigid rank ordering of the Eastern European regimes of the sort favored by the Nixon Administration. Assistant Secretary of State George Vest announced that American policy was designed "to recognize and support the sovereignty and individuality of *each* Eastern European nation in its domestic and foreign affairs."[11] PD-21, moreover, said that either foreign or domestic efforts at autonomy would be given equal weight in determining Washington's willingness to have productive relations with the regime involved. Perhaps most significantly, the Carter Administration moved away from a strictly "reactive" policy and instead supported American initiatives for normalization in anticipation that they would result in future domestic or foreign policy independence in Eastern Europe.

Despite the ostensible changes in American policy discussed above, it should be noted that President Carter's approach to Eastern Europe continued to involve a measure of prioritization, in practice if not in theory. Thus, the Administration's implicit goal was to bring Hungary into the "favored group" that already included Romania, Poland, and, of course, Yugoslavia (symbolized, for example, by the decision to return the Holy Crown of St. Stephen to Budapest). Carter's policy toward Poland was particular evidence that as far as Eastern Europe was concerned some "were more equal than others." An indication that this was to be the case was the fact that the President's first foreign trip in December 1977 was to Warsaw. There was also the putative influence of his National Security Adviser's being himself of Polish extraction (not to mention Carter's later Secretary of State, Edmund Muskie). In any case the United States was notably generous in economic assistance at the time to Poland: the Commodity Credit Corporation granted Warsaw some $500 million in credits in 1979 and increased this by almost $200 million in 1980. As of that year, some 37 percent of CCC credits worldwide were held by the Polish regime.[12]

The Reagan Administration, despite its ostensibly strong anti-Communist stance, has pursued essentially the same policies established by its predecessors. Assistant Secretary of State Rozanne Ridgway in 1985 testimony to the House Foreign Affairs Committee went into some detail on the criteria behind the

Administration's own differentiation policy: besides the usual reference to independent foreign policies, there was specific mention of tolerance of emigration, increased political and economic exchanges with the non-Communist world, economic decentralization, encouragement of political expression, and a general respect for fundamental human rights. This represented a greater refinement and specific explication of the standards for differentiation than had previously been offered.[13] Early in Reagan's term some consideration was given to establishing more stringent criteria in terms of both foreign and domestic policy practices by the East European states in return for favorable treatment by the United States, but this was eventually dropped in the National Security Council Directive (NSDD-54) of August 1982. NSDD-54 provided that policy would be continued as before, although it would app•ar that in the Reagan years there has been greater emphasis on the East Europeans demonstrating in advance what we have called their bona fides before the United States itself adopts conciliatory policies. This tendency toward a "reactive" differentiation was suggested by Assistant Secretary Lawrence Eagleburger in early 1981 when he said Washington would be guided by the degree to which the "Eastern European governments demonstrate both the desire and ability to reciprocate our interests in improved relations, and demonstrate sensitivity to U.S. interests."[14]

To the extent that the Reagan Administration's policy toward Eastern Europe may be substantively distinguished from that which preceded it, the main difference has been the willingness, even the insistence, of Administration spokespersons on frankly and publicly advertising the premises of the American approach to East Central Europe. Thus, in a speech in Vienna on September 21, 1983, Vice-President George Bush specifically stated that American policy "is one of differentiation." He cited Romania and Hungary as countries that had pursued either autonomous foreign policies or domestic liberalization and thus were deserving of "dialogue and cooperation" with the United States. On the other hand, East European regimes that stressed either belligerent foreign policies or the maintenance of closed societies could not be expected to be "rewarded" by favorable American attention. Bush made particular reference in this context to Bulgaria, Czechoslovakia, and East Germany. This surprising display of candor created some evident discomfort among East European elites, who didn't welcome a statement that in return for American favors they had to make a point of their deviance from Moscow—a step that might well backfire and undermine whatever limited independence they had managed to obtain. The uneasiness that Bush's comments aroused in Eastern Europe was presumably increased by his favorable reference to the Polish poet Czeslaw Milosz's description of the Russians as a "wild and primitive" people.[15]

In a later tour of various East European capitals—Bucharest, Belgrade, and Budapest—in December 1985, Secretary of State George Shultz elaborated on the themes enunciated by Vice-President Bush. He stressed the necessity of Eastern

European leaders openly accepting the importance of domestic or foreign policy independence if they desired favorable treatment by the United States. The reaction was similar to that extended to the Bush speech. One Hungarian diplomat emphasized that the Hungarian social system and ties with Moscow remained a "fact of life and a point of departure," and would remain constant regardless of Budapest's interests in good relations with the United States. Shultz's insistence on a public exegesis of American policy toward Eastern Europe once again raised a basic diplomatic concern. A Czech official put it bluntly: "Shultz's visit may make life more difficult within the bloc for the Hungarians and Romanians."[16] The point is that both Bucharest and Budapest were willing to accept the tacit premises of their relatively open relationship with Washington; they were highly reluctant, however, to offer a public analysis of the bases of this "special relationship" for the further enlightenment of Moscow.

THE MEANS OF NORMALIZATION

So far we have been discussing the purposes and goals of the normalization strategy in American policy toward Eastern Europe. Some attention ought also to be given to the techniques by which these goals are ostensibly to be achieved, especially since the debate over "means" has at times been as contentious as that concerning, say, the wisdom of prioritization. It perhaps needs no reiteration that the normalization option rules out the use or even the threat of force to attain its goals. Even the rather limited paramilitary covert operations of the late 1940s and early 1950s that we have described are evidently no longer given serious consideration by Washington. This leaves a variety of nonviolent policy measures.

President Johnson in his bridge-building speech indicated that the bridges referred to would be those of travel, trade, and humanitarian assistance. An analysis of Washington's stance on human rights and general humanitarian questions in Eastern Europe was offered in an earlier section of this study, as was a discussion of the use of trade as a tool of political leverage in Eastern Europe. Suffice it to say here that what we have called the "quid pro quo" school of thought is closely connected to the notion that normalization should be "reactive," that is, carried out in response to prior policy initiatives by the East European regimes desirous of American economic concessions. In contrast, the "spillover strategy" underlies the position of normalization activists, those who believe that the United States ought to take the initiative in creating an atmosphere for improved American-East European relations. President Johnson plainly aligned himself with the activists. In February 1965 he established a Special Committee on U.S. Trade Relations with Eastern European Countries and the Soviet Union, generally referred to as the Miller Committee after its Chairman, J. Erwin Miller. Johnson applauded the following language contained in the Miller Committee report: "Trade with the communist countries is politics in the broadest sense. . . . In this intimate engagement men and nations will in time be altered by the engagement itself. We do not fear this. We welcome it. . . . If we do our part, time and change will work for us and not against us."[17]

Several specific issues or controversies in the debate over the manner of implementing normalization deserve at least brief mention here. The first of these concerns the American adherence to the Helsinki Final Act. The U.S. role in the Conference on Security and Cooperation in Europe presents something of a paradox from the perspective of normalization theory. On the one hand, the American willingness to recognize postwar European territorial arrangements would seem to have contradicted the general American policy of normalization. Because the basic thrust of that policy is gradually to alter the prevailing Soviet hegemony in Eastern Europe, it appeared quixotic that Washington would give its own imprimatur to Soviet territorial gains following World War II. In another sense, however, the Helsinki process may be regarded as intimately related to the purposes and aspirations of normalization. The essential tradeoff at Helsinki, of course, was Western concessions in Basket One on the European territorial status quo in return for a willingness by the Soviet Union (and the East European regimes themselves) to allow a much broader range of communications and interaction in the areas of trade, technology, journalistic activities, and human rights, as represented in Baskets Two and Three. The provisions of Baskets Two and Three are basic to most conceptions of how normalization can best be pursued. The issue that continues to arouse debate centers around a basic cost-gains calculation: did the West give up more than it achieved at Helsinki? Did the concessions in Basket One outweigh the putative opportunities contained in the other sections of the Helsinki accords? The debate is complicated, of course, by the fact that the Soviet Union in particular has attempted to limit the effect of Basket Three (and Principle VII) as much as possible. Those who are united on the overall wisdom of the normalization strategy have argued heatedly among themselves on these very questions.

The State Department, for example, in an analysis of the Helsinki Final Act two years after its signing, showed an obvious sensitivity to the charge about an American "sellout" on European territorial issues. The department did admit rather defensively that the Soviets had "sought to obtain" recognition of the territorial status quo in Eastern Europe, but it went on to emphasize that, even though the inviolability of frontiers was accepted at Helsinki, the real thrust of the Final Act was to establish once again the inadmissibility of armed aggression as well as the principle that frontiers could be changed peacefully. The department's somewhat ingenuous conclusion was that the "CSCE Final Act has no effect on longstanding U.S. positions on European frontiers."[18] Although this was technically correct, it did not address the important political symbolism of the United States' formally accepting at Helsinki what had been only implicit policy until 1975.

We have referred to the "broader range of communications" promised at Helsinki. This concept raises another aspect of the debate over the implementation of normalization in Eastern Europe: the role of what we have called the Western "information offensive" in the region. In a sense, something like improved travel opportunities for citizens of Western countries in Eastern Europe—a specific provision of the Helsinki Final Act—might itself be regarded as one aspect of a campaign to introduce alternative economic and political concepts to the nations of the region. Presumably there is at least some residual effect in closed societies of the continued presence of significant numbers of individuals from more open polities. It is perhaps not entirely coincidental, for example, that the gradual improvement of Western relations with Eastern Europe in the 1960s was accompanied by a substantial increase in Western tourism to the area. In the period from 1958 to 1967, for example, American tourism to Bulgaria and Hungary increased sevenfold, with three times as many Americans going to Poland and over ten times as many to Romania. The upsurge in West European visits to the East was even more impressive, with some half-million West Germans traveling throughout Eastern Europe by 1967.[19]

The long-term effects of this phenomenon would merit extended consideration in its own right.[20] For present purposes, however, we might refer back again to the one institution that is most prominently mentioned in discussion of the means by which Western ideas can penetrate the Marxist-Leninist systems of Eastern Europe, that is, Radio Free Europe (RFE).

The relevance of Radio Free Europe to the general process of normalization is a matter of some speculation and controversy. One of the most distinguished students of American policy toward Eastern Europe—himself committed to the broad tenets of normalization—has suggested that the United States should focus considerable effort on reaching the East European populations. A promising strategy, he argues, would be "to simultaneously conduct a prudent policy of detente with the Eastern European regimes and of active entente with the Eastern European masses, who . . . still yearn for eventual self-determination without entertaining illusions about the immediate prospects of release from hegemony."[21] The testimony of former National Security Adviser Zbigniew Brzezinski is also of some interest in this regard. He felt strongly that RFE offered the "best means for influencing the internal political transformation of Communist systems." He stressed that the radios should not be used to foment insurrections in Eastern Europe, but should be used as a deliberate instrument for offering alternatives to the current domestic policies of the Communist systems of East Central Europe. In order to do so, they had to be freed from "excessive" political control, especially from the State Department, which Brzezinski felt was overly concerned about an aggressive use of RFE in Eastern Europe.[22] It may be that "excessive political control" can undermine the potential effectiveness of RFE broadcasts, yet the challenge remains of shaping RFE editorial policy so that it reflects the basic incrementalism inherent in normalization strategy.

CAGING THE BEAR

In discussing the techniques by which normalization can be or has been pursued in Eastern Europe, we ought, finally, to consider the American performance in reacting to, and in some cases perhaps deterring, actual Soviet military intervention in the region. This is a conundrum that in some ways lies at the heart of hopes for normalization. After all, this strategy attempts to achieve a gradual loosening of the Soviet-East European connection without at the same time provoking a violent Soviet reaction (thus the emphasis on "moderating" rather than overturning the Eastern European Marxist systems). It is extremely difficult in this instance to arrive at any definitive conclusions as to how the United States ought to proceed. The main events that would need to be considered in any systematic examination of the matter (only some of which we discuss here) would be the abortive East German uprising in 1953, the Polish and Hungarian crises of 1956, the brief Dubček period in Czechoslovakia in 1968, and the Polish events of 1980-81. One might also include Soviet threats against Yugoslavia after 1948 and rumors of intervention against Romania and Yugoslavia following the Warsaw Pact invasion of Czechoslovakia.

Two general conclusions do seem appropriate. First, Soviet decision-making on intervention depends importantly on the momentum and context of the deliberations within the Politburo itself, which may be relatively unaffected by outside pressures or considerations. Thus, the Soviet move into Hungary in 1956 was significantly affected by the personal political position of Nikita Khrushchev at the time. The Soviet leader had still not fully consolidated his power, and several of the Stalinist figures in the Soviet elite held him responsible for the turmoil in Eastern Europe which followed his denunciation of Stalin before the Twentieth Party Congress in February 1956. In this sense, Khrushchev may have decided on intervention in part to demonstrate his bona fides as a defender of the Leninist faith. There is also evidence that the rivalry between Leonid Brezhnev and Alexei Kosygin played some part in persuading Brezhnev to support advocates of intervention against Dubček (Kosygin being regarded as relatively more moderate on the Czech situation).[23] Even setting aside the factor of personal power struggles, it seems fair to conclude that Moscow will decide on intervention basically in terms of its own definition of the situation, in particular the degree of perceived threat to Soviet domination of its East European security system presented in specific instances.

Soviet calculations here have also been heavily influenced by their analysis of the "objective" circumstances (to use a favorite Marxist term) obtaining in a given crisis. In particular, to what degree is military intervention likely to meet substantial resistance and involve the Soviet regime in a protracted struggle? A common assumption about the Soviet move into Afghanistan, for example, is that Moscow anticipated a relatively brief period of opposition to its presence. The same analysis may have proved crucial to the interventions against Hungary in 1956 and Czechoslovakia in 1968. Given the relatively limited capabilities of the armed forces of both regimes, it was reasonable to expect that a reestablishment of Soviet hegemony could be achieved at minimal cost. By contrast, it is generally assumed that a major deterrent to Stalin's use of the military option to suppress Tito's heresy in the late 1940s was the impressive Yugoslav military record in World War II, complemented in major part by the extremely difficult terrain that the Soviet bloc forces would have had to operate in. The same theory has been advanced to explain the lack of a military move against Poland in both 1956 and 1980-81, to wit, that the relatively unified and capable Polish military would actively resist Soviet incursions into their country.[24]

What role has the United States played—or can it play—in influencing Soviet decision-making on the question of intervention? For present purposes, it might be instructive to examine two basic categories of crises in Eastern Europe, the first of which results in Soviet military intervention and the other which does not.

Czechoslovakia stands as a prime reference point for the first category. Many analysts would assert that the Johnson Administration's position at the time of the Czech crisis in 1968 constitutes a virtual paradigm of how not to proceed. Even after the Soviet intervention the President was eager to proceed with his proposed state visit to the Soviet Union. He instructed the American Embassy in Moscow to give the Soviet leaders the following message: "I'm ready. Are they?" We have also referred to veiled and not so veiled hints to Soviet authorities prior to August 21, 1968, that the United States would not regard a Soviet move against Dubček as necessarily leading to a crisis in Soviet-American relations. The tenor of American policy at the time was perhaps summarized in the strict orders given to the U.S. military command in Europe not to increase air or ground patrols along the Czechoslovak border or to engage in any activity that might appear to the Soviets to be supportive of the Dubček government.[25] This is not to suggest that, even with a more vigorous American opposition to intervention, the Soviets would have stayed their hand in moving against Czechoslovakia. On the other hand, a firmer stance in Washington, or at least a posture of studied ambiguity, might well have been at least one additional complicating factor affecting the evidently delicate intra-Politburo deliberations on how to react to the Prague Spring.

What about the American role in those situations in which Moscow did not opt for military intervention? Stalin's lack of a military response to Tito's defection in 1948 may have been determined by "objective" circumstances, but there is also some reason to suppose that the rapid and public decision by Washington, together with allies such as Britain and France, to throw its weight behind the Yugoslav effort at independence played some role in Moscow's caution. Moreover, even though we have questioned the Johnson Administration's relative passivity in the face of Soviet threats to Czechoslovakia in 1968, it is also true that shortly after that intervention the President openly warned about unleashing the "dogs of war" elsewhere in Eastern Europe (widely interpreted to mean Soviet moves against Romania or Yugoslavia).[26] For whatever reason, the Politburo decided against any additional adventurism in Eastern Europe at the time.

The case of Poland in 1980-81 stands as perhaps the most interesting example of the potential influence of the United States in deterring Soviet military intervention in East Central Europe. The Carter Administration received indications in the first two weeks of December 1980 that the Soviets were seriously considering a military solution to the Solidarity challenge. Sections of the Polish-East German and Polish-Soviet border had been sealed off, and Soviet troops had been placed in offensive positions. On Friday, December 5, the Central Intelligence Agency asserted that in its judgment the Soviets would invade Poland the following Monday. In response, President Carter issued a public statement warning of the serious consequences of such a Soviet action for East-West relations. He sent a private message over the hot line to First Secretary Leonid Brezhnev along the same lines, and he suggested that the United States would transfer "advanced weaponry" to the People's Republic of China in the event of a Soviet military move.[27] Prime Minister Indira Ghandi of India was scheduled to visit Moscow at the time, and additional pressure was put on her to dissuade the Soviet Union from radical action. The President's National Security Adviser later recalled that he personally "through my own channels" sent messages to the Solidarity leadership warning of a possible military move by the Soviets, and he also called the Pope in Rome to discuss the deteriorating situation. The four goals of American policy at the time were described as being to eliminate the Soviet achievement of surprise, to encourage the Poles to resist if invaded, to organize international pressure against such an invasion, and—perhaps somewhat ironically—to disabuse the Solidarity leaders of any illusions they may have had that the Soviets would balk at a military resolution of the crisis.[28]

As National Security Adviser Brzezinski himself put it, "there is no way of knowing whether in fact the actual decision to intervene had been reached by the Kremlin and then rescinded because of this massive reaction."[29] An American correspondent resident in Moscow during this period argues that "the Kremlin was much more reluctant to resort to the use of its own military might than most Western analysts had assumed." He argues that the Soviets realized an invasion would unite the Polish people, who would offer serious military resistance to Warsaw Pact forces.[30] Nevertheless, a serious threat of intervention did exist (another "war scare" occurred in March 1981), but for whatever reason it did not materialize.[31] It would be risky to draw too many conclusions from this non-event—the Jaruzelski regime's ability to impose and sustain martial law was obviously a critical factor in the situation—yet presumably there are some lessons for American policy nonetheless. Perhaps the most prudent and balanced lesson is that the United States does have some capacity to influence Soviet calculations on the most drastic alternative open to Moscow for maintaining its current dominance in Eastern Europe, that is, use of military force. It also has to be said that American leverage in this regard—assuming that the United States continues to rule out use of its own military forces to deter Soviet pressure on the region— remains somewhat on the margins. The distinctly ambiguous character of this assessment is in its own way a prime testament to the general ambiguities and dilemmas attendant on the normalization strategy in American dealings with Eastern Europe.

A QUESTION OF DIRECTION

We might conclude this discussion of the normalization option by raising one final "dilemma" inherent in this strategy. Simply put, does the road to Eastern Europe lie through Moscow, or can the road to Moscow perhaps lie through Prague, Warsaw, Budapest, and so on? As a general matter, a reasonable criticism of American policy toward Eastern Europe over the last forty years is that it has often treated that policy only as a relatively minor adjunct of its relations with the Soviet Union itself. Approached in these terms, it seems fair to say that the United States has sometimes deprived itself of real opportunities for improving the American-East European relationship because of its tendency to mortgage that relationship to the ups and downs of the Soviet-American competition.

This observation, however, does not fully answer the question of how the United States generally should deal with the complex policy triangle involving Moscow, Washington, and the East European regimes. It is hard to deny that the current atmosphere in Soviet-American relations does affect the opportunities the United States has for openings in Eastern Europe itself. As Raymond Garthoff (former American Ambassador to Bulgaria) has said, "Given the particular symbolic importance of the United States in Eastern Europe and the sensitivity of Soviet reactions to American influence, the American-Soviet detente [of the early 1970s] permitted development of a much more forthcoming relationship with countries of Eastern Europe than would otherwise have been possible."[32] As already noted, the deterioration in Soviet-American relations in the early 1980s made several East European regimes more cautious about their options in dealing with Washington, the assumption being that Moscow was now much less prone to allow manifestations of foreign policy independence in the region.

On the other hand, there are troublesome implications in the propensity of both the Carter and Reagan administrations to use, say, the "China card" to pressure the Soviet Union into accepting a broader American presence in Eastern Europe. We have referred to Carter's threat to transfer advanced weapons to the People's Republic of China (PRC) in retaliation for any Soviet moves against Poland. Washington has also been accused of encouraging Chinese overtures to countries such as Romania and Yugoslavia on the assumption that this reduces the credibility of Soviet threats against either Bucharest or Belgrade. Given Soviet paranoia about the "threat" from the PRC, such measures would be rather problematic, and indeed might be essentially counterproductive.

Perhaps one of the most interesting points in assessing the American-Soviet-East European triangle concerns the very purposes of American normalization policy. All advocates of this approach would agree that a prime consideration is to create opportunities for more independent domestic and foreign policy behavior on the part of the Eastern European regimes. This begs the question, however, of why such a development should be seen as important to the United States and the West more generally. A partial answer would be that Eastern Europe would be better off under such an arrangement—with more opportunity for expressions of national pride and self-determination, for increased observation of basic human rights, for improved economic performance. All are laudable goals, but it may not be unduly cynical to suggest that governments are not eleemosynary organizations, at least when it comes to making foreign policy. From the narrower self-interest perspective of the West, the rationale of normalization may be twofold.

On the one hand, any loosening of the bonds between Moscow and Eastern Europe promises certain tangible strategic benefits. Ironically, both liberation and normalization theorists are united on this point, the only difference (and admittedly a substantial one) being in the degree to which it is anticipated Eastern Europe can be removed from the Soviet sphere of influence. In any case, mention has already been made of the military-industrial resources of East Central Europe, and the fact that any lessened Soviet call on these resources has to be a consummation devoutly to be wished by Western policymakers. There is, however, a more subtle potential rationale for the strategy of normalization, and in this instance the premise is that the road to Moscow may indeed lie at least partially through the countries of Eastern Europe. In other words, the object may be or could be to modify over time the Soviet Union's own policies via the constructive influence of its East European allies. This may seem like a startling scenario given our perception of Soviet dominance of bloc affairs, but the evidence suggests that the Soviet-East European relationship has evolved significantly in recent years. It would be premature to speak of a genuinely collegial association between the two, but there is no question that in forums such as the Warsaw Treaty Organization and COMECON there is something resembling negotiation and even disagreement on various policy issues, certainly when compared to an earlier era.[33] This provides the logic for a Western stance of encouraging policy innovation in Eastern Europe in the hope that there might be a "spillover effect" on the Soviet Union itself. From another perspective, the very closeness of the Soviet-East European relationship may provide substance for the notion that the Soviets are open to influence from their partners in the WTO and COMECON.

The idea that Eastern European influence on Moscow might ultimately prove beneficial can be traced as far back as Franklin Roosevelt. As noted, Roosevelt accepted the reality that the Soviets would initially dominate postwar Eastern Europe, but he went on to speculate that ten or twenty years of European influence might help to soften or mitigate Soviet hegemony in the region.[34] Brzezinski saw the same possibility long before he assumed a position of official responsibility. "East Europe, while not breaking away from the Soviet Union, may pull the Soviet Union forward by moving ahead of it, thereby cumulatively preparing the ground for a better East-West relationship."[35] Specific instances of the ostensible role which more creative policy by East European states might have in the Soviet Union include Tito's efforts in the middle 1950s to persuade Nikita Khrushchev that Soviet tolerance of greater polycentrism in Eastern Europe would be to the Soviets' own benefit, as well as the supposed interest which Moscow has displayed in the success of the Hungarian economic reforms in more recent years.[36] The point here is that the West supported Yugoslav autonomy, and thus its opportunity to be an independent voice, and has also done what it could to encourage continued Hungarian innovation in the economic sphere. It is well not to be overly optimistic about the tutelary opportunities of the East European regimes in dealing with Moscow—Soviet leaders have indicated that what may work for Hungary may not be relevant to the much larger Soviet economy—yet the notion of bringing the Soviet Union more firmly "into Europe" may be one of the more tantalizing prospects that one can hold out for the overall strategy of normalization.

NOTES

1. U.S. Department of State, FOREIGN RELATIONS OF THE UNITED STATES 1949, Vol. 5: Eastern Europe; the Soviet Union (Washington: GPO, 1976), 44.

2. A classic study of the incrementalist model of decision-making is David Braybrooke's and Charles Lindblom's A STRATEGY OF DECISION (New York: Free Press, 1963).

3. U.S. Department of State, FOREIGN RELATIONS OF THE UNITED STATES 1948, Vol. 4: Eastern Europe; the Soviet Union (Washington: GPO, 1974), 1079-1081.

4. U.S. Department of State, BACKGROUND NOTES: YUGOSLAVIA (Washington: GPO, 1964), 7.

5. U.S. Department of State, Bureau of Public Affairs, "U.S. Policy Toward the U.S.S.R., Eastern Europe and Yugoslavia," Statement by Assistant Secretary of State for European Affairs Lawrence Eagleburger before the Subcommittee on Europe and the Middle East of the House Foreign Affairs Committee, June 10, 1981 (Washington: GPO, 1981), 5.

6. Ibid., "U.S. Policy and Eastern Europe," Address by Deputy Assistant Secretary of State for European Affairs Robert L. Barry before the Cleveland Council on World Affairs, April 22, 1980 (Washington: GPO, 1980).

7. Lyndon Baines Johnson, THE VANTAGE POINT (New York: Holt, Rinehart and Winston, 1971), 471.

8. Cited in Alexander J. Groth, "United States Policy Toward Eastern Europe, 1969-1973," in U.S. FOREIGN POLICY IN A CHANGING WORLD, ed. Alan M. Jones, Jr. (New York: David McKay Co., 1973), 128.

9. Henry Kissinger, WHITE HOUSE YEARS (Boston: Little, Brown and Co., 1979), 930.

10. Raymond Garthoff, "Eastern Europe in the Context of U.S.-Soviet Relations," in SOVIET POLICY IN EASTERN EUROPE, ed. Sarah Meiklejohn Terry (New Haven, Conn.: Yale University Press, 1984), 322.

11. U.S. Congress, House of Representatives, Committee on Foreign Affairs, Subcommittee on Europe and the Middle East, HEARINGS, July 12, 1979, Statement of George S. Vest, Assistant Secretary of State for European Affairs, 96th Congress, 1st Session, 12; Zbigniew Brzezinski, POWER AND PRINCIPLE (New York: Farrar, Straus and Giroux, 1983), 296.

12. Brzezinski, POWER AND PRINCIPLE, 299; Jerry Hough, THE POLISH CRISIS: AMERICAN POLICY OPTIONS (Washington: Brookings Institution, 1982), 15-16.

13. U.S. Congress, House of Representatives, Foreign Affairs Committee, Subcommittee on Europe and the Middle East, U.S. POLICY TOWARD EASTERN EUROPE AND YUGOSLAVIA, Testimony by Rozanne L. Ridgway, Assistant Secretary for European and Canadian Affairs, October 2, 1985, 99th Congress, 1st Session, 3.

14. Garthoff, "Eastern Europe in the Context of U.S.-Soviet Relations," 338; Eagleburger, "U.S. Policy Toward the U.S.S.R., Eastern Europe, and Yugoslavia," 4.

15. DEPARTMENT OF STATE BULLETIN (November 1983), 22.

16. William Erickson, "US-East Europe Ties Face Test on Shultz Tour of Region," CHRISTIAN SCIENCE MONITOR (December 12, 1985).

17. Johnson, THE VANTAGE POINT, 472.

18. "Conference on Security and Cooperation in Europe," DEPARTMENT OF STATE BULLETIN (September 26, 1977), 406.

19. Groth, "United States Policy Toward Eastern Europe, 1969-1973," 126.

20. One of the best series of studies available on the issues involved here is Herbert Kelman, ed., INTERNATIONAL BEHAVIOR (New York: Holt, Rinehart and Winston, 1965), especially Ithiel De Sola Pool's "Effects of Cross-National Contact on National and International Images," 104-29; and Anita L. Mishler's "Personal Contact in International Exchanges," 548-64.

21. Bennett Kovrig, "The United States: 'Peaceful Engagement' Revisited," in THE INTERNATIONAL POLITICS OF EASTERN EUROPE, ed. Charles Gati (New York: Praeger Publishers, 1976), 146.

22. Brzezinski, POWER AND PRINCIPLE, 300.

23. Jiri Valenta, SOVIET INTERVENTION IN CZECHOSLOVAKIA 1968 (Baltimore: Johns Hopkins University Press, 1979), 47-48.

24. A very valuable and perceptive study of the factors governing Soviet decision-making on Eastern Europe is Michael Tatu's "Intervention in Eastern Europe," in DIPLOMACY OF POWER, ed. Stephen S. Kaplan (Washington, Brookings Institution, 1981); see also William Potter and Jiri Valenta, eds. SOVIET DECISIONMAKING FOR NATIONAL SECURITY (London: George Allen and Unwin, 1984).

25. Valenta, SOVIET INTERVENTION IN CZECHOSLOVAKIA 1968, 132.

26. NEW YORK TIMES (August 29, 1968), 1.

27. Jimmy Carter, KEEPING FAITH (Toronto: Bantam Books, 1982), 584-585.

28. Brzezinski, POWER AND PRINCIPLE, 463-468.

29. Ibid., 468.

30. Andrew Nagorski, RELUCTANT FAREWELL (New York: Holt, Rinehart and Winston, 1985), 155. Given their analysis of the difficulties of a military solution to the Polish crisis, the Soviet leaders were, according to Nagorski, almost in a state of "panic" about developments in that country.

31. Andrew Cockburn argues that basic problems of logistics and organization were a major deterrent to a Soviet military move against Poland, in particular the supposed chaos that accompanied the attempted callup of reserves in the Western military districts of the Soviet Union. Andrew Cockburn, THE THREAT (New York: Random House, 1983).

32. Garthoff, "Eastern Europe in the Context of U.S.-Soviet Relations," 324.

33. See, for example, Christopher D. Jones, SOVIET INFLUENCE IN EASTERN EUROPE (New York: Praeger, 1981).

34. Robert I. Gannon, THE CARDINAL SPELLMAN STORY (New York: Doubleday, 1962), 222.

35. Zbigniew Brzezinski, ALTERNATIVE TO PARTITION (New York: McGraw-Hill, 1965), 136-137.

36. Richard Lowenthal, WORLD COMMUNISM (New York: Oxford University Press, 1966), ch. 4; Eric Bourne, "Hungary Serves as Sounding Board for Possible Soviet-Bloc Reforms," CHRISTIAN SCIENCE MONITOR (April 18, 1983).

18.
Concluding Reflections

In this survey of problems in American foreign relations with respect to Eastern Europe, a consistent theme has been that the American-East European relationship presents the United States with considerable and perhaps surprising tests of its maturity as a nation in the international arena. There is nothing more frustrating for a society than to feel that it has important interests in a particular area and yet seemingly has a limited capacity to protect or pursue those interests. The national trauma over the Iranian hostage crisis stands as a prime example. Presumably the protection of one's own nationals, especially official representatives of one's government, is central to national pride and sense of worth. As it turned out, however, the United States was forced to accept the humiliation, extending over a period of many months, of not being able to "solve" this particular affront to the national psyche. American frustrations in Eastern Europe have perhaps rarely been as dramatic as this—save for the occasional crises such as Hungary in 1956 or Poland in 1981—but they nevertheless have been substantial enough.

The chief criterion for a "mature" response to frustration is the ability to adjust one's own expectations in the face of evidence that goals and dreams may be beyond achievement.[1] At the same time, it can be argued that a total abandonment of these goals and dreams converts utopianism into sterile cynicism. If this study of American policy toward Eastern Europe has had any one informing purpose, it has been to argue that the United States ought to be "mature" in its attitude toward the region, that is, recognize that our reach will for the foreseeable future be beyond our grasp. On the other hand, an equal premise of our analysis is that it would be both unnecessary and ethically unbecoming for this country to surrender all hope of contributing to a brighter and more rewarding future for a group of nations that have had their full share of historical calamity.

TWO ISSUES

In considering the theme of maturity in foreign policymaking, we might have reference to one general controversy and one specific controversy that have affected the development of American diplomacy toward Eastern Europe.

Throughout the forty years since the end of World War II, a major obstacle to a more productive American-East European relationship has been an ideological hostility in this country toward Communist regimes generally. Few could quarrel with the notion that there are basic issues of human dignity and personal freedom fundamental to the struggle between the Marxist-Leninist and democratic systems. Yet the overall anti-Communist predilection in this society has played a dolorous role in various administrations' attempts to develop a coherent and productive policy toward Eastern Europe. President Lyndon Johnson is an interesting source of evidence on this score, for he waged what might be called his own crusade in Southeast Asia against communism. The Johnson Administration's almost obsessive involvement in the Vietnam struggle receives very little support from liberal students of American foreign policy today (and not a great deal at the time either). Still one needs to recall that it was Johnson, after all, who introduced the possibility of a fundamentally altered American-East European relationship, despite his absorption in Communist aggression against South Vietnam. Johnson himself directly addressed the seeming contradiction between his policies in one place and those in another. "I resented as much as anyone what the Russians, Czechs, Poles and others were doing to help North Vietnam," the President admitted. "But it made no sense for the United States, because of that, to tie its own hands in trying to develop a coherent policy toward another important segment of the world." In fact, Johnson argued, American policy in Vietnam and Eastern Europe had an organic relationship. "We had to show that there was an alternative to confrontation. . . . We were using reason where we could and force where we must, in both cases working toward the stable and orderly world that was our goal."[2]

One may question Johnson's own analysis of the situation in Southeast Asia without at the same time doubting that in the case of Eastern Europe he was demonstrating an admirable ability to set aside the issue of Communist regimes per se in order to establish a more realistic policy. His example should be taken into appropriate consideration in any contemporary discussion of American policy options in Eastern Europe, especially since, as Congressman Lee Hamilton noted in a recent analysis, there seems to be a renewed attack on American policy as being "too soft on communist governments" and a renewed questioning of why we should treat the Eastern European regimes any differently than the Soviet Union itself.[3]

A more specific controversy in American-East European relations, one not unrelated to the general issue outlined above, concerns the matter of the so-called Sonnenfeldt Doctrine. In mid-December 1975 in London, State Department Counselor Helmut Sonnenfeldt addressed a meeting of American ambassadors to

Europe. In that speech, Sonnenfeldt referred to the desirability of a more "organic" relationship between the Soviet Union and the countries of Eastern Europe. The term *organic* may have not been the most felicitous choice of expression, as Sonnenfeldt himself later came to admit, and given subsequent events he had considerable cause to rue its use. Some three months later columnists Rowland Evans and Robert Novak published a piece in which they asserted that Sonnenfeldt had proposed a permanent organic union between the Soviet Union and Eastern Europe in order to avoid World War III. The column suggested that some members of the Ford Administration were "appalled" by the Sonnenfeldt doctrine, because it seemed to undercut the efforts of Eastern nationalists such as Nicolae Ceausescu of Romania to pursue independent policies vis-à-vis the Soviet Union.[4] On April 6, 1976, the *New York Times* published a leaked summary of Sonnenfeldt's remarks, which added fuel to the fire. A number of subsequent press reports referred to an American "sellout" of Eastern Europe. The furor was sufficiently great that Sonnenfeldt was asked to appear before the House Committee on International Relations a week later to defend himself.

The whole controversy surrounding Sonnenfeldt's remarks on Eastern Europe is a fascinating case study of the tendency in this country to regard realism toward the region as tantamount to a surrender to Soviet imperialistic designs. A close examination of Sonnenfeldt's remarks as reported in the *Times* (and which he accepted as being basically accurate) reveals that in this instance there was far less than met the eye. The crux of Sonnenfeldt's thesis concerning Soviet-East European relations may be briefly summarized as follows. It was tragic that "in this area of vital interest and crucial importance it has not been possible for the Soviet Union to establish roots of interest that go beyond sheer power." In view of this "unnatural relationship" between Moscow and the East European countries, there is a continuing prospect that they may one day "explode, causing World War III." The implications for American policy, then, were that the United States should "strive for an evolution that makes the relationship between the Eastern Europeans and the Soviet Union an organic one. . . . Our policy must be a policy of responding to the clearly visible aspirations in Eastern Europe for a more autonomous existence within the context of a strong Soviet geopolitical influence." Sonnenfeldt—rather ironically in view of subsequent events—mentioned Poland as an example of an Eastern European country that had been able to overcome its "romantic political inclinations" in developing a national identity without at the same time inviting a strongly negative Soviet reaction.[5]

Several points stand out about this analysis, and in each case they may be regarded as unexceptional to serious students of American-East European relations. An elementary point is that the Soviet Union does regard Eastern Europe as an essential geopolitical factor in its own security position and will take whatever steps are necessary to protect that position. At the same time the "un-organic" Soviet domination of Eastern Europe does raise the potential of continuing political crises that could lead to a general international confrontation. Do attempts to make the Soviet-East European relationship more "organic" (again, an unfortunate choice of words) imply a permanent acquiescence in Soviet domination of the region? Nothing in Sonnenfeldt's remarks would lead reasonably to this conclusion. On the contrary, as he later testified before Congress, the United States did not accept a Soviet sphere of influence in Eastern Europe to the extent that it denoted an "exclusive preserve of some power." Instead, the idea was to persuade the Soviets to alter their policy toward East Central Europe so that it was based on a more "natural" foundation implying the "broad set of relationships involving the normal intercourse between states." Two benefits would flow out of such an evolution: a reduced danger of international conflict arising from Eastern European instability and very positive benefits in the form of increased self-determination for the East Europeans themselves. The essence of the Sonnenfeldt analysis was that the United States should convince the Soviets that what was in the interest of Eastern Europe and the international community more generally was also in the interest of the Soviet Union itself—what the game theorists refer to as a "positive sum game." Sonnenfeldt was especially criticized for taking Soviet "sensibilities" so much into account in discussing Eastern Europe. His response again was straightforward, that is, in dealing with a "competing power of great magnitude" one had to conduct oneself necessarily with "restraint and responsibility."[6]

The reality is that the so-called Sonnenfeldt doctrine was a thoughtful statement of the premises and eventual goals of the "normalization strategy" that has been at the core of American policy toward Eastern Europe for twenty years now. Sonnenfeldt rejected any American efforts to encourage armed uprisings in Eastern Europe as "irresponsible." Instead, the policy had to be one of working, together with America's European Allies, toward a gradual evolution of the artificial Soviet-East European relationship that had existed since World War II. Interestingly, during the subsequent Polish crisis in 1980 members of the Carter Administration adhered to Sonnenfeldt's theses about American policy toward Eastern Europe, even if—for obvious reasons—they did not claim to be applying the "Sonnenfeldt Doctrine" to Polish affairs. As noted earlier, National Security Adviser Brzezinski argued that one purpose of sending warnings to both Moscow and Warsaw about a potential Soviet military intervention in Poland was to disabuse Polish Solidarity leaders of any illusions they might have had that the Soviets would refrain from a military solution to the Polish crisis. "Here in effect we have a common interest with the Soviets," Brzezinski concluded, "for they too may prefer to intimidate the Poles to a degree" [i.e., intimidate rather than actually invade].[7]

Of course, such "intimidation" is in itself repugnant, but the real issue in the American approach to Eastern Europe is not how to remove all the unpleasant aspects of Soviet behavior but how to minimize these to the degree possible. Evans and Novak, in a further column on the controversy over Sonnenfeldt's doctrine, reported that Representative Edward Derwinski of Illinois had said that the doctrine was "the straw that broke the camel's back," particularly given

American "concessions" at the Helsinki conference.[8] Whether or not Representative Derwinski actually phrased it this way, unquestionably the "Sonnenfeldt doctrine" constituted one of the major public controversies in the history of American-East European relations since 1945. That it should have been so says a good deal about what I have called the continuing lack of "maturity," at least in some circles, concerning those relations.

THE SHADOW OF YALTA

One reason why Sonnenfeldt's remarks in London aroused such a sensitive and tendentious reaction is that to many they seemed to confirm their worst suspicions about the Yalta accords of 1945. Varying interpretations of the Yalta agreements among Stalin, Roosevelt, and Churchill have been a perennial issue in discussions of American diplomacy since that time, especially as that diplomacy has involved the countries of Eastern Europe. The "worst case analysis" of Yalta is a familiar one: the United States and Britain cynically traded away the freedom of Eastern Europe at Yalta in return for putative concessions by Stalin on other matters (participation in the war against Japan, the structure of the United Nations, etc.). More specifically, the Western powers granted the Soviet Union a permanent hegemony in Eastern Europe in return for these concessions.

The Yalta controversy has shadowed the American political process and the careers of individuals for some forty years now, even if the passions that it originally aroused have faded somewhat as time passed. Thus, one reason many were prone to accept the notion that Alger Hiss was a Soviet agent was his having served in a minor capacity at the Yalta conference. One of the most distinguished of American diplomats, Charles Bohlen, found his nomination as Ambassador to the Soviet Union in 1953 under severe attack in the Senate because he, too, had served as an adviser to Roosevelt at Yalta.[9] The Republican party platform in 1952 contained a clause specifically repudiating the Yalta accords, even if President Eisenhower subsequently declined to do so himself. In perhaps the most bizarre example of Yalta's being employed for political purposes, Governor George Wallace of Alabama, not heretofore known for his interest in the subtleties of foreign policy, referred to Yalta in his 1968 presidential campaign as a means of discrediting his principal opponents. He reiterated the standard theme that Yalta represented a betrayal of Eastern Europe, and he pointed out that Richard Nixon and Hubert Humphrey "in their days of early apprenticeship in the Congress supported the Yalta agreement that today is really the plague of Czechoslovakia and Hungary and all of Eastern Europe." Even somewhat more sophisticated observers of the international scene, such as former Chancellor Helmut Schmidt of West Germany, have referred disparagingly to Yalta as a plan "practically to divide Europe into spheres of influence."[10]

Any discussion of future American policy options with respect to Eastern Europe presumably has to give at least some attention to the ghost of Yalta. An analysis of the meaning of Yalta, if we set aside the more flamboyant emotions or political maneuvering that Yalta has led to, does provide an interesting framework for considering those options. An instructive, and in some ways perhaps surprising, attempt to relate Yalta to contemporary policy was a speech by President Reagan to a group of Polish-Americans commemorating the fortieth anniversary of the Warsaw uprising against the Nazis in 1944. Given this particular President, and perhaps this particular audience, it would not have been unexpected if the President had joined the chorus of voices denouncing the Yalta accords as such. Instead, Reagan stressed that these accords had been "misinterpreted" to imply "American consent for the division of Europe into spheres of influence." On the contrary, the President said, the United States did not and never had accepted the "permanent subjugation of the people of Eastern Europe." As Soviet specialist Robert C. Tucker put it, in a sense Reagan was "coming to the defense of Roosevelt's Government.[11]

In rejecting the preferred interpretation of some of his conservative supporters, President Reagan argued that the Yalta agreements provided a positive foundation for the two superpowers' relationship with Eastern Europe. "We see that agreement as a pledge by the three great powers to restore full independence, and to allow free and democratic elections in all countries liberated from the Nazis after World War II. There is no reason to absolve the Soviet Union or ourselves from this commitment." A White House aide later indicated that the Administration's attitude toward Yalta was the same one it had toward the Helsinki accords of 1975 and thus did not represent any change in policy. A State Department spokesman stressed that the United States had no plans to embark on a "liberating" scheme in Eastern Europe, but instead would rely on the terms of Yalta and Helsinki as the basis for American policy.[12]

There may be some reason to question Reagan's own interpretation of Yalta as providing for the "full independence" of the Eastern European countries, but on balance there was considerable merit in his argument that Yalta and Helsinki as well provide a framework for American policy toward East Central Europe. In each instance, the relevant accords were a pragmatic recognition of the Soviet power position in the region and the inability or unwillingness of the United States to challenge this position by force. At the same time, both Yalta and Helsinki contain other provisions obtained in return for American acquiescence in the security interests of the Soviet Union in Eastern Europe. At Yalta, the much-maligned Declaration on Liberated Europe, which called for freely elected regimes in the liberated countries, provided at least a potential moderating force to the sheer impact of Soviet power. Numerous provisions of the Helsinki Final Act have the same function.

It would be idle to argue that the Soviet Union has a particularly impressive record of being "restrained" by either of these agreements. The real point is a different one: both Yalta and Helsinki establish as basic American policy that this country will not accept a permanent Soviet military hegemony in Eastern Europe, and that even within the context of acknowledging obvious Soviet security concerns this country will work over time for greater autonomy and humane polities in Eastern Europe. Equally important is the fact that the two accords provide a legitimate and enduring rationale for the United States remaining concerned about Eastern Europe, for in both instances the Soviet Union offered its own consent, however reluctant, to such a stance. The testimony of Jacek Kuron is a rather compelling, and poignant, affirmation of this interpretation. In an interview with an editor of the *New York Times*, Kuron, a leading figure in the Solidarity movement, insisted that what he wanted was not a revisal but a renewal of Yalta. Perhaps the free elections called for in 1945 are not currently possible, Kuron admits, but other forms of democratization, especially with respect to independent trade union activity, are now conceivable because of the Polish people's will to defend such activity. Kuron was arguing for a Western-induced program of reform in Eastern Europe, and he apparently saw little contradiction between this aspiration and the original Yalta formulations. As Theodore Draper rightly observes, "If Kuron's view prevails, Yalta may someday represent a historical weapon against the Soviet oppression of Poland, rather than the sellout it is supposed to have been."[13]

The real burden on American policy is to accept the fact that Yalta and Helsinki are only pointers to a better future for Eastern Europe, but at the same time to continue to work toward making all the provisions of both agreements more of a reality. The challenge here, as already discussed, is not to let frustration slip into cynicism, not to abandon both Yalta and Helsinki as a framework for our preferred vision of Eastern Europe.

A FINAL NOTE: ANOTHER MESSAGE FROM HELSINKI?

Throughout this book we have made numerous references to the Helsinki Final Act. In establishing the "preferred vision" of Eastern Europe referred to above, there is another piece of guidance that Helsinki can provide us. In this case the lesson relates to the whole course of Finnish foreign policy since 1945, in particular the relationship Helsinki has had with the Soviet Union. The term *Finlandization* has been used in a generally pejorative sense in discussion of European security questions in the last several decades, at least from the perspective of Western analysts. The spectre conjured up is of a clear Soviet military dominance in Europe, the withdrawal of American military forces from the continent, a series of leftist European governments wary of defying Moscow, and most likely the fracturing of the European integration movement.

Not surprisingly, Finnish spokesmen generally express some displeasure at the above use of Finlandization, implying as it does a negative verdict on their own foreign policy. This is not the place to assess the likelihood or the details of a Finlandized Western Europe. The point here is a somewhat different one, which is that the Finlandization of *Eastern Europe* may be a promising model for future political developments in the region.

It is necessary to define just what this model consists of. Basically, the Finns have general autonomy in their domestic policy in return for considerable discretion in the foreign policy sphere, at least as far as issues of importance to the Soviet Union are concerned. Even in the domestic area there are limits to Finnish independence. Thus, it is a more or less accepted fact of life within the country that no regime can be allowed to come to power which is avowedly rightist and anti-Soviet in character. Potential challenges to this unwritten rule have in the past occasioned brief but significant crises in Soviet-Finnish relations (for example, in 1961). Within these broad parameters, however, Finland is able to maintain an essentially free press, a competing party system, and all the other accoutrements of an open society. As noted, the price for this is a relative passivity in Finnish foreign policy on major issues of East-West relations. Helsinki is not necessarily required publicly to support the Soviet position on all major questions, but at the same time there are definite limits to any public criticism of Soviet policy. Moreover, Finland requires implicit or sometimes explicit Soviet permission before associating politically with any other state (e.g., membership in the Nordic Council, delayed until 1955).[14]

Several prime ingredients have contributed to this rather unique relationship. The legal framework is contained in the 1948 Soviet-Finnish Treaty of Friendship, Cooperation and Mutual Assistance, which recognizes Finland's neutral status and obligates each party to go to the aid of the other in the case of aggression by Germany or allies of Germany. Finland's foreign trade is also heavily oriented toward the Soviet Union, and a number of Finnish workers find employment on Soviet construction projects. There has also been a history of pragmatic working relationships and evident respect between the major Finnish and Soviet personalities, for example, President Urho Kekkonen and General Secretary Nikita Khrushchev, which has been instrumental in overcoming the occasional turmoil in the relations between the two countries. Finally, there is the fact of Soviet military power: there are no Soviet forces on Finnish soil, but there are massive Soviet military capabilities within close proximity, a reality that obviously commands Finnish attention.[15]

How did Finland manage to escape conversion to an outright Soviet satellite in the immediate postwar years and even today how does it maintain a relatively broad-based independence? There are lessons here that may be of some significance for the future of Eastern Europe, especially since Moscow had the naked power in the late 1940s to impose whatever arrangement it wanted on the Finns. One factor was that after 1945 the United States was generally regarded as having a special interest in the fate of the Finns. This country had admired the relatively democratic prewar politics of Finland—certainly when compared to other countries in Eastern Europe—and hadn't forgotten that Finland alone had paid in full its debts to the United States in the interwar period.[16] Finland was also blessed with unusually talented and flexible leadership as the war drew to a close. Finnish Prime Minister Joho Paasikivi played a particularly prominent role at the time.

He concentrated on making necessary concessions to Stalin (e.g., on reparations and leasing of naval facilities to the Soviet Union), while at the same time insisting on an irreducible core of continued Finnish independence. Stalin was reported to have developed a grudging admiration for this type of tough pragmatism and to have commented that what he needed to settle matters in Poland was a "Polish Paasikivi."[17] To be sure, one shouldn't exaggerate Stalin's sentimentality about interpersonal relations. Perhaps a more important factor in the dictator's mind was his perception of Finnish fighting capabilities—and willingness to use those capabilities—particularly as demonstrated in the "Winter War" of 1939-40, in which Finnish forces for a time held at bay the much larger Soviet military contingent.

If a series of Finlands, or at least countries enjoying some rough equivalent of the Finnish relationship with Moscow, could be established from the Baltic to the Adriatic, this would seem to represent a desirable outcome. It would not constitute the actual "liberation" of Eastern Europe; there would still be significant constraints on the freedom of action of the involved East European regimes. Yet, compared to the current status of most of the countries in the region, the prospect of Finlandization, at least from the perspective of the majority of the population, must seem attractive indeed. How likely is such a scenario? There is no immediate prospect that Moscow will agree to a general duplication of its special relationship with Helsinki in its relations with other East European capitals. Ironically, Moscow has expressed the same lack of enthusiasm for the Finlandization of Eastern Europe as those in the West have demonstrated about the Findlandization of Western Europe. The geographic factor has to be taken into account. Finland has had the good fortune to be located outside the main invasion routes into the Soviet Union. Presumably, this has helped persuade Moscow to take a somewhat more relaxed attitude toward Finnish policy.

Still, perhaps some intriguing pointers may be derived from the Finnish example for the broader Soviet-East European relationship. For instance, Finland exists in what is called a "soft" sphere of influence, that is, it maintains a fair degree of autonomy but at the same time accepts the limits to its independence without requiring the periodic overt demonstration of Soviet military power to reinforce this reality.[18] It is precisely the fact that Moscow believes the Finns do understand and accept the premises of their relationship that makes the USSR relatively relaxed in its attitude toward Helsinki. There is also what might be called the law of diminishing returns for the Soviet Union itself. In other words, in order to take Finland within its "hard" sphere of influence, where, say, Czechoslovakia dwells today, the costs to Moscow would likely exceed whatever gains could be had from such an operation, particularly when there is a reasonable degree of return from the current "soft" relationship.

What are the possible lessons for aspiring new Finlands in Eastern Europe—and for Western policy toward the region? The main lesson seems to be that further Finlandization is not totally ruled out, provided there is (1) a frank acceptance of at least a "soft" sphere of influence for the Soviet Union; (2) a willingness to abandon any lingering romantic notions about eliminating Soviet influence from the national life; (3) a stress on firm but pragmatic leadership; (4) a demonstrated willingness in the final analysis to defend by force at least limited sovereignty; (5) nonprovocative but definite expressions of commitment by the Western powers to limited sovereignty for the East European regimes. The leitmotif in all this is gradually to convince the Soviet Union that the law of diminishing returns has come to apply to all of Eastern Europe, not just Finland.

Our suggestion that the West generally and the United States more specifically adopt a long-range strategy oriented toward the Finlandization of Eastern Europe will arouse strong, if rather different, types of criticism from what we have called the disengagement, liberation, and destabilization theorists. The first will reject the idea because of its excessive ambition; the second will dispute it on the basis of its acceptance of a continued heavy Soviet presence in the region; and the third will ask why we should make the Soviet-East European relationship more stable. None of these critiques should be taken lightly, and all deserve respectful attention.

Nevertheless, I would close this analysis by suggesting that students of the American-East European relationship might do well to take at least one trip along the Vyborg-Helsinki Highway. Driving north from Leningrad, Vyborg is the last major city one passes through before reaching the Soviet-Finnish frontier. Generally, it takes several hours for the Western traveler to pass through customs and passport formalities at the frontier before being allowed to cross over into Finland, where the same formalities consume perhaps five minutes. To experience Finnish openness and self-confidence after the often oppressive atmosphere of the Soviet Union itself is in its own way perhaps the best argument for the merits of Finlandization. It is to be hoped that, as the future unfolds, there will be equivalents of the Vyborg-Helsinki Highway into other areas of Eastern Europe.

NOTES

1. For a discussion of alternative responses to "cognitive dissonance," see James E. Dougherty and Robert L. Pfaltzgraff, Jr., CONTENDING THEORIES OF INTERNATIONAL RELATIONS, 2d ed. (New York: Harper and Row, 1981), 284-287.

2. Lyndon Baines Johnson, THE VANTAGE POINT (New York: Holt, Rinehart and Winston, 1971), 473.

3. U.S. Congress, CONGRESSIONAL RECORD, December 16, 1985, 99th Congress, 1st Session, E5638.

4. Rowland Evans and Robert Novak, "A Soviet-East Europe 'Organic Union'," WASHINGTON POST (March 22, 1976).

5. U.S. Congress, House of Representatives, Committee on International Relations, UNITED STATES NATIONAL SECURITY POLICY VIS-A-VIS EASTERN EUROPE (The "Sonnenfeldt Doctrine"), Hearings, April 12, 1976, 94th Congress, 2d Session, 42-43.

6. Ibid., 4, 19, 23.

7. Zbigniew Brzezinski, POWER AND PRINCIPLE (New York: Farrar, Straus and Giroux, 1983), 407.

8. Rowland Evans and Robert Novak, "The Sonnenfeldt Doctrine: Deflecting the Ruckus," WASHINGTON POST (March 30, 1976).

9. Ambassador Bohlen rather vividly describes his travails at the time in WITNESS TO HISTORY (New York: W. W. Norton and Co., 1973), 309-336.

10. Josh Barbanel, "Yalta, After 4 Decades, Is Still a Disputed Topic," NEW YORK TIMES (August 18, 1984), 4.

11. Ibid.

12. NEW YORK TIMES (August 21, 1984), 4.

13. Theodore Draper, "Neoconservative History," NEW YORK REVIEW OF BOOKS (January 16, 1986), 10.

14. Two good studies of Finnish foreign policy are George Maude, THE FINNISH DILEMMA (London: Oxford University Press, 1976) and Roy Allison, FINLAND'S RELATIONS WITH THE SOVIET UNION, 1944-1984 (New York: St. Martin's Press, 1985).

15. Adam M. Garfinkle, "FINLANDIZATION": A MAP TO A METAPHOR (Philadelphia: Foreign Policy Research Institute, 1978), 32-36.

16. Geir Lundestad, THE AMERICAN NON-POLICY TOWARD EASTERN EUROPE 1943-1947 (Oslo: Universitetsforlaget, 1978), 286.

17. Cited in Louis Halle, THE COLD WAR AS HISTORY (New York: Harper and Row, 1967).

18. Garfinkle, "FINLANDIZATION": A MAP TO A METAPHOR, 22-32.

Bibliography

PUBLIC DOCUMENTS

ASSEMBLY OF CAPTIVE EUROPEAN NATIONS. New York: Assembly of Captive European Nations, n.d..

Ambassador Max Kampelman. "The Madrid CSCE Follow-Up Meeting: An Assessment." Statement in Madrid on July 15, 1983.

_____. "Statement to the Conference on Security and Cooperation in Europe." Madrid, July 18, 1983.

Congressional Quarterly. HISTORIC DOCUMENTS OF 1980. Washington, Congressional Quarterly, 1981.

_____. HISTORIC DOCUMENTS OF 1981. Washington: Congressional Quarterly, 1982.

Congressional Quarterly Weekly Report. "Suspension of Poland's Trade Status Sought." Washington: Congressional Quarterly Weekly Report, October 16, 1982.

THE IMS 1984 AYER DIRECTORY OF PUBLICATIONS. Fort Washington, Pa.: IMS Press, 1984.

International Institute of Strategic Studies. THE MILITARY BALANCE 1985-1986. London: IISS, 1985.

NATIONAL PARTY PLATFORMS, 1840-1956. Compiled by Kirk H. Porter and Donald Bruce Johnson. Urbana: University of Illinois Press, 1956.

National Republican Heritage Groups (Nationalities) Council. "A Handbook for Heritage Groups." Washington: Republican National Committee, n.d..

NEW BOOK OF WORLD RANKINGS, ed. George Kurian. New York: Facts on File, 1984.

North Atlantic Treaty Organization. EXTERNAL ECONOMIC RELATIONS OF CMEA COUNTRIES: THEIR SIGNIFICANCE AND IMPACT IN A GLOBAL PERSPECTIVE. Brussels: NATO Economics and Information Directorates. April 1983.

Organization for European Cooperation and Development. "Recent Trends in the International Financial Situation of Eastern Europe." FINANCIAL MARKET TRENDS. Paris: OECD, March 1985.

_____. Department of Economics and Statistics. FOREIGN TRADE BY COM-
MODITIES. Vol. 1. Paris: OECD, 1985.

Polish National Alliance. IN THE MAINSTREAMS OF AMERICAN LIFE. Chicago: Alliance Publishers, 1976.

Republican National Committee. "Representing Ethnic Americans Within the
Republican Party." Washington: Republican National Committee, n.d..

United Nations, Department of Social and Economic Affairs. YEARBOOK OF
INTERNATIONAL TRADE STATISTICS 1974. Vol. 1. New York: UN,
1975.

_____, Department of Economic and Social Affairs, Statistical Office. STATIS-
TICS YEARBOOK 1982. New York: UN, 1985.

U.S. Advisory Commission on International Educational and Cultural Affairs.
THE EFFECTS OF THE CONFERENCE ON SECURITY AND COOPER-
ATION IN EUROPE ON THE CULTURAL RELATIONS OF THE UNITED
STATES AND EASTERN EUROPE. A special report to Congress, April
1976. Washington: GPO, 1976.

U.S. Agency for International Development. PROPOSED MUTUAL DEFENSE
AND DEVELOPMENT PROGRAMS: FY 1966. Washington: GPO, 1965.

_____. OPERATIONS REPORT: FY 1966. Washington: GPO, 1966.

U.S. Board for International Broadcasting, Radio Free Europe/Radio Liberty.
"Listening to Western Radio in East Europe, 1981-Early 1982." Washington: GPO, 1982.

_____. FOURTH ANNUAL REPORT 1978. Washington: GPO, 1978.

U.S. Commission on Security and Cooperation in Europe. BASKET THREE:
IMPLEMENTATION OF THE HELSINKI ACCORDS. Vol. IV: U.S.
POLICY AND THE BELGRADE CONFERENCE. Hearings, June 3, 1977,
and June 6, 1977. 95th Congress, 1st Session.

_____. CSCE DIGEST. June 8, 1983-January 1986. Washington: GPO, 1983-
86.

_____. FULFILLING OUR PROMISES: THE UNITED STATES AND THE
HELSINKI FINAL ACT. Washington: GPO, November 1979.

_____. THE HELSINKI PROCESS AND EAST-WEST RELATIONS: PRO-
GRESS IN PERSPECTIVE. Washington: GPO, March 1985.

_____. IMPLEMENTATION OF THE HELSINKI ACCORDS. THE OTTAWA
HUMAN RIGHTS EXPERTS MEETING AND THE FUTURE OF THE
HELSINKI PROCESS. Hearings, June 15, 1985. 99th Congress, 1st Session.

_____. THE MADRID CSCE REVIEW MEETING. Washington: GPO, March
1983.

_____. THE SITUATION OF ANDREI SAKHAROV AND UNOFFICIAL
PEACE GROUPS IN THE U.S.S.R. AND EASTERN EUROPE. Hearings,
May 22, 1984. 98th Congress, 2d Session.

U.S. Congress. CONGRESSIONAL RECORD. 94th Congress, 1st Session, 1975.

_____. CONGRESSIONAL RECORD. 98th Congress, 1st Session, 1983.

_____. CONGRESSIONAL RECORD, 99th Congress, 1st Session, 1985.

U.S. Congress, House of Representatives, Committee on Foreign Affairs. YUGO-
SLAV EMERGENCY RELIEF ASSISTANCE ACT OF 1950. Hearings.
81st Congress, 2d Session.

_____. Subcommittee on Europe and the Middle East. U.S. POLICY TOWARD EASTERN EUROPE AND YUGOSLAVIA. Testimony by Rozanne L. Ridgway, Assistant Secretary for European and Canadian Affairs. October 2, 1985. 99th Congress, 1st Session.

_____. Committee on International Relations. HEARINGS, July 12, 1979. Statement of George S. Vest, Assistant Secretary of State for European Affairs. 96th Congress, 1st Session.

_____. THE BELGRADE FOLLOWUP MEETING TO THE CONFERENCE ON SECURITY AND COOPERATION IN EUROPE: A REPORT AND APPRAISAL. Washington: GPO, May 17, 1978.

_____. UNITED STATES NATIONAL SECURITY POLICY VIS-A-VIS EASTERN EUROPE (The "Sonnenfeldt Doctrine"). Hearings, April 12, 1976. 94th Congress, 2d Session.

_____. Subcommittee on Europe and the Middle East. THE HOLY CROWN OF ST. STEPHEN AND UNITED STATES-HUNGARIAN RELATIONS. Hearings, November 9, 1977. 95th Congress, 1st Session, 1978.

_____. "Statement by William H. Luers, Deputy Assistant Secretary of State for European Affairs." September 7, 1978. Washington: GPO, 1978.

_____. Committee on the Judiciary. HUMAN RIGHTS AND U.S. CONSULAR ACTIVITIES IN EASTERN EUROPE. Washington: GPO, 1977.

_____. Committee on Ways and Means, Subcommittee on Trade. REPORT ON TRADE MISSION TO CENTRAL AND EASTERN EUROPE. Washington: GPO, March 29, 1984.

_____. Joint Economic Committee. EAST-EUROPEAN ECONOMIC ASSESSMENT. Part 2—Regional Assessments. Washington: GPO, July 10, 1981.

_____. EAST-WEST TECHNOLOGY TRANSFER: A CONGRESSIONAL DIALOG WITH THE REAGAN ADMINISTRATION. Washington: GPO, December 19, 1984.

_____. ISSUES IN EAST-WEST COMMERCIAL RELATIONS. Washington: GPO, January 12, 1979.

_____. Senate, Committee on Finance. TRADE ACT OF 1974. Washington: GPO, December 30, 1974.

_____. Committee on Foreign Relations. HUMAN RIGHTS ISSUES IN UNITED STATES RELATIONS WITH ROMANIA AND CZECHOSLOVAKIA. Washington: GPO, April 1983.

_____. THE PROMOTION AND PROTECTION OF HUMAN RIGHTS IN EASTERN EUROPE AND THE SOVIET UNION. Hearings, November 9, 1983. 98th Congress, 1st Session.

_____. UNITED STATES FOREIGN POLICY, USSR AND EASTERN EUROPE. Washington: GPO, 1960.

U.S. Department of Commerce. Bureau of the Census, 1970 CENSUS OF POPULATION. Subject Report 1A: "National Origins and Languages." Washington: GPO, 1970.

_____. 1980 CENSUS OF POPULATION. Table 2: "Ancestry of the Population by State." Washington: GPO, 1980.

_____. STATISTICAL ABSTRACT OF THE UNITED STATES 1946. Washington: GPO, 1946.

_____. STATISTICAL ABSTRACT OF THE UNITED STATES 1947. Washington: GPO, 1947.

_____.STATISTICAL ABSTRACT OF THE UNITED STATES 1971. Washington: GPO, 1971.

_____. STATISTICAL ABSTRACT OF THE UNITED STATES 1974. Washington: GPO, 1974.

_____. STATISTICAL ABSTRACT OF THE UNITED STATES 1975. Washington: GPO, 1975.

_____. STATISTICAL ABSTRACT OF THE UNITED STATES 1979. Washington: GPO, 1979.

_____. STATISTICAL ABSTRACT OF THE UNITED STATES 1985. Washington: GPO, 1985.

_____. Bureau of East-West Trade. SELECTED U.S.S.R. AND EASTERN EUROPEAN TRADE AND ECONOMIC DATA. Washington: GPO, May 1974.

_____. "East Europe." BUSINESS AMERICA. Washington: GPO, March 4, 1985.

_____. "Export Administration Amendments Act of 1985." BUSINESS AMERICA. Washington: GPO, September 2, 1985.

_____. Domestic and International Business Administration. OVERSEAS BUSINESS REPORTS. EAST-WEST TRADE UPDATE. Washington: GPO, November 1976.

_____. Industry and Trade Administration. OVERSEAS BUSINESS REPORTS. EAST-WEST TRADE UPDATE. Washington: GPO, September 1979.

_____. TRADE OF THE UNITED STATES WITH COMMUNIST COUNTRIES IN EASTERN EUROPE AND ASIA 1976-1978. Washington: GPO, December 1979.

_____. International Trade Administration. MOST FAVORED NATION TRADE STATUS. Washington: GPO, n.d..

_____. OVERSEAS BUSINESS REPORTS: MARKETING IN YUGOSLAVIA. Washington: GPO, April 1980.

_____. OVERSEAS BUSINESS REPORTS. UNITED STATES FOREIGN TRADE ANNUAL 1973-1979. Washington: GPO, July 1980.

_____. THE UNITED STATES ROLE IN EAST-WEST TRADE. Washington: GPO, August 1975.

U.S. Department of State, BACKGROUND NOTES POLAND. Washington: GPO, June 1983.

_____. BACKGROUND NOTES YUGOSLAVIA. Washington: GPO, 1964.

_____. CURRENT POLICY No. 169. "U.S. Policy and Eastern Europe." Address by Deputy Assistant Secretary of State Robert Barry, April 22, 1980. Washington: GPO, 1982.

_____. No. 198. "U.S. Commitment to Human Rights." Statement by Assistant Secretary of State Patricia Derian, June 13, 1980.

_____. No. 206. "Human Rights and the National Interest." Statement by Deputy Assistant Secretary of State Warren Christopher, August 4, 1980.

_____. No. 284. "U.S. Policy Toward the U.S.S.R., Eastern Europe, and Yugoslavia." Address by Assistant Secretary Lawrence Eagleburger, June 10, 1981.

_____. DEPARTMENT OF STATE BULLETIN. Washington: GPO,–.

_____. "Conference on Security and Cooperation In Europe." September 26, 1977.

_____. "Eastern Europe: A Region in Ferment." November 16, 1964.

_____. "Human Rights in Romania." Statement by Deputy Assistant Secretary of State Gary Matthews. August 1985.

_____. "Opening Statement of Ambassador Griffin Bell to Conference on Security and Cooperation in Europe at Madrid." November 13, 1980.

_____. "Project Democracy." March 1983.

_____. "Ten Years After Helsinki." Statement by Secretary of State George Shultz. October 1985.

_____. "The Helsinki Final Act." September 1, 1975.

_____. FOREIGN RELATIONS OF THE UNITED STATES 1948. Vol. 4. Eastern Europe and the Soviet Union. Washington: GPO, 1974.

_____. FOREIGN RELATIONS OF THE UNITED STATES 1949. Vol. 5. Eastern Europe; the Soviet Union. Washington: GPO, 1976.

_____. GIST: "Soviet Jewish Emigration." Washington: GPO, 1977.

_____. "Controlling Transfer of Strategic Technology." April 1985.

_____. HUMANE PURPOSES IN FOREIGN POLICY. President Carter at the Commencement Exercises of the University of Notre Dame. May 22, 1977. Washington: GPO, 1977.

_____. IMPLEMENTATION OF THE HELSINKI FINAL ACT. Eighteenth Semiannual Report, October 1, 1984-April 1, 1985. Washington: GPO, 1985.

_____. THE BATTLE ACT REPORT 1963. Washington: GPO, 1964.

_____. THE SECRETARY OF STATE. "Human Rights Policy." Secretary Cyrus R. Vance on Law Day Before the University of Georgia's Law School. April 30, 1977. Washington: GPO, 1977.

Vienna Institute for Comparative Economic Studies. COMECON FOREIGN TRADE DATA 1982. Westport, Conn.: Greenwood Press, 1983.

_____. COMECON FOREIGN TRADE DATA 1983. Westport, Conn.: Greenwood Press, 1984.

BOOKS

Acheson, Dean. POWER AND DIPLOMACY. Cambridge, Mass.: Harvard University Press, 1958.

Adler-Karlsson, Gunnar. WESTERN ECONOMIC WARFARE 1947-1967. Stockholm: Almqvist and Wiksell, 1968.

Allison, Roy, FINLAND'S RELATIONS WITH THE SOVIET UNION, 1944-1984. New York: St. Martin's Press, 1985.

Ambrose, Stephen. RISE TO GLOBALISM. Baltimore: Penguin Books, 1971.

Amnesty International. AMNESTY INTERNATIONAL REPORT 1985. London: Amnesty International Publications, 1985.

Angell, Norman. THE GREAT ILLUSION. New York: Garland Publishing, 1972.

Bahr, Howard, Chadwick, Bruce, and Strauss, Joseph. AMERICAN ETHNICITY. Lexington, Mass.: D.C. Heath and Co., 1979.

Baldwin, Robert E., and Richard, J. David. INTERNATIONAL TRADE AND FINANCE. Boston: Little, Brown and Co., 1974.

Beamish, Tufton, and Hadley, Guy. THE KREMLIN'S DILEMMA: THE STRUGGLE FOR HUMAN RIGHTS IN EASTERN EUROPE. San Rafael, Calif.: Presidio Press, 1979.

Bennett, Marion T. AMERICAN IMMIGRATION POLICIES. Washington: Public Affairs Press, 1963.

Berger, Morroe, Abel, Theodore, and Page, Charles, eds. FREEDOM AND CONTROL IN MODERN SOCIETY. New York: D. Van Nostrand Co., 1954.

Bernstein, Morris, Gitelman, Zvi, and Zimmerman, William, eds. EAST-WEST RELATIONS AND THE FUTURE OF EASTERN EUROPE. London: George Allen and Unwin, 1981.

Bicanic, Rudolf. ECONOMIC POLICY IN SOCIALIST YUGOSLAVIA. London: Cambridge University Press, 1973.

Birnbaum, Karl, and Andren, Nils, eds. BELGRADE AND BEYOND: THE CSCE PROCESS IN PERSPECTIVE. Rockville, Md.: Sijthoff and Noordhoff, 1980.

Bohlen, Charles. WITNESS TO HISTORY. New York: W. W. Norton and Co., 1973.

Borowiec, Andrew. YUGOSLAVIA AFTER TITO. New York: Praeger, 1977.

Braybrooke, David, and Lindblom, Charles. A STRATEGY OF DECISION. New York: Free Press, 1963.

Brookings Institution. ECONOMIC RELATIONS BETWEEN EAST AND WEST. Washington: Brookings Institution, 1978.

Brzezinski, Zbigniew. ALTERNATIVE TO PARTITION. New York: McGraw-Hill, 1965.

————. POWER AND PRINCIPLE. New York: Farrar, Straus and Giroux, 1983.

Caldwell, Dan, ed. SOVIET INTERNATIONAL BEHAVIOR AND U.S. POLICY OPTIONS. Lexington, Mass.: Lexington Books, 1985.

Carter, Jimmy. KEEPING FAITH. Toronto: Bantam Books, 1982.

Chittick, William. STATE DEPARTMENT, PRESS AND PRESSURE GROUPS. New York: Wiley-Interscience, 1970.

Cockborn, Andrew. THE THREAT. New York: Random House, 1983.

Cohen, Bernard. THE PUBLIC'S IMPACT ON FOREIGN POLICY. Boston: Little, Brown and Co., 1973.

Colburn, David R., and Pozzetta, George E., eds. AMERICA AND THE NEW ETHNICITY. Port Washington, N.Y.: Kennikat Press, 1979.

Corson, William. THE ARMIES OF IGNORANCE: THE RISE OF THE AMERICAN INTELLIGENCE EMPIRE. New York: Dial Press, 1977.

De Conde, Alexander. ENCYCLOPEDIA OF AMERICAN FOREIGN POLICY. New York: Charles Scribner's Sons, 1978.

Diggins, John P. MUSSOLINI AND FASCISM: THE VIEW FROM AMERICA. Princeton: Princeton University Press, 1972.

Divine, Robert. FOREIGN POLICY AND PRESIDENTIAL ELECTIONS 1940-1948. New York: New Viewpoints, 1974.

————. FOREIGN POLICY AND PRESIDENTIAL ELECTIONS 1952-1960. New York: New Viewpoints, 1974.

Dougherty, James E., and Pfaltzgraff, Robert L. CONTENDING THEORIES OF INTERNATIONAL RELATIONS. 2d ed. New York: Harper and Row, 1981.

Dragnich, Alex. TITO'S PROMISED LAND. New Brunswick, N.J.: Rutgers University Press, 1954.

Draskovich, Slobodan. TITO, MOSCOW'S TROJAN HORSE. Chicago: Henry Regnery Co., 1957.

Gaddis, John Lewis. STRATEGIES OF CONTAINMENT. New York: Oxford University Press, 1982.

_____. THE UNITED STATES AND THE ORIGINS OF THE COLD WAR, 1941-1947. New York: Columbia University Press, 1972.

Gannon, Robert I. THE CARDINAL SPELLMAN STORY. New York: Doubleday, 1962.

Garrett, Stephen A. IDEALS AND REALITY: AN ANALYSIS OF THE DEBATE OVER VIETNAM. Washington, D.C.: University Press of America, 1978.

Gati, Charles, ed. THE INTERNATIONAL POLITICS OF EASTERN EUROPE. New York: Praeger, 1976.

_____. THE POLITICS OF MODERNIZATION IN EASTERN EUROPE. New York: Praeger, 1974.

Gerson, Louis. THE HYPHENATE IN RECENT AMERICAN POLITICS AND DIPLOMACY. Lawrence: University of Kansas Press, 1964.

Giffen, James Henry. THE LEGAL AND PRACTICAL ASPECTS OF TRADE WITH THE SOVIET UNION. New York: Praeger, 1971.

Glazer, Nathan, and Moynihan, Daniel. ETHNICITY: THEORY AND EXPERIENCE. Cambridge, Mass.: Harvard University Press, 1975.

Goldman, Marshall. DETENTE AND DOLLARS. New York: Basic Books, 1975.

Grub, Philip D., and Holbik, Karel, eds. AMERICAN-EAST EUROPEAN TRADE. Washington: National Press, 1969.

Haig, Alexander. CAVEAT. New York: Macmillan Co., 1984.

Halle, Louis. THE COLD WAR AS HISTORY. New York: Harper and Row, 1967.

Hero, Alfred. AMERICAN RELIGIOUS GROUPS VIEW FOREIGN POLICY. Durham, N.C.: Duke University Press, 1967.

Higham, John, ed. ETHNIC LEADERSHIP IN AMERICA. Baltimore: Johns Hopkins University Press, 1978.

Johnson, Lyndon Baines. THE VANTAGE POINT. New York: Holt, Rinehart and Winston, 1971.

Jones, Alan M., Jr., ed. U.S. FOREIGN POLICY IN A CHANGING WORLD. New York: David McKay Co., 1973.

Jones, Christopher D. SOVIET INFLUENCE IN EASTERN EUROPE. New York: Praeger, 1981.

Kaiser, Robert. RUSSIA. New York: Washington Square Press, 1984.

Kaplan, Stephen, ed. DIPLOMACY OF POWER. Washington: Brookings Institution, 1981.

Kelman, Herbert, ed. INTERNATIONAL BEHAVIOR. New York: Holt, Rinehart and Winston, 1965.

Kennan, George. MEMOIRS 1950-1963. Boston: Little, Brown and Co., 1972.

_____. THE DECISION TO INTERVENE. New York: Atheneum, 1967.

Kertesz, Stephen, ed. THE FATE OF EAST CENTRAL EUROPE. Notre Dame, Ind.: University of Notre Dame Press, 1956.

Kissinger, Henry. WHITE HOUSE YEARS. Boston: Little, Brown and Co., 1979.

_____. YEARS OF UPHEAVAL. Boston: Little, Brown and Co., 1982.

Kovrig, Bennett. THE MYTH OF LIBERATION. Baltimore: Johns Hopkins University Press, 1973.

Leacacos, John P. FIRES IN THE IN-BASKET. Cleveland: World Publishing Co., 1968.

Leiss, Amelia C., ed. EUROPEAN PEACE TREATIES AFTER WORLD WAR II. Boston: World Peace Foundation, 1954.

THE LETTERS OF THEODORE ROOSEVELT. Vol. 3. Cambridge, Mass.: Harvard University Press, 1954.

Levcik, Friedrich, and Stankovsky, Jan, eds. INDUSTRIAL COOPERATION BETWEEN EAST AND WEST. White Plains, N.Y.: M. E. Sharpe, 1979.

Levering, Ralph. THE PUBLIC AND AMERICAN FOREIGN POLICY 1918-1978. New York: William Morrow and Co., 1978.

Lowenthal, Richard. WORLD COMMUNISM. New York: Oxford University Press, 1966.

Lundestad, Geir. THE AMERICAN NON-POLICY TOWARD EASTERN EUROPE 1943-1947. Oslo: Universitetsforlaget, 1978.

Macesich, George. YUGOSLAVIA: THE THEORY AND PRACTICE OF DEVELOPMENT PLANNING. Charlottesville: University Press of Virginia, 1964.

Mamatey, Victor. THE UNITED STATES AND EAST CENTRAL EUROPE. Princeton: Princeton University Press, 1957.

Maresca, John. TO HELSINKI: THE CONFERENCE ON SECURITY AND COOPERATION IN EUROPE 1973-1975. Durham, N.C.: Duke University Press, 1985.

Maude, George. THE FINNISH DILEMMA. London: Oxford University Press, 1976.

Merli, Frank, and Wilson, Theodore, eds. MAKERS OF AMERICAN DIPLOMACY. New York: Charles Scribner's Sons, 1974.

Meyer, Cord. FACING REALITY. New York: Harper and Row, 1980.

Nagorski, Andrew. RELUCTANT FAREWELL. New York: Holt, Rinehart and Winston, 1985.

Nelson, Daniel, ed. SOVIET ALLIES: THE WARSAW PACT AND THE ISSUE OF RELIABILITY. Boulder, Colo.: Westview Press, 1984.

Osgood, Robert. IDEALS AND SELF-INTEREST IN AMERICA'S FOREIGN RELATIONS. Chicago: University of Chicago Press, 1953.

Pavlak, Thomas J. ETHNIC IDENTIFICATION AND POLITICAL BEHAVIOR. San Francisco: R&R Research Associates, 1976.

Philby, Kim. MY SECRET WAR. New York: Dell, 1968.

Pisar, Samuel. COEXISTENCE AND COMMERCE. New York: McGraw-Hill, 1970.

Potter, William, and Valenta, Jiri. SOVIET DECISIONMAKING FOR NATIONAL SECURITY. London: George Allen and Unwin, 1984.

Ra'anan, Uri. ETHNIC RESURGENCE IN MODERN DEMOCRATIC STATES. New York: Pergamon Press, 1980.

Rosenau, James, ed. DOMESTIC SOURCES OF FOREIGN POLICY. New York: Free Press, 1967.

Rositzke, Harry. THE CIA'S SECRET OPERATIONS. New York: Readers Digest Press, 1977.

Ryan, Alan A. QUIET NEIGHBORS. New York: Harcourt Brace Jovanovich, 1984.

Said, Abdul Aziz, ed. ETHNICITY AND FOREIGN POLICY. rev. ed. New York: Praeger, 1981.

Scammon, Richard, and Wattenberg, Ben J. THE REAL MAJORITY. New York: Coward, McCann and Geohegan, 1970.

Schlesinger, Arthur, Jr. A THOUSAND DAYS. Boston: Houghton Mifflin, 1965.

Seabury, Paul. POWER, FREEDOM AND DIPLOMACY. New York: Vintage Books, 1967.

Singleton, Fred. TWENTIETH-CENTURY YUGOSLAVIA. New York: Columbia University Press, 1976.

Smith, Gordon B., ed. THE POLITICS OF EAST-WEST TRADE. Boulder, Colo.: Westview Press, 1984.

Snetsinger, John. TRUMAN, THE JEWISH VOTE AND THE CREATION OF ISRAEL. Stanford, Calif.: Hoover Institution Press, 1974.

Spanier, John, and Uslaner, Eric. HOW AMERICAN FOREIGN POLICY IS MADE. New York: Praeger, 1974.

Spiegel, Steven. THE OTHER ARAB-ISRAELI CONFLICT: AMERICA'S MIDDLE EAST POLICY FROM TRUMAN TO REAGAN. Chicago: University of Chicago Press, 1985.

Stebbins, Richard, ed. THE UNITED STATES IN WORLD AFFAIRS 1954. New York: Harper and Row, 1955.

Stern, Paula. WATER'S EDGE. Westport, Conn.: Greenwood Press, 1979.

Terry, Sarah Meiklejohn. SOVIET POLICY IN EASTERN EUROPE. New Haven: Yale University Press, 1984.

Thernstrom, Stephen, ed. HARVARD ENCYCLOPEDIA OF AMERICAN ETHNIC GROUPS. Cambridge, Mass.: Harvard University Press, 1980.

Tyson, James L. INTERNATIONAL BROADCASTING AND NATIONAL SECURITY. New York: Ramapo Press, 1983.

Valenta, Jiri. SOVIET INTERVENTION IN CZECHOSLOVAKIA. Baltimore: Johns Hopkins University Press, 1979.

Van Horne, Winston, ed. ETHNICITY AND PUBLIC POLICY. Madison: Board of Regents, University of Wisconsin System, 1982.

Wandycz, Pyotr. THE UNITED STATES AND POLAND. Cambridge: Harvard University Press, 1980.

Weed, Perry L. THE WHITE ETHNIC MOVEMENT AND ETHNIC POLITICS. New York: Praeger, 1973.

White, Theodore H. THE MAKING OF THE PRESIDENT 1960. New York: Atheneum Publishers, 1964.

———. THE MAKING OF THE PRESIDENT 1972. New York: Atheneum, 1973.

Wilson, Woodrow. HISTORY OF THE AMERICAN PEOPLE. New York: Harper and Brothers, 1902.

Wise, David, and Ross, Thomas B. THE INVISIBLE GOVERNMENT. New York: Random House, 1964.

Wolf, Thomas A. U.S. EAST-WEST TRADE POLICY. Lexington, Mass.: D. C. Heath, 1975.

Wolff, Robert Lee. THE BALKANS IN OUR TIME. Cambridge, Mass.: Harvard University Press, 1956.

ARTICLES AND MONOGRAPHS

Adamek, Joseph. CENTRALLY PLANNED ECONOMIES. Economic Overview 1983. A Research Report from the Conference Board. Brussels: The Conference Board, 1983.

Andelman, David. "The Road to Madrid." FOREIGN POLICY (Summer 1980).

Bailey, George. "Where Titoism Was Tried." THE REPORTER. July 1, 1965.

Bucy, J. Fred. "Technology Transfer and East-West Trade." INTERNATIONAL SECURITY (Winter 1980/81).

Byrne, Robert. "Before and After Helsinki." REVIEW OF POLITICS 37 (October 1975).

CHRISTIAN SCIENCE MONITOR. 1976-1985.

Cook, Don. "Belgrade: Spinning a European Web." THE ATLANTIC (November 1977).

Czechoslovak Society of Arts and Sciences. BULLETIN (January 1983).

Dimitrijevic, Vojin. "The Place of Helsinki on the Long Road to Human Rights." VANDERBILT JOURNAL OF TRANSNATIONAL LAW 13 (Spring-Summer 1980).

Draper, Theodore. "Neoconservative History." NEW YORK REVIEW OF BOOKS (January 16, 1986).

Evangelista, Matthew. "Stalin's Postwar Army Reappraised." INTERNATIONAL SECURITY (Winter 1982/83).

Fascell, Dante. "The Helsinki Accords: A Case Study." ANNALS OF THE AMERICAN ACADEMY OF POLITICAL AND SOCIAL SCIENCE 442 (March 1979).

_____. "Did Human Rights Survive Belgrade?" FOREIGN POLICY (Summer 1978).

Fuchs, Lawrence. "Minority Groups and Foreign Policy." POLITICAL SCIENCE QUARTERLY 76 (1959).

Garfinkle, Adam. "FINLANDIZATION": A MAP TO A METAPHOR. Philadelphia: Foreign Policy Research Institute, 1978.

Garrett, Stephen A. "On Dealing with National Communism: The Lessons of Yugoslavia." WESTERN POLITICAL QUARTERLY (September 1973).

Gati, Charles. "Polish Futures, Western Options." FOREIGN AFFAIRS (Winter 1982-83).

Goldberg, Arthur. "Letter." FOREIGN POLICY (Fall 1980).

Granick, David. "The Hungarian Economic Reform." WORLD POLITICS (April 1973).

Handler, M. S. "Dogma and Practice in Jugoslavia." FOREIGN AFFAIRS (April 1952).

Heneghan, Thomas. "Human Rights in Eastern Europe." WORLD TODAY (March 1977).

Hough, Jerry. THE POLISH CRISIS: AMERICAN POLICY OPTIONS. Washington: Brookings Institution, 1982.

Hufbauer, Gary Clyde, and Schott, Jeffrey J. ECONOMIC SANCTIONS IN SUPPORT OF FOREIGN POLICY GOALS. Policy Analyses in International Economics No. 6. Washington: Institute for International Economics, October 1983.

Jones, Maldwyn. THE OLD WORLD TIES OF AMERICAN ETHNIC GROUPS. London: H. K. Lewis and Co., 1976.

Kamm, Henry. "Radio Free Europe, the In Sound from Outside." NEW YORK TIMES MAGAZINE (September 26, 1972).

Kaplan, R. D. "Rumanian Gymnastics." THE NEW REPUBLIC (December 17, 1984).

Kaplan, Stephen. "United States Aid to Poland 1957-1964: Concerns, Objectives and Obstacles." WESTERN POLITICAL QUARTERLY (March 1975).

Kirkpatrick, Jeane P. "Establishing a Viable Human Rights Policy." WORLD AFFAIRS 143 (Spring 1981).

Kohler, Daniel F. ECONOMIC COSTS AND BENEFITS OF SUBSIDIZING WESTERN CREDITS TO THE EAST. Santa Monica, Calif.: Rand Corporation, July 1984.

Korbonski, Andrezej. "Detente, East-West Trade, and the Future of Economic Integration in Eastern Europe." WORLD POLITICS (April 1973).

Korey, William. HUMAN RIGHTS AND THE HELSINKI ACCORDS. New York: Foreign Policy Association, 1983.

_____. "Sins of Omission." FOREIGN POLICY (Summer 1980).

Laqueur, Walter. "The Issue of Human Rights." COMMENTARY (May 1977).

Leary, Virginia. "The Right of the Individual to Know and Act upon His Rights and Duties: Monitoring Groups and the Helsinki Final Act." VANDERBILT JOURNAL OF TRANSNATIONAL LAW 13 (Spring-Summer 1980).

Lefever, Ernest. "The Trivialization of Human Rights." POLICY REVIEW (Fall-Winter 1978).

Magner, Thomas. "Yugoslavia and Tito: The Long Farewell." CURRENT HISTORY (April 1978).

Maynes, Charles W. "The Domestic Requirements of a Successful Foreign Policy." PROCEEDINGS OF THE NATIONAL SECURITY AFFAIRS CONFERENCE. Washington: National War College, July 14-15, 1975.

Mihajlov, Mihajlo. "Human Rights: A Means or an End?" THE NEW LEADER (November 3, 1980).

Molineu, Harold. "Hanging on to Helsinki." Paper prepared for the annual meeting of the International Studies Association (March 1984).

NEW YORK TIMES. 1961-85.

Pechota, Vratislav. "East European Perceptions of the Helsinki Final Act and the Role of Citizen Initiatives." VANDERBILT JOURNAL OF TRANSNATIONAL LAW 13 (Spring-Summer 1980).

Pienkos, Donald. "The Polish American Congress—An Appraisal." POLISH AMERICAN STUDIES 36, no. 2 (1979).

Remak, Joachim. " 'Friends of the New Germany': The Bund and German-American Relations." JOURNAL OF MODERN HISTORY 29, no. 1 (March 1957).

Sherer, Albert, Jr. "Goldberg's Variations." FOREIGN POLICY (Summer 1980).

Sherer, Carroll. "Breakdown at Belgrade." THE WASHINGTON QUARTERLY 1 (Autumn 1978).

Silberman, Laurence. "Yugoslavia's 'Old' Communism." FOREIGN POLICY (Spring 1977).

Skilling, Gordon. "CSCE in Madrid." PROBLEMS OF COMMUNISM (July-August 1981).

Tyson, Laura D'Andrea. ECONOMIC ADJUSTMENT IN EASTERN EUROPE. Santa Monica, Calif.: Rand Corporation, September 1984.

WASHINGTON POST. 1976-84.

Weil, Martin. "Can the Blacks Do for Africa What the Jews Did for Israel?" FOREIGN POLICY (Summer 1974).

Yergin, Angela Stent. EAST-WEST TECHNOLOGY TRANSFER. *The Washington Papers*, Vol. 8, no. 75. Beverly Hills, Calif.: Sage Publications, 1980.

_____. "East-West Technology Transfer: The West's Search for Consensus." THE WORLD TODAY (November 1984).

Index

About the Author

STEPHEN A. GARRETT is a professor at the Monterey Institute of International Studies and an Adjunct Professor at the Naval Postgraduate School. He holds a Ph.D. from the University of Virginia.